A LIBERAL IN CITY GOVERNMENT

My Experiences as Mayor of Milwaukee

Frank P. Zeidler

The efforts of many people were involved in bringing this book to publication. Special thanks are due to John Gurda, Christine Andrade, Milly Andrade, Alfred Bader, Daniel Bader, Thomas J. Nitschke, Christine Bjorklund Reynolds, Jonathan Reynolds and Rick and Sachiko Reynolds for their help and support. Special thanks are also due to Frank's daughter Clara for lighting the idea that began this project.

The publication of this book was made possible through the invaluable assistance of the Milwaukee Public Library, which houses the collected papers of Frank P. Zeidler and Carl F. Zeidler. We wish to extend our deepest gratitude to the staff of the Milwaukee Public Library, with special thanks to Virginia Schwartz and Tom Olson.

A LIBERAL IN CITY GOVERNMENT

My Experiences as Mayor of Milwaukee

Frank P. Zeidler

*Dedicated to
the many Milwaukee people
who built a fine city.*

Table of Contents

Introduction

Frank Zeidler wrote this book in 1962. Now, more than four decades after it was created, his account appears in print for the first time.

Frank Zeidler served as mayor of Milwaukee for three terms—from 1948 to 1960—before deciding not to run for a fourth term. Many of the reasons for that decision are explained here in this book.

Although this work was created when Kennedy was president and Khrushchev ruled the Soviet Union, the issues explored in these pages are still relevant today. Can governments find ways to put aside conflicts and achieve genuine cooperation? Can vital services and resources be shared fairly among vastly different communities? Can third party candidates position themselves to win public office, and if so, can they provide effective leadership without the support of a powerful party machine? Can government be kept free of graft and corruption? Can the public interest be served if government hears only the voices of powerful special interest groups while ignoring the needs of individuals who are too weak to have a voice?

While this book examines these larger issues, it also reveals much about a unique period in America's history. In the years following World War II, the country was struggling to rebuild itself from within. Like many other cities, Milwaukee faced an acute housing shortage and a backlog of overdue public improvements. Suburban sprawl was underway as people sought new homesites and lower property taxes. At the same time, Americans were trying to adapt to life under the constant threat of nuclear destruction. Postwar anti-Communist sentiment soon developed into paranoia and McCarthyism, which led many people to fear that the enemies of America might lurk in their own neighborhoods.

Despite increasing Cold War tensions following World War II, the majority of Milwaukee voters knew they had no reason to fear electing a Socialist mayor. The city had previously elected many successful Socialist leaders, among them Dan Hoan and Victor Berger. Milwaukee's Socialists were often known as "Sewer Socialists" because they advocated public ownership of city functions and had succeeded in achieving municipal ownership of the sewer system, as well as the waterworks, the harbor facilities and the city's trash incinerator. In a book about the history of the Sewer Socialists, Frank Zeidler notes that the name is not applied today in a derogatory sense:

> Rather it reflects a time when the practical Socialists of Wisconsin were held in some derogation by Socialist theoreticians, especially in the eastern states, who said the Milwaukee Socialists were incapable of great theoretical thinking and were content to see that rubbish was collected and sewers installed. The Milwaukee Socialists readily accepted the label as an answer to their detractors whom they considered impossibilists who could not win any elections.[1]

Milwaukee Socialists were driven both by ideals and by a determination to achieve practical solutions. Zeidler observes that local Socialists were "inspired by the hope of a brotherhood of workers, the *Cooperative Commonwealth*; by a fierce opposition to war; by a belief in the rights of people; by a passion for orderly government; and by a contempt for graft and boodling."[2] In addition, local Socialists advocated improved housing and the need for green spaces within a city. Their efforts to build a better society did not always meet with success; Milwaukee Socialists tried and failed to achieve municipal ownership of the mass transit system and the electric utility. Historian John Gurda writes,

> Faced with limits on their programs, local Socialists stressed instead their principles. Hoan and company made honesty, efficiency, and innovation Milwaukee trademarks, and they worked to instill something even larger in the populace: a sense that the welfare of one was vital to the welfare of all. Although it was frequently couched in radical rhetoric, the heart of their message was a compassionate commonality.[3]

It is this "compassionate commonality" which resonates throughout Frank Zeidler's work.

Zeidler chose to title this book "A Liberal in City Government" rather than "A Socialist in City Government," even though he considers himself both a liberal and a

Socialist. Here in this book Zeidler offers a definition of liberalism as a "willingness to accept new ideas" and "sympathy with the many rather than the special interests."[4] He also defines his brand of democratic Socialism:

> I did not, nor do I now, subscribe to the theory of the inevitability of Socialism as described by Marx, nor to his kind of Socialism. I am and was a democratic Socialist who believed that freedom and liberty are important to all individuals and that public ownership and socialist controls are sometimes necessary to achieve the greatest freedom and greatest liberty for people.[5]

Zeidler, like many other local Socialists, was inspired by the ideal of cooperative commonwealths, yet his Socialism is fundamentally pragmatic in its immediate ambitions. He says in this book that he has no intent to socialize businesses such as the corner grocery store. However, he does strongly advocate public ownership wherever private enterprise fails to serve the interests of the people. The severe housing shortage, for example, demonstrated the need for government to take an active role in creating public housing.

When Zeidler ran successfully for mayor in 1948, he did so as a member of a newly established coalition of liberals called the Municipal Enterprise Committee rather than under the banner of the Socialist Party, which had all but disappeared from the political landscape, even in Milwaukee. The Municipal Enterprise Committee was created in order to build a consensus among liberals around a core principle—public enterprise should take charge wherever private enterprise failed. It was in this way that Frank Zeidler came to be elected mayor of Milwaukee—as a candidate seeking consensus and common ground. And this fact sheds light on his choice for the title of this book.

Throughout his 12 years of service as mayor, Frank Zeidler was isolated politically. While he did have some liberal allies, he was a lone Socialist in city government. Far from having a powerful party machine, Zeidler was in many ways a party of one. His Socialist philosophy was viewed by many as anachronistic—even as mayor, he found no one in his administration willing to convert to the cause of the Socialist Party. His brand of democratic Socialism was often misconstrued or misrepresented, sometimes slurred as Communism during an era of intolerance and fear. Although Zeidler's party affiliation may have been more of a political liability than an asset, he remained consistently and proudly devoted to Socialism and its principles, as well as his own internal sense of fairness.

This book is divided into three chapters. In the first, Zeidler discusses his successful campaign for mayor despite strong opposition from business interests and the press. The *Milwaukee Journal*, in its company history published in 1981, confessed that its coverage of the 1948 race had not been completely objective and impartial. The *Journal* was in fact so committed to seeing Zeidler defeated that it was secretly involved in writing the press handouts of Zeidler's opponent. Unknown to *Journal* management, Zeidler's press handouts were aided by the volunteer efforts of a veteran *Journal* reporter, Hale Champion. A number of workers at the *Journal* were sympathetic to Zeidler's candidacy and some even attempted a minor revolt until they were threatened with dismissal from their jobs. The *Journal's* efforts to defeat Zeidler ultimately proved ineffective. Author Robert W. Wells noted, "Around the newsroom, it was felt that the *Journal's* heavy-handed tactics had backfired."[6]

In the second chapter, Zeidler discusses some of the various problems he faced during his three terms as mayor. He also describes the day-to-day duties and burdens of serving as the leader of a major American city. For Zeidler, foremost among those duties is a constant dedication to a strict set of ethical standards.

The third chapter recounts the city's ambitious efforts to expand its territory despite vigorous suburban opposition. Although the last such conflict in Milwaukee County officially ended in 1962, annexation battles are still fought today among cities, towns and villages in outlying areas of Wisconsin, and these struggles are often filled with the same sort of drama, bitterness and strong language. The third chapter also describes the local fight between municipalities over water and sewers. This fight, of course, remains with us today, and Zeidler's work offers a valuable glimpse into the historical origins of the current issues, which have yet to be resolved.

The subjects of annexation and water supply were closely connected during Frank Zeidler's years as mayor. Many of the suburbs surrounding Milwaukee had grown and prospered without making sufficient accommodations for water service; they instead chose to rely on Milwaukee's waterworks. Milwaukee, for its part, wanted to use water to encourage annexation and thereby shore up its eroding tax base as the city's industry moved to the suburbs. The issue became fiercely contested. Business leaders soon joined the fray, ostensibly to achieve reform in the operations of government in the metropolitan Milwaukee area. In a 1965 book about the formation of the Milwaukee Metropolitan Study Commission, the authors revealed the true impetus behind the movement for change:

> Water in particular served to trigger off the new interest. Hot, dry summers in 1953 and 1955 graphically demonstrated the incapacity of Milwaukee city's water system to serve the growing needs of the area, while the resulting restrictions on water use greatly irritated suburban customers as they surveyed their parched lawns and burnt-out shrubbery.[7]

Political wrangling was ultimately brought to a head by a particular group of suburban customers—namely, Milwaukee business leaders who were unhappy about water problems at their own homes in the suburbs. A delegation of Greater Milwaukee Committee leadership decided to go to the governor to demand a solution:

> The group stressed the need for examining the water problem, a subject that GMC leaders regarded with particular interest at the

time. Many of them lived in north shore communities which were dependent on the City for their water supply. The acuteness of the problem had been brought forcibly to their attention by personal experiences with chronic water deficiencies. . . . When a solution did not appear to be forthcoming through local political channels, they turned to other means. This incident represents one of the few instances in recent Milwaukee history where the community's top influentials personally involved themselves and actively intervened in a metropolitan governmental issue.[8]

The suburbs ultimately maneuvered their forces to a victory in the water war. As noted by historian Frederick Olson, the north shore suburbs formed a water utility of their own, while other suburbs, "partly as a result of successful legal action brought by Wauwatosa, gained wholesale access to the water intake system of the City of Milwaukee while maintaining their separate distribution facilities."[9]

When Frank Zeidler wrote this book in 1962, he originally included an additional chapter detailing the struggle for better housing and urban redevelopment in Milwaukee during his tenure. He considered these issues, which played out against a backdrop of growing racial tensions, to be central to his 12 years of service as Milwaukee's mayor. The length and breadth of Zeidler's exploration of these issues require the publication of a separate book, which will be available in the coming year.

One of the most compelling features of *A Liberal in City Government* is its author. Frank Zeidler was born in Milwaukee in 1912, the son of a barber and the third of four children in a German Lutheran family. He grew up in the Merrill Park neighborhood on Milwaukee's near west side. After graduating from West Division High School and attending classes at Marquette University, he found himself compelled by the Depression to seek employment. He worked as a surveyor and topographical engineer from 1931 to 1948.

Despite the hardships of the Depression, Frank Zeidler continued to educate himself by studying extensively at the Clybourn Street branch of the Milwaukee Public Library. There he read the works of many prominent Socialists and found himself attracted by their ideals. He joined the Socialist Party in 1932 and became the secretary of the party in Milwaukee in 1937. He met his wife Agnes through work for the party and they married in 1939.

As mayor of Milwaukee from 1948 to 1960, Frank Zeidler played a pivotal role in Milwaukee's growth, more than doubling the land area of the city while fighting the forces of suburban sprawl. He led the city's postwar urban renewal effort that saw the advent of public housing and numerous other improvements including the construction of a new expressway system, museum, arena and civic center. At the same time, he succeeded in advancing the tradition of honest and efficient government established by Milwaukee Socialists in the first half of the century.

While serving as mayor, Frank Zeidler often took a streetcar or a bus to work. Sometimes he rode a bike. He never drove a car because he never sought a driver's license due to poor vision. He says that the people of Milwaukee are better off that he does not drive.

After leaving office in 1960, Frank Zeidler chose to devote his time and energy to recording the major events of his three terms as mayor. Whether or not the finished product saw publication, it was important for Zeidler to create this historical record if only for the sake of creating it. Even so, his account is filled with valuable observations and analysis, and the reader gains special insights not only into history and politics and Milwaukee, but into the passion and vision of a man devoted to building a better community based on principles of justice and compassion.

In a recent conversation, Frank Zeidler talked about how and why he wrote this book:

> It took me quite a while to write it. I didn't have any income, so I had to live on what savings I had. That was in 1962.
>
> Much of the book was written at Brisbane Hall, which was at 536 W. Juneau Avenue, which was the office of the Socialist Party. They had a library of books and a wonderful collection of pamphlets, many from the time of the Great Depression. I was out of office, and I didn't have a job, but I did have a very large collection of notes, and the pamphlets from the office, and I worked from those notes and newspaper clippings and other sources to develop the book. And a lot of it reflects my memory of the events at the time.
>
> It occurred to me that in the 1950s Milwaukee had made some very great strides. The city more than doubled its size during my administration, we started the freeway system, we began the public museum, we expanded the library system, we started a completely new waterworks.
>
> One of the reasons I wrote the book was that my mind was full of these activities, and I thought it would be interesting just to record them for myself, if not for anybody else, so that they would stay in my mind as to how things developed. I was glad that I reported it, that I wrote it all down, as a record of some historical value.

Since leaving office, Zeidler has continued to pursue activities geared toward achieving social justice. He has worked as an arbitrator, college instructor, consultant, historian and activist. In 1976, he ran for president as the Socialist Party candidate.

Today, Frank Zeidler continues to reside on Milwaukee's near north side with his wife Agnes in the home they have shared since 1946. In the 1950s, rumors were circulated that the mayor was planning to move to a luxurious home he was building in the suburbs, but during the course of the past five decades Frank has shown those rumors to be unfounded.

While many things may have changed in the world since Frank Zeidler entered politics, he remains very much the same man who joined the Socialist Party in 1932 — idealistic, crusading, committed to principle, devoted to his community and his country, and determined to help create a better world for all humanity.

Dean Andrade and James Reynolds

1. Introduction by Frank Zeidler. Elmer Axel Beck. *The Sewer Socialists: A History of the Socialist Party of Wisconsin, 1897-1940*. Fennimore, WI: Westburg Associates Publishers, 1982.
2. Ibid.
3. p. 302. John Gurda. *The Making of Milwaukee*. Milwaukee: Milwaukee County Historical Society, 1999.
4. p. 18. Frank Zeidler. *A Liberal in City Government*. Milwaukee: Milwaukee Publishers, 2005.
5. p. 29. Ibid.
6. p. 353. Robert W. Wells. *The Milwaukee Journal: An Informal Chronicle of Its First 100 Years*. Milwaukee: Milwaukee Journal Company, 1981.
7. p. 73. Henry J. Schmandt and William H. Standing. *The Milwaukee Metropolitan Study Commission*. Bloomington: Indiana University Press, 1965.
8. p. 80-81. Ibid.
9. p. 70. Frederick Olson. "Trading Post to Metropolis: Milwaukee County's First 150 Years." Ralph M. Aderman, editor. Milwaukee: Milwaukee County Historical Society, 1987.

Chapter 1

Campaigning for Office on a Liberal Platform

America is an urban nation. More people live in cities than in rural areas. Americans are becoming more conscious of their cities and are beginning to study their workings. Many students of human life believe that cities hold the secrets of the future.

Cities have held an irresistible fascination for millions of people over the centuries. Some people are attracted to the business life of a city, some may like the industrial life, others may be captivated by a city's entertainment world. I was attracted in great curiosity to the political life of a city — my home city of Milwaukee.

This curiosity ultimately brought me to the position of mayor of that city for three terms from 1948 to 1960.

As mayor, I was able to get a perspective of city life that one does not get from any other position. At the focal point of the mayor's office many of the events of the city swirl. It is this fascinating, neverending and sometimes tragic swirl that draws people into this position of mayor from which they cannot escape except that they are changed in mind and spirit, and except that they also change and influence the course of society around them.

Much of our political literature centers on the role of the president and of national political leaders or statesmen. Considerably less is written about state leaders and governors, and the literature about municipal leaders is meager.[1] This is unfortunate because the position of mayor is oftentimes harder to handle successfully than the positions of state or national responsibility. The tempo of a mayor's activity tends to move faster and more turbulently than that of a senator or congressman. In addition, the mayor is more closely scrutinized, easier to reach and more intimately connected with the people. The strain of holding this office is great, the political life is often relatively short and it is harder to reach the political heights than it is from state or federal office. Reputations are destroyed faster and oblivion is closer in the position of mayor, yet there seldom is a dearth of candidates for the position in most cities. Why do people run for the job?

My campaign for the office of mayor of Milwaukee in 1948 illustrates the difficulty a person with a liberal and, in my case, a democratic Socialist background faces in United States elections.

I happened to become a candidate for mayor of Milwaukee for the first time in 1944. I was the crusading type. I carried the banner of my party, the Socialist Party of Milwaukee, in the 1944 election.

I became a member of the Socialist Party in 1932 when I joined one of its ward branches while I was unemployed. I began by peddling campaign literature, helping run meetings and other "Jimmy Higgins" work, as party work by ordinary members was described. I later came to serve the Socialist Party of Milwaukee County for some years as secretary, beginning in 1937, when it was not a party on the ballot.

The Socialist Party seemed attractive to me because of the philosophy and ideas in the writings of Norman Thomas, Harry Laidler and other Socialists. I was opposed to war and it seemed to me that the Socialist ideals of cooperation and brotherhood might help to prevent future wars. The Socialist concept of public ownership seemed to offer possibilities for ending the severe Depression.[2]

Socialists had achieved some record of success in Milwaukee's municipal elections beginning in 1904 with the election of Milwaukee's first Socialist aldermen. The first Socialist mayor of Milwaukee, Emil Seidel, was elected in 1910. Seidel went into office with Socialists for treasurer, city comptroller and city attorney. There was also a sizeable contingent of Socialists in the Milwaukee Common Council.[3]

Seidel was elected on a party ticket in the municipal elections, but in the 1911 session of the Wisconsin Legislature the Republicans and Democrats succeeded in eliminating party elections in municipal races. This permitted a Republican-Democratic coalition, thereafter known as the "non-partisans," to defeat Seidel in 1912.

Incidentally, Seidel's secretary during this two-year term was a former news reporter, Carl Sandburg.

After Seidel's defeat, only one other Socialist remained in a citywide office in Milwaukee. He was Daniel Webster Hoan, a 31-year-old labor attorney who had been elected city attorney in 1910. The tall, gangling, Lincolnesque Hoan was re-elected as city attorney in 1912 and 1914. When he ran for the office of mayor in 1916 as the Socialist candidate, he won.[4] This was the beginning of a long career in which Hoan was re-elected six more times as mayor for 24 consecutive years.[5] Hoan was a colorful mayor, fighting the press, the bankers, the utilities, the corrupt elements and pillorying his opponents on the public platform to cheering crowds.

The Socialist Party was at the peak of its strength in Milwaukee at this time. It had elected Hoan as mayor and with him a city attorney, Max Raskin, and a city

2

treasurer. Enough Socialists had been elected aldermen to enable a Socialist to become president of the Common Council. This group served from 1932 to 1936, when the non-partisans regained power by claiming most city offices, but not that of the mayor.

During this time, Wisconsin had four different political parties: Republican, Democratic, Progressive and Socialist. Both the Republican Party and the Democratic Party were conservative. The Progressive Party, led by Bob LaFollette, Jr., and his brother Phil, was a liberal party, closer to the New Deal in philosophy than the Wisconsin Democrats.

The Socialist Party, in response to pressure from Wisconsin labor leaders who felt that important labor legislation was being lost in the Legislature because of the existence of four parties, voluntarily retired from the ballot in 1935 and maintained their organization as an educational group. Many of their members joined a bloc within the Progressive Party called the Farmer-Labor Progressive Federation (FLPF) composed originally of nine constituent groups including farm and labor groups. The chief political activity of Socialist leaders was transferred to this pressure group within the Progressive Party. The conservative wing of the Progressives, which included the LaFollette brothers, stayed outside of this particular bloc.

The Socialist members of Hoan's following faltered in the years between 1936 and 1940 because they divided their energies between two different organizations: the Socialist Party, functioning as an educational group not on the ballot as a party, and the FLPF, operating as a caucus within the Progressive Party.

Hoan was defeated in 1940 by a young man of 32, my brother, Carl F. Zeidler. Carl was a non-partisan assistant city attorney when he decided to run. After trailing Hoan in the primary, Carl Zeidler caught the popular fancy and beat the still fiery Dan Hoan.

At the same time my brother was campaigning for mayor against the FLPF slate in the city, I was a candidate on the FLPF slate for the office of Milwaukee County supervisor. We did not attack each other and maintained good personal relations, but my brother Carl did vigorously attack Hoan, the Socialist office holders and the Socialist record. The Socialist label stuck to a man once he had it and it was a good target to shoot at as I came to learn for myself quite well. Hoan, himself, although he later became an active Democrat in the 1940s and was one at the time of his death, could not get rid of the Socialist label that was pinned on him as a tag of opprobrium by his political foes inside and outside of the Democratic Party.

I failed of election to the Milwaukee County Board at the time my brother Carl was elected mayor. A few months later in 1940 I was nominated by the FLPF to run as a Progressive candidate in the primary for state treasurer. The FLPF slate carried the Progressive primary with its candidates but failed in the general election before a resurgent Republican Party.[6]

A division developed within the Socialist Party following the defeat of Dan Hoan in 1940. One section of the Socialist Party called for separation from the weakening Progressive movement and sought to re-establish the Socialist Party ballot. Many Socialists were unhappy because the conservative wing of the Progressive Party had

3

failed to accept the newer Progressives with a Socialist background. At a state Socialist convention in Madison in May of 1941, the majority at the convention voted to separate from the Progressive Party.[7]

The Socialist Party returned to its own ballot but the party was greatly reduced in numbers and leadership. Despite the vote to separate from the Progressive Party, most of the prominent Socialists had chosen to stay with the Progressives, and many of the other Socialists were gravitating toward the Democratic Party. The Farmer-Labor Progressive Federation began to break apart and the remnants were absorbed by the Progressive Party. The Progressive Party itself ultimately went out of existence in 1946,[8] and most of the members went into the Democratic Party where they gave an infusion of liberalism into a party that was in some aspects as conservative in Wisconsin as the state's Republican Party.[9]

When the Socialists started their party all over again in 1942, they had little timber available for candidates. A few of us, therefore, stood as the party candidates. We were not an organization with a popular label, like the Republican or Democratic labels, and without a popular label, it was difficult to succeed in statewide party elections. The public votes frequently, although not always, by labels in such party elections. In non-party elections the public can often demonstrate a high degree of selectivity.

I was the Socialist Party candidate for governor of Wisconsin in 1942 and polled only 11,295 of 800,579 votes cast.

My brother Carl did not have a long tenure of office as mayor. The United States entered the Second World War and Carl volunteered for the Naval Reserve. Alderman John L. Bohn, the Common Council president, became acting mayor when Carl left for the war.[10] In October of 1942, after Carl had been on only one other voyage and shortly after his enlistment, the merchant ship on which he was an officer of the armed guard disappeared, *spurlos versenkt*, on a trip from the Canal Zone around Cape Horn to the Cape of Good Hope. The ship, the SS LaSalle out of Mobile, carried to their death a crew of splendid men, including my brother. Many promising lives were thus added to the monstrous total of the dead in the incomprehensible tragedy of the Second World War.

In 1944, I was selected by the Socialist Party to be its candidate for mayor of Milwaukee, since there was no FLPF slate. The Socialist Party put a full slate of citywide candidates in the field and a number of aldermanic candidates. Edwin W. Knappe was the Socialist candidate for city attorney. He had been an assistant city attorney under Max Raskin, the Socialist city attorney, from 1932 to 1936. Rudolph Beyer, an accountant and glass manufacturer, was the party candidate for comptroller, and Ervin A. Koth, an electrical engineer, the party candidate for city treasurer.

There were four principal candidates for mayor in the 1944 race. Mayor John L. Bohn was the incumbent. John A. Seramur, a personable police officer on my brother Carl's staff and later on Mayor Bohn's staff, was another candidate. Attorney Herbert L. Mount, a man with a Progressive background, was the third candidate. I was the Socialist candidate.

4

During this campaign for mayor, I was working for the Milwaukee Road Railroad doing surveying and related jobs. My ability to campaign was limited because I was working at what was considered an essential job in wartime, but I was pleased to have our small party organization ask me to carry its banner. Perhaps I was fired with the zeal of what the cause of a Socialist world brotherhood in the future meant, for I could see in our ideal of a world of cooperative commonwealths the hope of avoiding the terrible tragedies such as those inflicted on millions of people by the war. It always grieved me that the people of the world could not see our ideal and practice it, and it especially grieved me that our Socialist movement did not forestall the Second World War, but this is another subject.

The party drew up a municipal platform as it usually did in all its elections.[11] The plans naturally contained demands for municipal ownership of electric power and light facilities, the gas company and the public transportation system. The platform also called for municipal ownership and development of all docks and a municipal milk distribution system. The platform proposed that the city be made a garden spot and that slum areas be eliminated by municipal housing. The platform encouraged arts, craftsmanship and vocational learning for all students and the re-education of adults for new vocations. It proposed extension of free public education in the Milwaukee area to the junior college level and the teaching of the social sciences in the public schools. The platform supported vigilance in management of municipal finances and in all city departments and it proposed not to borrow money from the banks but to have the city remain debt-free. The party's platform also asked for a commission to devise ways and means of putting the city's unemployed to productive work, and it promised a fair tax system based on services to be rendered.

Two points were stressed by the Socialist Party in this campaign. One point was to have the city remain debt-free. For many years the Socialist Party had supported a program to have the city get rid of its municipal debt. Under the Hoan administration, the city began to reduce borrowing. It raised the cash levy for current expenditures, and put certain money into an amortization fund so that this fund could carry the city debt when the lessening amount of the debt was matched by the growing amount of the amortization fund.[12]

This remarkable objective of city financing came into actual existence in 1944 when the public debt of Milwaukee stood at a total of $10,162,000. The amortization fund at that time was at $10,092,105 and carried the debt until 1948 when, after a bitter struggle, the city's policy reverted to going into debt for capital improvements.

Mayor John L. Bohn, the non-partisan incumbent, to his credit in the 1944 election supported the debt-free status of the city as a means of conserving its money for improvements instead of paying out money in interest.[13]

Another issue stressed by the Socialist Party in 1944 was municipal housing for slum clearance, specifically targeting the blight surrounding Milwaukee's downtown. In my campaign I listed a proposed five-year housing development "in the blighted cordon that extends around Milwaukee's business district as of primary importance."[14] It is interesting to note that in the term of Socialist Mayor Seidel from 1910 to 1912 the achievements of the Social Democrats (as Socialists were then known) were claimed to be as follows: "Workingmen's homes being provided for through comprehensive scheme of city planning and platting" and a "general cleaning up of the slum districts."[15]

In other speeches around the city, I proposed public ownership of mass transportation, with lines radiating from the center of the city to connect to business in the outskirts in order to bolster declining central city property values. Public ownership of the transportation system did not develop during my years in office, but municipal housing and slum clearance, which had been growing steadily since the federal Public Works Administration programs of the early 1930s, were beginning to take root in Milwaukee successfully about this time.

In this political campaign I had the invaluable assistance of a man who was a major help to me in every subsequent campaign. Manuel Meyers, a former City Hall reporter of the *Milwaukee Leader*, a Socialist daily whose successor, the *Milwaukee Post*, expired in 1941, gave me advice on how to present issues and consented to prepare releases and literature. "Manny," with his cigar and his hat tipped over one eye, was a newspaperman in the best tradition with a warm heart and a feeling for humanity that appeared in his writings and in his treatment of the news.

Despite the help I received from many people, I failed in the primary, but my fellow candidates on the citywide slate were nominated.[16]

After the primary I pitched in to help the other Socialist candidates, but they too were handicapped by the meager party resources. Ervin Koth, Ed Knappe and Rudy Beyer had a difficult burden to run a campaign without a head to the ticket. In the election, each received about 25,000 votes out of a total of 140,000 cast.

The failing fortunes of the Socialist Party were demonstrated in the defeat of two fine men for aldermen—Alex Ruffing of the Seventh Ward and Edward H. Kiefer, state chairman of the party and alderman of the 20th Ward. Carl P. Dietz, who had been Socialist city comptroller and later Socialist alderman, was re-elected alderman of the 10th Ward as an independent.

The Socialist movement was terribly downhearted about the loss of its two aldermen. Alex Ruffing had been a great help to me in the campaign of 1944 and when I ran again in 1948 he was a principal source of encouragement and guidance. Ed Kiefer was a gentleman of courage. He had made a fine record as an assemblyman in the Wisconsin Legislature—he would not touch a penny of tainted money or take a favor and he proposed forward-looking legislation. Mr. Ruffing was a machinist and Mr. Kiefer a painter.

John L. Bohn was re-elected mayor in a sharp contest with John A. Seramur.[17] In this election, the votes of the liberals and labor people were split, some voting for Mayor Bohn and others voting for Mr. Seramur.

Several former Socialists and several Progressives who had been members of the FLPF ran more or less as independents in races for the County Board and were elected.[18] The strength of the Socialist Party, however, was still further cut down by these 1944 municipal elections.

The Socialist Party continued its political and educational activities, while many of its former members became more and more identified with the Democratic Party through the labor movement. The Socialist Party of Wisconsin qualified with enough votes to stay on the ballot until the elections of 1950 as a distinct party. In 1952 the party had to run its candidates in the presidential election as "Independent Socialist" candidates. In 1956 and 1960 the party put up no presidential candidate.

The weakening of the Socialist Party nationally occurred because the managers of the Democratic Party won the allegiance and support of American labor leaders by meeting their immediate demands for legislation. The Socialists, who were steeped in the labor movement, did not want to turn away from the mainstream of the movement and therefore suffered the decimation of their own party in order to advance labor's demands. This national condition resulted in a decline in the local party because new individuals interested in serving in public office could see no hope of election with the Socialist movement.

In Milwaukee County, the Socialist movement in the period from 1944 to 1947 addressed itself to the problems of housing, municipal ownership of utilities and international events, including the onset of the Cold War and the problem of the atomic destruction of cities and people. The Progressive movement was practically absorbed into the Democratic Party after the defeat of Senator Robert M. LaFollette, Jr., by Joseph McCarthy in the Republican Party primary of 1946. With the liberals in Wisconsin divided among the Democrats, Progressives, Republicans and Socialists, McCarthy and the right-wing Republicans won.[19]

A special situation of interest to liberals arose in Milwaukee following World War II. The debt-free status of the City of Milwaukee was a constant irritation to financial houses around America for it demonstrated what a city might do to free itself from the endless payment of interest. The opponents of the debt-free status used the backlog of public works that had developed during the war as a reason to demand an end to the debt-free status and the use of borrowed funds for all capital improvements in the future. Some of the community leaders fell victim to this type of argument, even though the city had a cash reserve fund of about $20 million to start its new program of public works. This money had been set aside during the war. To some people, including myself, it is iniquitous to be in debt to someone else, whether as a citizen of a municipality or as a private individual. To people in the business of lending, it is iniquitous for cities not to be in debt to them.

An attack was mounted against the city's debt-free policy that the Socialists had established. A group of estimable citizens, including men from banking and investment organizations, formed a group called the "1948 Corporation" (named for the state's upcoming centennial) with the idea of convincing the city to obtain funds for future capital improvements by borrowing and going into debt. Socialists, remembering Mayor Hoan's strictures and remembering the long struggle to free the city of debt, found the proposals unpalatable. Hoan used to tell at political meetings of the harsh terms the bankers put to him in the Depression days to finance city government and this stuck in the minds of his listeners.

7

The debt-free status of the city was the work of Hoan, his party and especially his advisor and secretary, Thomas M. Duncan. It was also the work of an able independent named Leo Tiefenthaler, an official of the City Club, to whom public borrowing meant an unnecessary waste of public funds. Thus in the battle over Milwaukee's debt-free status, Socialists found themselves fighting alongside a few independent individuals.

The issue was joined over a referendum of an advisory nature submitted to the voters in the spring election of 1947. The referendum was worded as follows: "Shall the city issue bonds for a program of public improvements?"

As an active member of the Socialist Party, I took an interest in this question and fought for the debt-free status. Lined up against those favoring a debt-free status were the large commercial interests, some labor leaders and both newspapers, which hammered away at the issue.

Two citizens' committees were formed to take active issue. One was extraordinarily well financed: "The Improve Milwaukee Now Committee." The other committee was a group, comprised of Socialists and independents, called the "Keep Milwaukee Debt-Free Committee," with almost no financial resources.

The *Milwaukee Journal*, which had formerly advocated the debt-free status,[20] and the *Milwaukee Sentinel*, a typical Hearst paper, repeatedly made strong editorial and special feature appeals for the city to abandon the debt-free status on the grounds that the backlog of public works left over from the Depression and the war required much borrowing. Some of the advocates of borrowing proposed financing all future capital improvements with borrowed funds, without using any cash for projects.

The advocates of borrowing were well financed and had plenty of literature and could advertise. Our party finances were drained, and my personal employment in my own surveying business was not enough to meet the expenses of my family with its five children at that time. We had to fight high-speed rotary printing presses of two metropolitan dailies with a mimeograph machine. Nevertheless, I took up the party's crusade.

Some people called the issue of trying to keep the city debt-free an out-of-date policy. However, the Socialists remembered the period of the Depression when the banks had squeezed the city. They also remembered how difficult it had been to finance city government by borrowing for all expenditures each year and then using the tax levy to pay off the indebtedness. It had been a painful process to switch to cash in advance for the city's budget, and the Socialists did not want to see the bankers once again compel the city to borrow for all purposes including current operations.[21]

In the course of the discussions, I joined forces with a civic-minded attorney, Samuil Nissenbaum. He and I went to meeting after meeting together to explain our side of the debt-free question in debate. The strain of events on Mr. Nissenbaum was such that he suffered a heart attack with lingering and fatal consequences. He was truly a martyr for civic betterment. I was greatly saddened by this occurrence and the sadness has not left me with the passage of time.[22]

I had been elected to the Milwaukee School Board in the spring of 1941 with a group of Progressives for a six-year term. In this position I tried to carry out my work conscientiously without too much dogmatism, but with independent liberal judgment based on a Socialist and public ownership background. I fought for better pay to compensate teachers, for pre-kindergarten training, for vocational guidance, for expanded scientific and technical studies and experimentations, for new schools, for school ownership and operation of the buses, for a school forest and other measures.

It was because of this independence that I sometimes found myself a minority of one, but I also endeavored to create personal harmony in a board traditionally split between members representing manufacturing and commercial interests and those representing labor. I had differences on principle but not on personalities.

I decided to stand again for the Milwaukee School Board in 1947. At the same time, I was working for the Keep Milwaukee Debt-Free Committee on the upcoming referendum question. The task of speaking at meetings on the school issues was added to my activity for the debt-free status.

To make the burden even heavier, my entire family, including myself, came down with a virulent attack of influenza in the spring of 1947 and for days every member of the family was seriously ill. The youngest child of the family at that time, Mary, was also taken ill, and my wife called me home because of her worsening condition, marked by a stiffening. We quickly called Doctor Sylvester Coffey, who at once diagnosed the condition as influenzal meningitis, which usually had fatal consequences. He injected an antibiotic, streptomycin, at once and sent the child to an isolation hospital. For weeks she was in danger and this sapped the nervous energy of myself and my wife. I did not care then what happened to my political causes so long as my child was saved. Thanks to the discovery of streptomycin, and to the work of Doctors Max Fox and George Wegman, whom Doctor Coffey brought into the case, the child was saved. It was an act of God but also the result of scientific advancement—in this case, antibiotics discovered by Selman Waksman of Rutgers University. The discovery of these disease destroyers has saved more lives than the military forces have been able to destroy and yet in few of our cities do we see statues to the great biologists, doctors and scientists.

The vote on the referendum question went in favor of the city going into debt— 54,036 to 40,909. The committee supporting indebtedness had spent $36,172 and our committee had spent about $145.[23] There is some kind of moral in that. Even a good cause has trouble against great financial odds.

In this same election I was re-elected to the Board of Directors of the Milwaukee Public Schools for a second term of six years. My vote total was the highest of the five persons elected to the board, and I always regarded this as curious because many of the people who favored the city going into debt, which I did not favor, must have voted for me as a school director.[24]

The prospects of the city government of Milwaukee leaving the traditions of liberalism and going into a period of ultra-conservatism as a result of the 1947 bond referendum was an unpleasant prospect to some of the liberals of the city—the

Socialists and former Progressives. Several other propositions reflecting a liberal trend were consistently defeated or thwarted in the Milwaukee Common Council. Many of the issues revolved around meeting the acute housing shortage. Since 1938, the Milwaukee Common Council, under the domination of an ultra-reactionary group of aldermen, had refused to establish a housing authority to build any public housing with federal aid.[25] A group of women who organized in 1944 succeeded in getting the Common Council to create a housing authority, but it was slow in getting started because of opposition of the real estate interests, builders and property owners. This opposition to public housing prevailed for the entire period of my stay in office and continued long after.

One matter of a housing venture worth noting here was a proposed project by a private redevelopment corporation. The idea was put forward by Henry S. Reuss, an attorney, a returned veteran and a member of a prominent Milwaukee family. He proposed to use a Wisconsin law that would give a tax freeze for clearing blight in order to construct some large apartment buildings in an area in Milwaukee's Fourth Ward near N. 10th Street and W. Michigan Street. There was a small park in this area that was known as the Red Arrow district, named after the 32nd Division of the Wisconsin National Guard, which had distinguished itself in the First World War. Around this park were some dilapidated buildings.[26] The redevelopment proposal of Reuss and his backers was vehemently and discourteously rejected for this was the reactionary mood of the Milwaukee Common Council at the time.[27] Mr. Reuss, by his activities, showed himself to be a knowledgeable and liberal person, as well as a potential candidate for public office because of his leadership.

The prospect of a change in city government came from an announcement in 1947 by Mayor John L. Bohn, who was then in his 80s but very alert, that he would not seek another term of office. Liberals in Milwaukee were thus presented with the hope of regrouping their shattered forces to again exert a constructive influence on city government. This prospect appeared difficult to attain due to the political landscape.

Since the turn of the century, elections in Milwaukee had demonstrated a division in voting between people oriented toward labor and people oriented toward private business and upper-income groups. This, of course, is a social phenomenon that persists in Milwaukee and many other industrial cities. The Socialist Party under the leadership of Victor L. Berger, an Austrian immigrant who had become a powerful Socialist editor, had garnered the support of much of the labor movement.[28] However, a non-Socialist element gradually began to appear within the labor movement, consisting of people who were uncomfortable with the Socialists' ideas of public ownership and occasional manifestations of anti-clericalism. This non-Socialist element was mostly Democratic and grew in strength with the presidential election of 1932, as labor began to follow President Franklin D. Roosevelt's lead in securing some of their immediate demands.

By 1947, the Democrats in Milwaukee had grown more influential in the labor movement than the Socialists and had drawn many former Socialists into their ranks. The liberal movement in Milwaukee was thus split between Socialists, former

10

Progressives and liberal Democrats. While the liberal Democrats were active in the Democratic Party, the conservative Democrats still held most of the public offices. As a result, the actual policies of local government as carried out by Democrats were not always distinguishable from Republican policies.

There was considerable communication between Socialists and their former associates who had gone into the Democratic Party. There was a bond of friendship between Socialists and many labor leaders who still paid Socialist Party dues. Many of the venerable old-timers of the labor movement were also Socialists of long standing. Small merchants, too, were friendly to the Socialist liberals.

The conservative and reactionary opposition consisted of the powerful utility lobbyists, the real estate interests and many of the leading merchants and industrialists. This group controlled the Milwaukee Common Council. In the years since Seidel's election in 1910, there had been a deep division in local government between Socialists and their combined Democratic and Republican opposition, which went under the name "non-partisan." The division was still manifest in 1947 although the remnants of the Socialists had been almost wiped out in the 1944 municipal elections. The leader of the non-partisans in the Milwaukee Common Council was Alderman Milton J. "Mickey" McGuire of the Third Ward.[29]

Although Mayor Bohn's decision to leave office at the end of his term presented liberal forces with an opportunity to gain representation in city government, the Socialist Party did not appear strong enough to do the job by itself. In addition, Socialists did not want to turn away from the mainstream of the labor movement, and they did not want to offend the many personal acquaintances who had left the Socialist movement and were at that moment politically adrift.

The summer of 1947 went by without any apparent consolidation of liberal forces. The names of Daniel W. Hoan, former mayor, and Andrew Biemiller, a former Socialist and later a Progressive assemblyman in the Wisconsin Legislature and still later a Democratic congressman, were mentioned as possible choices to head a ticket of liberal city officials. But there was no cohesive organizing force.

A suggestion was made by a south side Milwaukee merchant, John J. Schupp, that an attempt be made to formally institute an organization of liberals which would back liberal candidates and which would include Socialists, Progressives, liberal Democrats and members of trade unions. Such a group would meet the criticism that the Socialist movement always had to face in municipal elections, namely that they were participating as a party in what was said to be a non-partisan election.

The question was raised as to what was the common ground of political philosophy upon which all the liberals would meet. One of the keenest issues at the time was public housing. The liberals were for it and the conservatives against it. Public housing was frequently referred to as Socialistic and for many near-liberals this label was enough to scare them away from supporting public housing. In order to reach a common ground, Schupp suggested that the name of the organizing committee be the Municipal Initiative and Enterprise Committee. The idea behind this title was that it was a commonly agreed principle among liberals that if a public need was not being met by private initiative and enterprise, or not being met well enough, then public initiative and enterprise were needed. In the informal discussions of this group of liberals the name was finally shortened to the "Municipal Enterprise Committee." A convening committee, of which Stanley Budny was secretary, issued a call to the "forward-looking and progressive citizens and voters of Milwaukee" to attend a public meeting at the Milwaukee Turners Hall on November 26, 1947. The call stated further:

> The purpose of this meeting is to aid in the formation and development of a *MUNICIPAL ENTERPRISE* Committee for the purpose of participating in the *spring elections* of 1948.
>
> *The city of Milwaukee is in danger* from a combination of selfish and reactionary interests led by the two large newspapers. These interests would plunge the city into debt, would sidetrack housing and slum clearance, and would continue to harass the organized labor movement so that the profit motive might seize the city in its grasp as it has seized practically every large city in the nation.
>
> In order to establish a city and county government which has the interests of the toilers and producers of this city at heart, we are calling this meeting to promote municipal enterprise where it is socially needed.[30]

To accompany this mimeographed call, a statement was issued explaining why the eight members of the convening committee had issued it. The statement noted that the city faced a time of expansion and that special privileged groups would likely capture the city government by default. The statement said, "Already the utilities are pushing their prices upward unchecked by a vigilant administration, housing is being checked, slum clearance relegated to a minor position, and the city's debt-free status thrown away."

The statement took aim at the newspapers. It said that Milwaukee had been brought to the peak of American cities by the Socialist Party and the Farmer-Labor Progressive Federation with a platform democratically drawn up, but now the city's newspapers saw in such organizations the threat to their own domination of municipal life on behalf of special and privileged groups. The statement said that the newspapers had succeeded in driving out or silencing the advocates of municipal ownership and enterprise by placing in public office people without any philosophy of government other than that of opposition to municipal ownership and enterprise.

The statement further argued that the Milwaukee metropolitan area was too big to function without a liberally inclined endorsing vehicle in so-called non-partisan elections; without a democratically established committee to build a municipal platform, to endorse or select candidates, no group of men and women could be elected to public office with a constructive and coherent philosophy of government beneficial to the poor, the exploited and the toilers. The committee stated that municipal governments would go by default to the managers of corrupt machines or special privileged groups. The statement proposed to build a progressive platform on the basis of municipal ownership and enterprise and to support candidates who favored this platform.[31]

The meeting was held as scheduled and a platform committee was selected.[32] This committee consisted of Edward C. DeBriae, a teacher and union member; James Fitzpatrick, another teacher; Milton M. Cohn, an attorney; John J. Schupp and myself. A rough draft was discussed and improved by the committee. This was the beginning of the Municipal Enterprise Committee, which later became the Public Enterprise Committee.

The hopes and prospects of organizing liberal forces with a possible inclusion of most liberals almost immediately encountered adversity. Max Raskin, a Democrat and state CIO attorney, called a meeting between Henry S. Reuss, the veteran active in promoting urban redevelopment, and myself shortly after the meeting of the newly formed Municipal Enterprise Committee. Mr. Raskin hoped to accomplish the same purpose as the committee, namely to get a candidate for mayor.

The meeting was held in Mr. Raskin's office. I had not made up my mind to run at the time; I had only made up my mind to try to get a liberal slate of candidates for city offices, and that I would as an individual back such a slate. With my tiny income, large family and dim prospects of election, I was not keen about the personal sacrifice my family would have to make, but I felt strongly then, as I do at the time of this writing, of the necessity of liberals, few in number, keeping themselves together on a common program.

The meeting was a failure. Mr. Reuss apparently regarded the Municipal Enterprise Committee as a vehicle unacceptable for his candidacy, as the personal vehicle of Frank Zeidler or as a vehicle that would include the remaining Socialists. Probably all three factors were in his mind when he announced his candidacy for mayor a few days later.

Mr. Reuss' announcement was carried in the *Milwaukee Journal* of November 30, 1947, in a front-page story.[33] The story said that Mr. Reuss would bid for labor support but that this bid would be complicated by Zeidler's probable candidacy. The *Journal* reported that "the attempted coalition between Reuss and Zeidler failed because of disagreement over methods, according to Zeidler. Reuss plans to make the campaign run as an individual, while Zeidler proposes to prepare a slate of candidates for city offices who would work together as an organization." The story reported that both of us had met in the office of Mr. Raskin who was quoted as saying that the purpose of the meeting was to "get a clear field for one liberal candidate . . . we hoped that either Reuss or Zeidler would withdraw, but both are determined to run."

The same story carried the announcement that on the next Wednesday, December 3, 1947, a group known as the New Milwaukee Committee would stage a rally to promote the candidacy of Henry W. Maier.

On the same page and adjacent to the announcement of Mr. Reuss' candidacy, the *Journal* carried a story on the developing activities of the Municipal Enterprise

Committee.[34] The article reported that a platform would be drafted by Socialists and non-Socialists who had banded together as the Municipal Enterprise Committee, which was open to all "liberally inclined persons." The newspaper story carried a quotation from the statement at the November meeting as to why a liberal group was needed. The newspaper quoted me as saying that the Socialist Party had been criticized for endorsing candidates in "non-partisan" elections and that the committee was formed to avoid such criticism. If the committee did not succeed in bringing liberals together, the Socialists would go back to party endorsement. The article also commented at length on the decline of the Socialist Party and reported that it currently had no aldermen in office.

Mr. Reuss found it necessary to comment on the failure of the meeting in Mr. Raskin's office, and on my comment on the reasons for the failure. In an article in the *Milwaukee Journal* the next day, Mr. Reuss stated that the attempt to draw into an accord two liberal candidates for Milwaukee's mayoralty failed because of a disagreement over two matters of policy.[35] This story reported, "'I have a high regard for Zeidler,' Reuss said, 'but I draw the line when it comes to two basic planks in his platform in 1948.'" Reuss objected to the idea of the municipality not borrowing money; he called it a "Socialist dogma that interest is evil." He also objected to the idea that public enterprise should take over private business that failed to make a proper showing. The story quoted me as saying that the liberal coalition had failed because Reuss wanted to run for mayor as an individual and had refused to "submit to the discipline" of the newly organized Municipal Enterprise Committee. The story also said that the committee planned to endorse a slate of 20 candidates.

The *Milwaukee Journal*, an independent Democratic paper, of course observed all these doings closely. It had fought for many years to bring the Hoan administration to an end and eliminate most Socialists from public office, although it occasionally endorsed a Socialist aldermanic candidate. The *Journal* was not anxious to have another Socialist mayor, for the obvious reason that Socialist mayors were thought to hurt private business and the city's business reputation elsewhere in the world. This was not an unnatural policy for this paper to follow. In fact, Socialists would have been unreasonable to expect anything other than strict opposition from both the *Journal* and the Hearst-owned *Milwaukee Sentinel*.

The editors of the *Journal* found it desirable and perhaps even necessary to write an editorial warning the Milwaukee people about the formation of the Municipal Enterprise Committee. In an editorial appearing on December 1, 1947, entitled "Zeidler's Straw Man," the following comment was made:

> The Socialist group to be known as the Municipal Enterprise Committee, which was apparently organized to run Frank Zeidler for mayor, starts out with the old political trick of setting up a straw man. The committee statement said, "The two large newspapers in this city finally succeeded in driving out or silencing the advocates of municipal ownership or enterprise and in placing in office public

officials without any philosophy of government other than opposition to municipal ownership and enterprise."

We shall let others speak for themselves, but as for the *Journal*, it had done no such thing. Its record is clear and not subject to perversion.

The *Journal* has supported the right of every community to have municipal ownership of utilities if that is what the people want. We regard a utility as primarily the people's business. Our view is that municipal ownership falls well within the lines of democracy and in no way conflicts with what is truly private business.

We have not taken the view that municipal ownership is good per se, or that it ought to be adopted as part of a political doctrine. This is what irks the Socialists. They want municipal ownership everywhere, whether a community can handle it or not, and regardless of whether the people are going to get something better or worse than the so-called "private" ownership. This is no good, in our view.

The editorial continued that "successful municipal ownership requires willingness on the part of people to set up a good system of management and to be alert to keep politics out." The editorial stated that the *Journal* had supported municipal ownership of the waterworks as well as a bill to create a metropolitan transit authority in the last Legislature. The *Journal* also said it had supported the Tennessee Valley Authority as the only sensible way to deal with a river as a unit.

The editorial stated that "we dwell on this present incident because it is important to start right on the city campaign that lies ahead." There were too many big issues, the editorial stated, to have Milwaukee waste time on straw men. Yet, it was on this issue of public enterprise and on "socialism" that the final campaign revolved, despite the comment by editors of this paper that they had an open mind on municipal ownership.

Immediately after this editorial appeared, Mr. Reuss had a campaign meeting at which his candidacy was launched. His program for the city included a policy of annexation, a modern building code, 4,200 public housing units and limited dividend corporations to build homes.[36]

The *Milwaukee Journal* continued, however, to be disturbed by the existence of the Municipal Enterprise Committee. In an editorial on December 3, 1947, "Socialists Try a New Mask," it again struck at the organization.

What a fine bit of hocus-pocus the Milwaukee Socialists are trying to palm off now! They are not, they announced, going to be Socialists in the coming municipal election. They are going to be members of an outfit called the Municipal Enterprise Committee.

15

They are not, as Socialists, going to endorse candidates as they have always done in the past. Oh, no! But as Municipal Enterprisers they meet Saturday, write a platform and select 20 candidates for city offices.

As the Frenchman said, "It's all so different it looks exactly the same."

Take this Municipal Enterprise Committee. A nice new, shiny name, indeed. But behind it are the same old Socialist faces, Frank Zeidler,[37] Stanley Budny, William Buech, Alex Ruffing, Walter Bubbert—it sounds like a roll call of the Socialist inner guard of a few years ago.

This new organization will be a fine vehicle for liberals, Mr. Zeidler says. Fine, indeed! Liberals can sit in the back seat, help pay for the gas and oil, and enjoy the ride as the Socialists, hands firm on the steering wheel, try to get back into power in the city.

The insincerity of the whole business is shown by Zeidler's frank admission that if this venture doesn't work in 1948, the Socialists may resume the old practice of acting as a party in endorsing candidates.

The editorial further said that the citizens were tired of the Socialist Party and that the Socialists had dreamed up the Farmer-Labor Progressive Federation, which the editorial claimed had not fooled Milwaukeeans. Now there was a new name, said the editorial, and if it did not work the party would go back to its former self. Milwaukeeans would not be fooled: "The whiskers show too plainly," as the last line of the editorial stated.

It became clear that the *Journal's* idea of liberalism did not include Socialists and that the newspaper would fight a Socialist reappearance in government. This editorial and the one preceding always impressed on me the idea that conservatives fear democratic Socialists more than Communists or Fascists. I was not surprised, therefore, to find that in the late 1950s and early 1960s the supposed drive against totalitarian Communists by the extreme right wing in the United States was not a drive against Communism, but against democratic Socialism, the British Labor Party and the Swedish Social Democratic Labor Party platforms.

On December 3, 1947, the New Milwaukee Committee held a rally at the Milwaukee Auditorium at which it announced its support of Henry W. Maier as a candidate for mayor. The supporters of Mr. Maier represented a group of young but quite conservative people who were seeking to emulate the style of my brother, Carl F. Zeidler, in putting on the same kind of showy campaigning that Carl was able to do so effectively.

After a shower of confetti, Mr. Maier made a speech, to the 100 persons his committee had assembled, in which he used strong language. He called the Common Council "a cross-breed of drifting dunces and bumbling buzzards" and declared war on the man "who masquerades as mayor." He denounced unnamed people as "self-appointed Gestapo" and "vicious, underhanded politicians," whom he called "wholly incompetent and morally corrupt." He said, "City Hall is an old haunted house, inhabited by ghouls, ghosts, bats, bugs and mice for 100 years."[38] This and other strong language was directed against the incumbents in the city government, but Maier's program and philosophy and that of his backers was much the same as the people he was denouncing, for he demonstrated later in the campaign that he too did not want liberalism to apply to municipal government. The *Milwaukee Journal* found this type of histrionic campaigning objectionable. In an editorial on December 4, 1947, entitled "Let's Quit the Circus Stuff," the editors expressed disapproval of the "hokum" of Maier's rally, which reminded them of Pappy O'Daniel and Gene Talmadge, but they carefully stated they were not passing judgment on Mr. Maier's program.

The Municipal Enterprise Committee met for the adoption of its platform on December 6, 1947, at the Milwaukee Turners Hall. About 50 people attended. The platform was adopted after discussion, item by item. The platform was built around the themes of planning and progressive administration. The platform called for carrying out a master plan, for clearing 160 acres of blight in the next four years, for reducing population density in slum areas, for 10,000 low-rent homes, for financing the city as nearly as possible by pay-as-you-go methods, for harbor development, for public ownership of gas and electric utilities, for collective bargaining for public employees, for encouragement of consumer co-operatives, for a citizens' civil rights committee, for establishment of a metropolitan government, for the establishment of a county manager and for an integrated traffic program.

The platform was entitled "Platform for Milwaukee's Future."

The *Milwaukee Journal*, in reporting this event, acknowledged that non-Socialists as well as Socialists were present in the meeting, and this paper listed political, union and occupational activities of the various participants, but the paper emphasized the role of Socialists in the meeting.[39]

After the platform was adopted, $46.52 was raised to finance initial expenses. A functioning subcommittee was set up to introduce the program to various organizations and to propose a slate of candidates to advance the platform.

The functioning subcommittee made inquiries of various prospects for liberal candidates, including Daniel W. Hoan and Andrew Biemiller, to see if there could be a substantial agreement by such prospective candidates on backing a liberal platform. The editorials of the *Milwaukee Journal* had accomplished their objectives. No candidates could be found who would support such a program of liberalism, for it appeared to be an almost foregone conclusion that the powerful *Journal* would defeat any such candidate who tried for office.

While all these activities were going on within the liberal segment of the city's political spectrum, other well-known individuals and some lesser-known people had decided to enter the mayor's race. Ultimately 15 candidates entered. These candidates included Arthur S. Ehrmann, a popular assistant city attorney; John J. Fleming, a former alderman and well-known leader among some of the more conservative people; Sheriff George Hanley; another candidate who was a Stalin Communist; a Trotsky Communist, among others. The widest political choice ever presented to the Milwaukee voters in a municipal election was presented in this 1948 municipal election.

Mayor John L. Bohn finally declared himself definitely not a candidate for re-election after he had seemed to consider the idea, and Daniel W. Hoan, former mayor, later consented to run early in February at the insistence of his friends.[40] This further tended to split the liberal vote.

When the subcommittee of the Municipal Enterprise Committee sought candidates of any type to support its platform, it could secure no unanimity of action among liberals. At a meeting early in December, the Municipal Enterprise Committee decided to ask me if I would be its standard bearer in the race for mayor and I said that I would.[41] The subcommittee then sought candidates for the other city offices to support its program and platform but again none would stand because the Municipal Enterprise Committee had drawn heavy editorial and news column fire. Once more the liberals in Milwaukee failed to unite their forces to present a common front in an election. The overwhelming strength of the press in a non-partisan election was too much for the divided liberals. The subcommittee ultimately gave up its search for candidates early in January of 1948.[42]

While this activity was going on in the Municipal Enterprise Committee, Henry W. Maier, candidate of the New Milwaukee Committee, challenged me to a radio debate. This debate took place on December 21, 1947, on radio station WEMP. The principal bone Maier had to pick with me was on the issue of liberalism. Mr. Maier, in this debate, claimed that the word "liberal" had a meaning only in national politics and not in local government. I maintained that liberalism had a place in municipal elections and gave my definition of liberalism as a "willingness to accept new ideas" and "sympathy with the many rather than the special interests." I gathered later that Mr. Maier was picking his ground very carefully, for he wanted to be able to claim both the liberal vote and the conservative vote and therefore objected to having any other candidate point out a division between the two.

Mr. Maier accused me of not being liberal on the debt policy and he asserted I was introducing "false issues" into the campaign by expressing "labor's viewpoint." I replied that one of the major issues in the previous mayoral campaign in 1944 was each candidate's attitude toward the organization of city workers, an issue that was to appear in subsequent municipal campaigns.

Mr. Maier claimed that "a city has no power to propose either liberal or conservative legislation in the accepted sense. Public ownership can and should be decided on economic merit." This statement is of interest, for when Mr. Maier was elected a Democratic state senator he was strongly pro-labor and for this reason received immense financial support from labor organizations. When he was later elected to succeed me as mayor of Milwaukee, he reverted back to his original position of submerging labor and liberal interests in order to gain the support of conservatives.

In this debate I said, "Municipal government is not purely housekeeping. It involves a philosophy of government. If the 1948 Corporation can represent the interests of bankers and industrialists, labor has a right to express its needs in municipal elections."[43]

While these events were unfolding, Mr. Reuss' proposal for veterans' housing was before the Milwaukee Common Council. The proposal received rough going and devious treatment. It was finally defeated in February of 1948, by a vote of 14 to 13, after Mayor John Bohn came out against it.

Opposition to the plan came from several sources. People in the area involved did not relish being forced to look for new homes at the time of an acute housing shortage. The aldermen did not like the property tax freeze involved in the project. Many of the aldermen were against any kind of housing program as socialistic. And many of them thought Reuss too liberal and they did not like his candidacy for mayor.[44]

The *Milwaukee Journal*, which had heavily backed the proposal, published the strongest kind of editorials and called for the defeat of the aldermen who had opposed it for being "wreckers."[45] The project had merit and most of the problems that were raised might have been readily solved, but it remained for the Stalin Communist candidate, Sigmund Eisenscher, to raise the question that has accompanied every Milwaukee public or private housing project. He asked Mr. Reuss whether this project in an all-white neighborhood would be rented under an open occupancy policy.[46]

The struggle over the Red Arrow housing project was taking place while the mayoral candidates and their campaign committees were busy talking about this project and other issues. The issues the candidates spoke on were usually solid and many good proposals on planning, traffic control, housing and utility control were offered. There was a surprisingly liberal tone to the political campaign in the primary.

The Municipal Enterprise Committee had few financial resources, but it gathered strength in members as it held weekly meetings on Saturday afternoons during the winter of 1947-1948 at the Milwaukee Turners Hall. The public was invited to these meetings and all business was openly discussed.

Financial strength of the organization was weak. There were no big contributors. It was reported in the minutes of December 20, 1947, that $26.11 was on hand.[47] Mr. Harold Klitzke, the manager of a company that printed campaign literature and labor publications, offered to print our platform. Subscription cards were prepared for obtaining donations of any amount, however small, from workmen in shops and other places where people congregated. These small contributions of a quarter, half dollar or one dollar helped the organization through the primary election.

Many people helped circulate nomination papers. These people included union members, Progressives, liberal Democrats and former Socialists. A retired elderly man, Max Starke, volunteered with an unemployed woman, Pearl Holzknecht, to keep open a campaign office at 536 W. Juneau Avenue in Milwaukee. Melvin Schneider, a welfare worker, volunteered to take me to meetings in his automobile since I did not drive and had to go to meetings by streetcar and bus. William Buech, an insurance

19

man who had been a School Board member, became head of the Municipal Enterprise Committee. A businessman, Edward E. Matthes, a former Socialist and later a Progressive, was the treasurer of the committee. Stanley Budny, then manager of the Milwaukee Turners, headed the campaign committee.[48]

The Milwaukee public was very interested in the numerous candidates for mayor. Invitations to speak to public gatherings, unions, forums, smokers and rallies came in great numbers so that a fatiguing pace was set for all the candidates. In addition, in this era before widespread television, the main medium for reaching large numbers of people outside of press accounts was the radio, and so the candidates needed to spend time preparing radio speeches.

The platform of the Municipal Enterprise Committee was of immense value. It was something that could be placed in people's hands for them to read and comprehend, and this platform helped win the first endorsements I received from organized labor groups, beginning with the International Association of Machinists, District Council No. 10.

As far as I know now, none of the other candidates had bothered to prepare a written platform for distribution, although later in the campaign Mr. Reuss claimed he did but I never saw any platform.[49] Issues were picked up as they seemed appropriate by the candidates, or as they strove for a single winning idea.

My experiences in the many years of previous campaigning for public office, especially my work for the 1947 referendum on the debt-free status, were immensely helpful in giving me familiarity with municipal problems, so that I was as familiar with them as any of the candidates who had been in the government itself.

Manuel Meyers, the former City Hall reporter, was especially helpful. Almost daily he and I talked over each new idea in a program and tested it. He had many helpful suggestions that he could make from detached observation. It was my feeling to present a positive approach on all issues, avoiding as much as possible criticizing the other candidates, while promoting the Municipal Enterprise Committee platform and my own ideas of city government within the framework of this platform. Occasionally, if I deviated from this pattern and started swinging at another candidate, Manny would point out the error. In following this pattern of constructive campaigning a candidate can build a consistent picture of his ideas, and he can come out of an election, winning or losing, without having left a trail of too many enemies nursing personal grievances for his assaults. It is safe to say that without Manuel Meyers' consistent advice the campaign for office would not have been successful.

On the basis of the platform, I began to win endorsements from various groups in addition to the Machinists District Council. Ultimately I received the endorsement of the American Federation of Labor-Federated Trades Council of Milwaukee County and the Milwaukee County Industrial Political Action Committee.[50] Mr. Reuss and I were called the two most liberal candidates by a union, Ampco Local 210, United Farm Workers Equipment Workers, CIO.[51]

Five of my colleagues on the Milwaukee School Board endorsed my candidacy also and this was a tremendous help. They were Dr. Emmet F. Cook, Albert Boyer,

Martin C. Baumann, Paul C. Baumann and John F. Seramur, the father of the candidate for mayor in 1944. These endorsements served to answer the later accusations of the press that I was irresponsible, that I was a menace to democracy and that I could not get along with an elected body such as a city council.[52]

Of course, friendship and a long-standing acquaintance with liberals helped my candidacy. I believe that the existence of a platform which spelled out a program also persuaded many people to give me an endorsement. The platform was a rallying point for liberals. I tried to and did faithfully adhere to the objectives spelled out in the platform. Many of these goals came into actuality after I was elected.

In the absence of money to pay for newspaper ads our committee decided on certain courses of action to make up for the deficiency. I would try to make as many public meetings as possible. I would give a press release on my views for every single edition of the morning and afternoon newspapers. I would make radio speeches whenever possible. The committee would print our own campaign paper to the extent of our money.

This method of campaigning was relatively effective. If the big industrialists and commercial interests had concentrated their money early, they might have nominated and elected a candidate. With the large number of candidates in the field, those big campaign contributors were undecided about which candidate to support. Reuss, Hoan, Zeidler and Ehrmann were too liberal. Ultimately some of the big funds went to one of the other candidates who was able to put up an estimated 60 billboards (a sizeable number for Milwaukee) but this candidate failed of the nomination by a few thousand votes.[53]

The Municipal Enterprise Committee had no billboards because it did not have funds. Instead the committee concentrated on window cards that were posted in hundreds of store windows throughout the city. The accumulated effect of such cards was helpful in impressing the name.

The day-by-day news releases of the various candidates revealed that every single one of the candidates favored the bond issues for public housing and slum clearance. This truly was a revolution, for the idea of public housing a few years back was strongly opposed by the Milwaukee Common Council's non-partisan majority.[54]

On the whole, the press statements of the candidates revealed a progressive program for the city, but some of the candidates took time out to denounce other candidates instead of pressing their own ideas, and this caused bad feeling between some of the contenders.[55] In our campaign all speakers of the Municipal Enterprise Committee stayed strictly away from attacking other candidates in the primary. When one of our campaign speakers made an adverse comment on Dan Hoan in a rally, I felt it necessary to state that this was a mistake and that I had high regard for Mr. Hoan's record. Manuel Meyers and I stayed up late one night, after an extensive series of public meetings, to carefully prepare a statement to restore the equilibrium.[56]

It was apparent during the primary race, and it was especially apparent to the other mayoral candidates, that the one candidate which the *Milwaukee Journal* would favor (and possibly later, the *Milwaukee Sentinel*) would be Mr. Reuss.

With a field of 15 candidates, a newspaper supporting one candidate could afford to ignore many of the minor candidates as they would receive too small a vote to have to be reckoned with. However, six or seven candidates appeared to have major strength and these the newspaper needed to dispose of editorially. Sheriff George Hanley drew first fire from the *Journal*. He was under attack for alleged gray-market activities in automobiles, and the *Journal* pointed this out in an editorial of January 13, 1948: "We Dare You, Sheriff Hanley."

The paper did not focus much direct attention on the mayoral race during the latter part of January and early February because it was lending its editorial support to the Red Arrow housing project of Mr. Reuss. The same non-partisan aldermen whom the *Journal* had defended against the Socialists, and whom the *Journal* had preferred to Socialists, now drew the paper's heaviest fire for refusing to support the Red Arrow project. The *Journal* attacked the aldermen, the mayor and the acting city comptroller, Virgil H. Hurless, for seeking to stop approval of the project.[57]

The Red Arrow project was rejected by the Common Council on February 2, 1948.[58] The next day in campaign meetings Mr. Reuss described this action as strangulation of his project and Henry W. Maier called it "stabbing."[59] On February 4, the *Milwaukee Journal* in an editorial called for support of 13 aldermen who backed the Red Arrow project. On February 5, in an editorial entitled "The Builders and the Wreckers," the *Journal* called for the defeat of 11 aldermen seeking re-election out of the 14 who had opposed the project. The *Journal*, having supported a reactionary Common Council in the past now had a taste of its own philosophy of 10 years earlier when it had opposed public housing. However, the paper had progressed greatly in those 10 years and a majority of the non-partisan aldermen had not.[60]

On February 17, 1948, the *Journal* attempted to editorially narrow the choice of candidates for its readers to four candidates. In an editorial "From Among Four Young Men," the *Journal* attacked Daniel W. Hoan by saying that he had been around too long and that the city had drifted under his administration. The *Journal* attacked Sheriff Hanley once again as a gray-market operator. The paper said that Frank Zeidler was "pleasant and able" but that he had the old Socialist crowd with him. The editorial recommended that the voters select from Arthur S. Ehrmann, John J. Fleming, Henry W. Maier and Henry S. Reuss.

In response to this editorial attacking me for my Socialist views, I made a public speech in which I said that Socialist doctrines were being pinned on those who favored a liberal municipal program. I asked the other candidates not to abandon proposals for housing, blight removal, parking, a public food terminal and transportation development because they were now in danger of being called Socialist.[61]

A strange editorial next appeared in the *Journal*. On February 23, 1948, the paper commended a public meeting in which I had appeared by invitation in the Town of Wauwatosa to discuss how municipal issues and a growing community affect city and township alike.[62] The idea of city and suburb struggling with each other was apparently more alarming to this metropolitan daily than the possibility of me receiving favorable notice. For this little editorial I have always been most grateful.

The newspaper on February 29, 1948, dealt an editorial blow at Arthur S. Ehrmann, the personable assistant city attorney, who had been promoted a few days earlier by the *Journal*. In an editorial "Mr. Ehrmann Tries a Fast One," the paper accused him of trying to avoid responsibility for lobbying in the Wisconsin Legislature for a law that enabled city officials to retire on pension. This lengthy editorial undoubtedly hurt Mr. Ehrmann's chances.

On February 28, 1948, the paper editorially attacked Hoan again. In an editorial "Some Vaudeville from Hoan," the paper charged that Hoan's dramatic methods of campaigning, which the paper claimed fooled some people, were being tried again.

This negative editorial attitude was then replaced by a more positive tone. In an editorial of March 1, 1948, the paper said that there was one question in the mayoralty: "Which of the various candidates is the best one to lead the city in a program of progress?"[63]

In the next weeks before the primary day of March 16, 1948, the *Milwaukee Journal* proceeded to give its answer to the question it posed. It ran four lengthy editorials on the qualifications, background and potential leadership of Mr. Reuss, winding up the last of these editorials on March 15, 1948, with an unprecedented half-column picture of Mr. Reuss in its editorial columns.[64]

The heavy editorial support of the *Milwaukee Journal* naturally provoked most other candidates and set them against Mr. Reuss, ultimately preventing them from throwing any of their support to him, so that they remained silent after the primary.

It became apparent that if the Municipal Enterprise Committee were to make any showing against the press support for Mr. Reuss, it would be desirable and necessary for the committee to get out a campaign paper for itself. Accordingly, it was agreed to prepare such a paper for the primary, giving the platform of the committee, describing the candidate and making general comments about the city's future and a program for it. More than 75,000 papers were ultimately printed and mailed to many voters before the primary. Not all voters were reached because the committee could not afford the costs.[65]

This campaign paper had the effect of making a better total impression on the reader than a series of paid advertisements. It described my background and the Municipal Enterprise Committee's program in detail. The paper was attractively edited by Manuel Meyers, who gave it a friendly tone. We had the assistance of Erwin Hess, a well-known cartoonist, and the technical advice of Harold Klitzke, whose publishing organization was engaged to produce the work. This campaign paper was favorably received.

Scores of campaign workers did the tedious job of addressing each paper and it took considerable effort to prepare it for mail distribution.

The paper, the many talks, the support of many rank-and-file liberals, the constructive platform, the good tone imparted to the campaign as Manuel Meyers insisted and the faithful help of volunteer workers, equally motivated as myself by liberal ideas, produced a surprising result in the primary of March 16, 1948. I led the field of candidates with 49,766 votes; Henry S. Reuss had 38,236 votes; John J. Fleming,

33,176 votes; Daniel W. Hoan, 21,918 votes; Arthur S. Ehrmann, 21,092; and Henry W. Maier, 9,567.

Immediately after the election, Dan Hoan announced his support for me and I thanked him for it.

The editorial board of the *Milwaukee Journal* claimed to be pleased with the results of the primary. In an editorial the day after the primary, on March 17, 1948, the paper immediately made known its views. In this editorial, "Here Are the Issues Between Mr. Zeidler and Mr. Reuss," the board stated, "In the fine job they did in the primary, Milwaukee voters created exactly the right situation in the mayoralty contest. The voters nominated two men who are personally qualified — as to intellect and home interest in the city. This takes out the personal element and leaves citizens free to concentrate on issues." The two major issues the paper raised were that I was opposed to borrowing and putting the city back into debt, and that I could not get teamwork from a non-partisan Common Council with my background from the old "Socialist Hoan crowd." These two issues, which were to become the major themes of the campaign, were thus at once sharply defined with no breathing space after a grueling primary. The candidates were off on their feet and running again.

The long years of contention between the Socialists and the *Journal* had again come to the fore. It was hardly to be expected that so prosperous and important a news and advertising medium as the *Journal* would espouse the cause of one who believed in public ownership as an essential part of liberalism. The opposition of this publication caused no disappointment in the Municipal Enterprise Committee. However, other than making a reference during the primary to the *Milwaukee Journal's* previous opposition to public housing in 1938, I had not mentioned it or the *Milwaukee Sentinel* adversely. I did not intend to do so, and this also was the opinion of Manuel Meyers. Instead, our campaigning would continue to discuss the issues, and if the press raised an adverse issue, we would answer it as politely and firmly as possible, mentioning only the issue, and not the press itself.

In another editorial, "Electorate Does a Good Job," also on March 17, 1948, the *Milwaukee Journal* said the voters had selected candidates outspoken on the need for civic improvements. The editorial said, "Henry Reuss and Frank Zeidler, nominees for mayor, now have the opportunity to give Milwaukee one of the cleanest and most informative campaigns in history," and then the editorial expressed its support of Mr. Reuss.

This same sentiment was echoed in a news story signed by a veteran *Journal* reporter, Lloyd Gladfelter.[66] In a report of the primary election, Mr. Gladfelter wrote, "The campaign from now until election day, April 6, promises to be one of the cleanest, most intelligent, and hard fought in the city's history. Both nominees indicated Wednesday that they would discuss the issues in a friendly manner and that there would be no 'mudslinging.'" This article also noted the vigorous campaigning Mr. Reuss and I did, even visiting small home groups in various neighborhoods as a means of reaching the people with a personal message.

In some of the news stories about myself, there appeared to be statements contradictory to what the editorials were saying about me. In a *Milwaukee Journal* news story of March 17, 1948, "One of These Will Be Mayor: Here Are Close-Ups of Rivals," the reporter said that although I was different from my brother, Carl, I possessed the same friendliness. It stated, "In sizing up the man Frank Zeidler, probably his most important characteristics are his friendliness, gentleness and moral courage," and that he is "a determined but not dogmatic thinker." This contrasted sharply with a later editorial attempt to portray me as a dangerous subversive. Mr. Reuss was favorably described also as one who blended study and action, a true observation.

The *Milwaukee Journal* of March 17, 1948, however, was not done with the matter of "Reuss versus Zeidler." It published a story, "Who Prodded Reuss to Run? Now It Can Be Told in Public." This article claimed that I had asked Henry Reuss to run. The article recounted the meeting we had in Mr. Raskin's office late in November to select a liberal candidate. In the summer of 1947 I had called on Mr. Reuss to find out if he would be part of a liberal slate. It was a friendly meeting, but I felt from the meeting that Mr. Reuss did not want to be too closely identified with my kind of liberalism and, as a matter of fact, he did not even want to be identified as a member of the Democratic Party. He was still making up his mind about the permanent cast of his political career.

All of these stories must have presented the voters with what appeared to them to be a confused situation with respect to the issues of liberalism and conservatism. Which of the two candidates was the liberal candidate and which the conservative candidate? Mr. Reuss' immediate backers were considered new liberals in the professions of law, public service and so on. Some of the real conservatives were therefore afraid of Mr. Reuss as being farther to the left than I was. On the other hand, I was a known Socialist who had joined forces with other long-time liberals. There was one further confusing issue—liberals were expected to favor government borrowing and going into debt and I favored what I thought was the real liberalism on this issue, namely the old Socialist principle of staying out of debt and keeping the city out of the hands of the bankers. Was this reactionary or liberal?

Apparently to dispel this indecision about the candidates the editorial board or management of the *Milwaukee Journal* is said to have issued orders to its staff writers early after the primary that in all news stories about the campaign Mr. Reuss' name would appear first with the word "non-partisan" afterward and my name would appear second with the word "Socialist." This would clearly identify Mr. Reuss as more conservative. This order caused some stir among the employees, some of whom objected, but the practice was followed to a great degree throughout the election. Members of the Municipal Enterprise Committee considered this unfair reporting. We could not object to the paper expressing its own editorial opinion, but we thought that it ought to treat the news as impartially as possible.[67]

The two main issues of the campaign began to be emphasized. One was the issue of the city going heavily into debt and the other was the issue of my Socialist background.[68] Mr. Reuss and I were substantially in agreement on most of our other programs.

In campaigning I stressed my belief that good liberal city government required staying as close as possible to the pay-as-you-go principle. This was a means of avoiding the waste of tax dollars on interest. I maintained that more public improvements could be obtained over the long run by staying away from debt than by going into debt. I objected to saddling future generations with a debt burden when they would have their own problems, and I stated that Milwaukee had enough cash on hand to meet the major improvements required of it.[69]

The *Milwaukee Journal* and Mr. Reuss took the position that Milwaukee needed so many improvements that it had to go into debt at once.[70]

To complicate matters, the existing Common Council had put six referendum questions on the ballot to borrow money for public improvements. The Common Council, in effect, had already cast the die to go into a program of borrowing. One of these questions asked for advice on borrowing $3.5 million for housing for veterans. Another dealt with a question of borrowing $2.5 million for slum clearance. Two more referendum questions asked for advice on borrowing for street widening. One question called for borrowing on parking projects and another called for borrowing $5 million for expressways. I took the position that in the absence of any direct budget appropriations for housing and slum clearance, both of which could not wait, I would support the expenditure of funds for these projects because the only other method of financing had been precluded by Common Council action. Borrowing for these projects was made unavoidable and was therefore the lesser of two evils, the greater of which would have been no housing program. The other issues were not urgent and could have been supported by direct levies. I did not favor borrowing for those projects.

Because of my position on taking the lesser of two evils, Mr. Reuss in a debate before the Milwaukee Young Democrats charged me with having changed my position on bonds. I replied that I had not changed my stand, but had been forced to a "second line of defense," because the Common Council had made no financial provision for housing and blight elimination. I asserted that these projects should have been jointly financed by a tax levy and use of the permanent improvement fund reserves.[71]

This position of mine provoked an editorial attack by the *Milwaukee Journal*. In an editorial entitled "Stand Still, Mr. Zeidler" on March 20, 1948, the *Journal* echoed the charge that I had switched positions on the public debt and claimed that I did not know where I stood.

While I was trying to meet the pressure of the issue of public debt, our Municipal Enterprise campaigners were discovering that the issue of Socialism was coming to the fore. It was necessary to meet the charge made against me that I could not cooperate with the Common Council. In a speech on March 19, 1948, I asserted that I could cooperate, and that I had worked well on the Milwaukee School Board with people of all shades of opinion. I charged that Mr. Reuss was now injecting a personal element in the campaign.[72]

Mr. Reuss and I participated in a radio debate on March 21, 1948, at radio station WTMJ, the *Milwaukee Journal's* own station. It was described by Edwin Bayley, *Journal* political reporter at that time, as the liveliest forum of the campaign. The issue of Socialism came up immediately after the opening statements of the candidates. Mr. Reuss on the previous day had said in a campaign speech, "My opponent's Socialism is the authentic Karl Marx variety. He thinks the city ought to be running the corner grocery store." A member of the radio studio audience then asked me if I thought the city should take over the corner grocery store.

"Emphatically not," I replied. "The corner grocery store is a business making a proper showing." I expressed my belief, however, that there must be government enterprise in housing and public transportation. Mr. Reuss countered by saying that public ownership of the utilities is not Socialism.

Mr. Reuss was asked by Russell Leitch, who was later to be a candidate for mayor in 1952, if he believed in the trends of the political party he belonged to, meaning the Democratic Party, and in the Americans for Democratic Action. Mr. Reuss declared that the Americans for Democratic Action, familiarly known as the ADA, was opposed to Communism. As to the suggestion that he belonged to the Democratic Party, he asserted it was not true. He was reported as saying, "When I returned from the Army, I was sent a membership card in the Democratic Party in the mail. I have many good friends among the Democrats, but I never paid dues or joined a ward organization. I have little control over incoming mail." Mr. Reuss apparently was not convinced either of the political potency of the Democratic Party in 1948 or of its essential liberalism. The party at that time still had some old guard elements who were to the right of Republicans on some issues.

When Mr. Reuss made his comments on the Americans for Democratic Action, to which he apparently belonged, I pointed out that the Socialist National Committee considered membership in the Socialist Party and the ADA compatible and not contradictory.

The discussion also revolved around whether people who supported public housing were supporting a Socialist position, and whether the Hoan administration was a good or corrupt one. I defended the Hoan administration, and I pointed out that former Socialists also were backing Mr. Reuss. The role of bankers in seeking to have the city leave the debt-free status was also debated.[73]

In order to further meet the issue of Socialism, which was now being fully raised in the campaign, I went to a campaign rally after the radio broadcast and there in a talk charged that Mr. Reuss was seeking to make Socialism "the phony issue of the campaign." I charged that my opponent was making a campaign of party labels and that he sought to divert the thinking of the citizens into emotional channels. I said that this type of campaigning would not aid Milwaukeeans in judging his platform. I pointed out that he also had Socialist backers and mentioned the roles these backers had played in the Socialist Party without mentioning their names. I stated that I stood on a platform that had appealed to all kinds of people. "They know," I said, "and the public generally knows that I will be a mayor for all Milwaukee, and that I will appoint the best qualified men and women to serve in positions of public trust. My record of impartiality on the School Board is evidence of this."

Then I said, "All that I ask from Milwaukee newspapers is that whatever they say in their editorials, they fairly and evenly present the opposing points of view in their news columns without giving either candidate preferred position or disproportionate space. They owe this in the spirit of fair play to the Milwaukee public." This statement, which Manuel Meyers and I jointly prepared and which I delivered in public, brought the issues into the open.[74]

The tempo of the editorial disagreements with my position now began to increase. On March 23, 1948, the *Milwaukee Journal* asserted that my fears about plunging the city into debt amounted to a bugaboo fading away because the city attorney, Walter J. Mattison, had said that the bond referendum questions were only advisory and that the city did not have to go into debt.[75]

The next day the *Journal* editorially attacked the respected City Club for also supporting a debt-free status for the city.

The issue of the origin of the terms "non-partisan" and "Socialist" were the subject of a story written by *Journal* reporter Lloyd Gladfelter on March 25, 1948. Mr. Gladfelter apparently was giving an explanation of the political situation that justified the use of "non-partisan" after Mr. Reuss' name and "Socialist" after my name in the *Journal* columns.[76]

The *Milwaukee Sentinel*, which had remained relatively quiescent in the primary and which was devoting its space to getting delegates for General Douglas MacArthur for the 1948 Republican convention, found the running issue of Socialism too much for a Hearst paper to ignore. It entered the campaign with an editorial on March 25, 1948, entitled "Milwaukee's Choice." This editorial stated that Reuss and I were intelligent, well educated, honest, vigorous and experienced in municipal affairs. Reuss, it stated, had a clean slate, free of the errors of the past. About me it said, "Zeidler is a Socialist. For years he has been the mainstay, the spokesman and the sparkplug of the Socialist Party of Milwaukee and Wisconsin."

The editorial said the Socialist Party was "an outmoded and discredited party, clinging stubbornly to the old Karl Marx dogma, which recently has become charged with new dangers." The city, this editorial said, survived Hoan without falling apart, but then he only preached Socialism; he didn't practice it. Frank Zeidler was different; the editorial alleged I was a practicing Marxist. "Twenty years ago a mayor like Frank Zeidler might have been a harmless novelty; today, with the world divided into two great camps, almost but not quite at war, he would be a constant threat to the safety of his city and nation." Henry Reuss, the editorial continued, believed in the American system, but Zeidler had no faith in it. "Zeidler would weaken America's hand in the hour when it needs greatest strength."

This outrageous, nauseating attack can only be appreciated when one looks at subsequent history. In 1960 when Mr. Reuss ran for mayor against Henry W. Maier, the *Sentinel* opposed Mr. Reuss and plumped heavily for Mr. Maier, whom it obviously regarded as the more conservative of the two. The *Sentinel* always had a corporate-state outlook on American politics, favored the big money interests, the militarists and the war party, and therefore could not tolerate a democratic Socialist, nor even a liberal Democrat.

The *Milwaukee Journal* did not quite get down to this level, but it did respond to my charge that the injection of Socialism into the campaign was a phony issue. In an editorial on March 25, 1948, the *Journal* listed a series of quotations of my speeches advocating Socialist measures and principles in government. The editorial asserted that the issue of Socialism in the campaign was valid.[77]

I sought to counter the charge that I was a menace to democracy as indicated in the two editorials of March 25, 1948. I spoke at a forum of the American Veterans of World War II along with Mr. Reuss. I pointed to the citizens who helped shape the platform on which I stood and asserted that this was democracy in action.

It is important to note here that the charge that I was a Marxian Socialist was not correct. I did not, nor do I now, subscribe to the theory of the inevitability of Socialism as described by Marx, nor to his kind of Socialism. I am and was a democratic Socialist who believed that freedom and liberty are important to all individuals and that public ownership and socialist controls are sometimes necessary to achieve the greatest freedom and greatest liberty for people.

Mr. Reuss apparently felt that he needed to make a stand on some issue of liberalism and proposed in a campaign talk that he would make the public transportation company, which was privately owned, pay for its use of the streets, an old Hoan Socialist issue.[78]

A surprising development then occurred. On March 26, 1948, there appeared the following news item in the *Milwaukee Sentinel* in six-point type, about the smallest they could use: "Al Hoffman and Joseph Weiss, president and secretary of the Independent Neighborhood Grocers Association here, said they were endorsing Zeidler." There was no better answer to the charge that I would socialize the corner grocery store.

The *Milwaukee Sentinel* did not like the looks of the trend of things apparently. It set one of its top feature writers and editorialists, a reporter whom many public officials then and later greatly feared, to attack me. William A. Norris wrote a two-column editorialized story saying that if the voters voted for me it would cost them $5 million a year because of my debt-free program.[79]

The remaining days of this campaign became something of a nightmare. The editorial charges began to come almost faster than I could answer them. The large number of forums, radio talks and the necessity of presenting fresh new ideas on a city program apart from the issues of Socialism and public indebtedness all taxed my strength and the efforts of the campaign committees. Under these attacks campaign workers nevertheless presented themselves in increasing numbers and the committees had to be organized to put their efforts to useful purposes.

Literature, hand cards and window cards had to be printed and distributed, for this was all that we had money for. Melvin Schneider faithfully accompanied me to meetings every night during the campaign, and sometimes we made five or six of them in one evening. Speakers were assigned to meetings that I could not attend. Often we ran into Henry Reuss at a forum or meeting and exchanged somewhat friendly greetings, for we grew to like him despite the heat of the campaign. It was like meeting an old opponent of one's high school track or football days.

The editorialists, however, did not let up. On March 29, 1948, the *Milwaukee Journal* felt it was necessary to answer the charge, which was now current among the people, that Mr. Reuss was the *Journal's* man. The editorial praised Mr. Reuss as clear-headed and stated that Zeidler, if elected, would result in four years of bickering at City Hall.[80]

On the same day the Milwaukee County CIO Political Action Committee announced it was unanimously endorsing Zeidler.[81]

In a meeting on the previous day, Mr. Reuss and I met at a forum of the American Veterans Committee. Both of us were subject to sharp and sometimes hostile questioning, but in the news stories it appeared that the AVC leaders were supporting Mr. Reuss. This may have served to give rise to a swiftly spreading rumor that Mr. Reuss was a "pink," a charge he later felt necessary to counter.[82] The AVC was a liberal group among veterans' groups.

The next few days Mr. Reuss and I spent discussing our methods of financing the city's improvement program and needs—good constructive campaigning. However, the *Milwaukee Sentinel* was preparing a particularly vicious assault, beyond the bounds of decent campaigning. On April 1, 1948, it published in a prominent place in the paper an article entitled "Zeidler Gets Red Pat on Back." This article was more in the nature of a display advertisement. It featured an enlarged copy of a Communist Party reprint attacking Mr. Reuss. Above the word "Communist" (in large type in the facsimile), my picture appeared with two arrows slanted alongside pointing to the word "Communist." Mr. Reuss' picture was printed opposite mine without such arrows. The text of the *Sentinel* editorial read:

> Milwaukee Communists have joined the old line Socialists in trying to keep Henry Reuss, non-partisan, out of the mayor's office. Below is a facsimile of a statement issued a few days ago by Communist Party headquarters. It shows that the Communists hate Reuss because he has denounced them, while they give Frank Zeidler a cautious pat on the back, believing that his Socialist theories run fairly close to their own party line.

I immediately reacted by a public speech in which I said my opponents were calling me a Communist to obscure their own attack on the city treasury. The Milwaukee Federated Trades Council helped me over this situation by endorsing me.[83]

On April 1, 1948, the *Milwaukee Journal* again praised Mr. Reuss editorially: "Reuss Will Get Things Done," the headline said.

The *Milwaukee Sentinel*, however, was not content with anything less than another strident editorial. On April 2, 1948, it printed an editorial entitled "Russia and Our Race for Mayor." This editorial said, "Henry Reuss, the non-partisan, is what might be called a moderate liberal. Frank Zeidler is a dogmatic, stubborn and conscientious Marxist Socialist." It added,

> Reuss' liberalism is well within the framework of our American democratic system. He believes in free enterprise, individual initiative and a vigorous but controlled capitalism.
>
> Zeidler's Marxist ideology places him close to the thin dividing line between radical, leftwing democracy, and Communist dictatorship. By the very nature of his Socialist theories, Zeidler is closer to Communism than is Reuss.
>
> And yet it is Reuss who has been called a Communist. It has not been done openly, but in a subtle, underhanded whispering campaign. . . .
>
> Zeidler himself is too decent and intelligent to have anything to do with it, but the same cannot be said for all of his followers and hangers-on. . . .
>
> In only one way can Communism be called an issue in this mayoralty campaign. If the election of either candidate would tend to weaken our traditional American system, to promote collectivism, to discredit capitalism, private property and individual freedom— then that candidate, as mayor, would sap some of America's strength in the ideological conflict between free-enterprise Democracy and Communism.
>
> The *Sentinel* believes that the election of Frank Zeidler would do exactly that.

The editorial pointed out that Zeidler believed in public ownership. "We repeat," it stated, "Frank Zeidler is no Communist, but in these dangerous times his Socialist collectivism would weaken our defenses against the collectivism of Stalin."

I always believed that this editorial was written to answer a possible lawsuit against them for the picture of myself with the arrows pointing to the word "Communist," which, incidentally, was in capital letters.

As the campaign stepped up, I became increasingly fatigued by the strain of the race and the same seemed to happen to Mr. Reuss. The editorials were particularly grievous to the spirit and would have been hard enough to take in normal conditions. It was a spiritual beating that I have never recovered from. I was to endure more of it from the press thereafter, especially from the *Milwaukee Sentinel* in the municipal campaign of 1956.

Because the burden of campaigning was more than the Municipal Enterprise Committee alone could carry, other campaign committees were formed. A youth committee, a veterans' committee and a group of non-partisans formed separate organizations to share the workload and to try to raise funds. Many loyal workers joined the campaign committees. The speed of the campaigning attracted the attention of the press. An account was written in the *Milwaukee Journal* of the pace Mr. Reuss and I had to keep to meet the requirements of the public.[84]

The almost overwhelming assault of both newspapers on my candidacy was most frustrating because I had no medium of public information to counter it. The newspapers had a right to their own editorial opinion; if I didn't like it I could print my own paper. That is exactly what we decided to do, just as we had done a month earlier for the primary. Once again, after a consultation between myself, Manuel Meyers, William Buech, Edward Matthes, Stanley Budny and others, we agreed that our only chance of winning was to try to answer all the charges made against the Municipal Enterprise Committee and myself in one issue of our own four-page campaign paper. Manuel Meyers again assumed the task of putting it together. He did a masterful job, reworking my public speeches and doing the major work on construction of an important editorial. [85]

The paper repeated the Municipal Enterprise Committee's views on public questions and my statements on the issues of debt, traffic, housing, culture and other issues. In addition, we featured an editorial, with my signature, taking issue with the way I had been treated in the news columns. We also ran a human interest story on how it feels to run for public office and be lambasted as un-American, as I had been by the *Sentinel*.

The editorial comment appeared in a special box above the publication's name, "The Voter's Digest." The title of the editorial was "The Election—and Milwaukee's Afternoon Newspaper." The editorial began, "Milwaukee's afternoon newspaper joined my position in requesting that this be the cleanest and most constructive campaign in the city's history." I then said I would keep my pledge. The editorial continued,

> Milwaukee's afternoon newspaper at times has fallen from the high plane of public discussion to one of personal attack. In all fairness to our city's afternoon newspaper, I must, however, ask the men on its editorial board if they do not realize the great harm they are doing to that newspaper's reputation for fairness in this community? Do they not recall they first suggested that this campaign be fought out *on the single issue of which candidate's program for the city was most worthwhile?*

The question was then raised as to whether the editorial writers knew of the protests of their own staff for interference with impartial handling and writing of news stories. I stated further, "If elected mayor, I shall look to people from all walks of life for constructive criticism and for suggestions for the proper conduct of municipal affairs. This includes editorial writers. I shall be fair with them and leave to their conscience whether they will be fair with me."

Our campaign paper further said that the fundamental issue was not who should be mayor but whether the judgment of six men on an editorial board, five of whom did not live in the city, should be substituted for the collective judgment of the people. The editorial concluded,

> The people of Milwaukee must recognize this threat to their sovereignty. No person or group of persons should aspire to a position of total power in a free society. A government can not be quitclaimed to an editorial board any more safely than to a Stalin or a Hitler. The broad diffusion of power and faith in the judgment of a free people is the only safeguard for democracy.

In an answer to the *Sentinel's* charges that I was a danger to democracy, there was an article that I drafted with Manuel Meyers entitled "How Would You Like to Run for Mayor, Folks? Here's Lowdown From a Fellow Who Knows." This article described how a man feels when he has to meet his wife after he is called a threat to the nation.

This editorial in our own campaign paper and the whole newspaper had a good effect. The paper was attractive, constructive and full of information. The folksy cartoons drawn by Erv Hess, who specialized in the American scene of the good old days, gave a nice flavor to the paper.

It was necessary to answer the *Sentinel* of April 2, 1948, which charged me with being close to the Communists. On the same day I spoke to a joint meeting of Locals 1053 and 309 of the Carpenters and Joiners Unions at Bohemian Hall in Milwaukee. I said, "I believe I yield to no man in Milwaukee on American principles. For years the Communists have bitterly opposed me. They fought me tooth and nail when I ran for mayor four years ago, and are endorsing neither candidate this election." I said that the Communists knew I detested and opposed dictatorship both of the Hitler and Stalin variety. They knew that I had spent my entire life fighting for freedom of speech, of the press and of religion.

It was announced on this same day that the Joint Council No. 50 of the Auto Truck Drivers Union, AFL, had endorsed me.[86]

The powerful effects of our campaign newspaper began to be felt in the newspaper office. The tone of the editorials became harder. In an editorial on the front page of the *Milwaukee Journal* on April 4, 1948, the paper charged that I had never held a position calling for administrative or executive ability and that I had done only theorizing and running for office.[87]

Mr. Reuss, about whom the charge had gone around that he was possibly a "pink," something more to be feared than being an open Socialist, declared that he was not a Communist or a Socialist. He also took issue with my campaign literature and denied that the news stories were slanted in his favor.[88]

On April 4, 1948, the *Milwaukee Sentinel* again made an editorial attack, using the line that I had changed my mind on public ownership, housing and other matters.[89]

The editorial pressure kept on, right up to the day before the election. On April 5, 1948, the *Milwaukee Journal* published two editorials, one on the front page and one in the inside editorial column, attacking me. The front-page editorial picked up the charge made by *Sentinel* writer William A. Norris that I would cause a boost in the tax rate.[90]

The inside editorial opined that I had done a perfect job of striking a martyr's pose.[91]

My response to all this was to fall back on the issue I had talked most about — getting more permanent improvements by not plunging the city into debt.[92]

The psychological and physical effect of this campaign was most tiring. Sometime after the primary, I felt completely unable to go on, but after treatment by a physician, Dr. S.E. Coffey, I regained enough strength to meet a few more radio engagements including the most important debate of all with Mr. Reuss on March 21, 1948, discussed earlier.

Campaign workers began to report that there was a favorable mood to be found among the people. The minds of the voters were beginning to shape into voting decisions. It looked as if victory were possible. However, I felt uncertain about the result and prepared messages for victory or defeat on election night, whatever might happen. I was prepared not to be unduly elated by victory, for I knew what a difficult time was ahead if I won, and I was not going to be unduly depressed by defeat.

On election day, April 6, 1948, the organization had a number of workers at the polls, but not nearly enough to man them as a more powerful organization might have done. The counting started as the polls closed after eight o'clock and the first election returns were inconclusive. Gradually I pulled ahead and about midnight it appeared that election was certain. I then appeared at a few radio stations to make my statement on victory in which I renewed my pledge for good government and thanked my workers. I met Mr. Henry Reuss in the editorial room of the *Milwaukee Journal*, where a radio broadcast was being made. He was very gracious. Both of us showed the physical effects of the beating we had taken in the campaign.

I then went to the Milwaukee Turners Hall where a number of campaign workers had gathered for a victory celebration. My father and mother, Michael and Clara Zeidler, came there with friends. They again showed some puzzlement as to how another of their sons had won the mayoralty of the City of Milwaukee. No doubt, the fate of their son, Carl, was in their minds, a tempering thought at this time. Many a worker talked to me about the problems of campaigning and I was most impressed by the number of people who sacrificed their time and effort for a cause of liberalism, of which I was the current symbol.

The Municipal Enterprise Committee had won a victory; the members realized the responsibilities they now faced of making good on their platform.

The final vote total was 124,029 to 97,277.

I had been elected to the office of mayor at the age of 35 years, as compared to the 32 years of age of my brother Carl when he was elected in 1940.

In the other citywide elections, no Socialists or former Socialists, or even members of the Municipal Enterprise Committee, were elected to any post. The other city officials were either liberal Republicans or conservative Democrats, and some of the conservative Democrats were far to the right of the liberal Republicans. I felt quite isolated except for three or four aldermen who were once Progressives.

Mr. Reuss in his message to me conceding my victory said, "Please accept my best wishes for a successful administration. I pledge you and the people of Milwaukee my continued efforts to make this a better city." This pledge he kept as a citizen, later as a Milwaukee School Board member and then as a Democratic member of Congress.

This narrative of a municipal campaign on the issues of liberalism and socialism cannot be concluded with the victory in the election. My election, more than Mr. Reuss' defeat, was grievous to the editorialists because they had made it such a personal thing. I felt I could expect no rest nor breathing space from the editors, but that they would press me immediately to show results. In this I was not mistaken. The *Milwaukee Sentinel* in a series of articles by William A. Norris warned me to go along with borrowing for public improvements. This disclosed to me that the issue for that paper was not to get Mr. Reuss elected, or perhaps even to get capital improvements for the city, but to see that such improvements were obtained through borrowed funds, so that the financial houses received their tribute.[93] The *Sentinel* said in its columns that the city had issued on me an order to this effect.

The deep division between myself and the *Milwaukee Journal* editors over this campaign never fully mended. On April 7, 1948, the *Journal* gave vent almost to despair in an editorial headline: "Only One Thing Counts—That Is the Future of This City." It stated, "No mayor of Milwaukee has faced more perplexing problems than now confront Mr. Zeidler," which was undoubtedly true up to that time.

On April 8, 1948, I resigned from the Milwaukee School Board with the congratulations of fellow board members. I pledged to them that my interest in education would not be neglected when I left the School Board. I carried out the pledge in supporting funds for new schools and aiding art education in Milwaukee. I also fought for educational television, for expanded vocational education, for adult education and for play spaces and playgrounds throughout the city.

To win an election, an individual has to have not only a well-run campaign but a certain amount of helpful breaks. Out of 15 candidates in the primary I was first on the ballot, an undoubted advantage. Although I did not own an automobile, a friend, Melvin Schneider, offered to drive me after working hours wherever I needed to go. The assistance of Manuel Meyers' advice was worth half the campaign. Harold Klitzke enabled us to employ rotary newspaper presses to good advantage in turning out our own campaign paper.

Mr. and Mrs. Stanley Budny's constant help and organizing ability in campaigning were unsurpassed in any other organization. The volunteer help of Max Starke and Pearl Esser made my primary victory possible. Milton Cohn and Mr. and

Mrs. Glenn Jirikowic managed one of the campaign committees. The help of Folke R. Peterson in writing radio talks relieved me of a great burden. The help of Louis Merz and Clement Stachowiak of the Machinists Union and Anthony J. King of the Plumbers Union proved invaluable. It was Arthur Urbanek who made and posted scores of campaign signs for election day, attorney Maurice Spracker who helped organize a non-partisan committee, Edward E. DeBriae who helped shape the platform and Edward Matthes who handled most of the finances. William Buech served as the chairman of the Municipal Enterprise Committee and its members worked many hours on all sorts of jobs.

The participation of each individual connects the candidate to them and helps shape his outlook and attitude toward issues that confront him in his job. It is from these people that a public official often draws advice and spiritual aid. The people who engage in a campaign by their very association with the candidate tend to help shape public policy later, because the candidate, when elected, thinks of what they think about his acts.

The campaign put a considerable strain on my wife Agnes and our six small children. It was a trying circumstance for them for their lives were much disrupted. Mrs. Zeidler helped in the campaign committees and also participated with me on radio programs in which we talked over problems of the government of interest to families. One of the factors that tended to dispel the charges of my being a menace to democracy was a picture published in the *Journal* of Mrs. Zeidler and myself walking on Second Street near our home with the six little children.

A public official comes out of a certain milieu and social background. He has developed loyalties and ideas of values that profoundly affect his decisions on matters of public interest. This fact was as true of me as of any other person ever elected to a position of responsibility and my subsequent actions reflected again and again the background of liberalism from which I had come. No matter how hard the press attacked me, I could not desert the principles and values of liberalism I had acquired in the previous years, and my campaign was unique only in that I was a member of the Socialist Party running on a liberal platform. I was a member of a political group that had found it almost impossible to win election to public office in recent years despite the splendid record of municipal honesty of Socialist officials.

We started with ideals and a mimeograph machine. We had no paid workers, except that Manny Meyers received a small amount for his masterpieces of campaign papers. We had no professional publicity agents, we could not mount razzle-dazzle campaigns, we could not afford billboards. We did have tested liberals, we knew our city and its people, we had speakers, we had the issues and we had the resources of information, so that the charges made against our platform and program could be answered. But above all we had ideals and the philosophy of liberalism that caused our fight for the people against the special interests to take on the nature of a crusade for better government and a better city.

A candidate is really a team of people, for whom the candidate is the spokesman. Without the help of Melvin Schneider, I could not have gone to the meetings as I needed. Without the help of Stanley Budny, who organized the circulation of nomination papers and the distribution of literature, I could not have been nominated. Without the help of Pearl Holzknecht Esser and Max Starke, we could not have maintained our headquarters. Without the help of Edward Matthes, we would not have been able to keep our limited financial resources working most effectively. Without the help of John Schupp and later Sig Zarning, we could not have organized a south side headquarters that was essential to our success. Without the help of Manuel Meyers, we could not have handled our press commitments. Without Harold Klitzke's advice, we could not have created presentable literature. Without Louis Merz and Clem Stachowiak, we could not have gained labor support. Without Maurice Spracker, we could not have gained non-partisan liberal support, and so the list grows.

As the campaign went on, hundreds and hundreds of people helped whom I cannot expressly name here with my thanks for I still would do injustice by omitting some names and some deeds.

If I had one regret it was that my opponent was Henry Reuss who subsequently demonstrated himself as a great national liberal and a man of progressive views, but the campaign possibly drew public attention to his ability and made his later election to the Milwaukee School Board and to the Congress more feasible.

NOTES FOR CHAPTER 1

1. Accounts of municipal officials include a book by Carl Lorenz, *Tom L. Johnson, Mayor of Cleveland* (New York: Barnes, 1911); Ernest H. Crosby's *Golden Rule Jones* (Chicago: Public Publishing Company, 1906), an account of Samuel Milton Jones, mayor of Toledo; and *Robert W. Speer, A City Builder* (Denver: Denver Common Council, 1919). These were reform mayors. Daniel W. Hoan, long-time Socialist mayor of Milwaukee, produced a volume, *City Government* (New York: Harcourt, Brace, 1926). Fiorello La Guardia, mayor of New York is the subject of a book by Ernest Cuneo, *Life With Fiorello* (New York: Macmillan, 1955). It is widely alleged that Mayor James Curley of Boston is the basic character portrayed in Edwin O'Connor's book, *The Last Hurrah* (Boston: Little, Brown, 1956).

2. Much of my information on economic and political issues came from the small Clybourn Street branch library of the Milwaukee Public Library. This library at N. 35th Street and W. Clybourn Street in the Merrill Park area of Milwaukee was a source of help to many young unemployed persons in the early 1930s. I was one of the unemployed. This library served to lead to the greater collection of volumes at the Milwaukee Public Library. The library was my university and I have had a profound gratitude for it since. The books of Norman Thomas, Harry W. Laidler and Kirby Page especially influenced me during the formative years of 1930 to 1937. Among these books, as I remember, were the following:

   Norman Thomas:
   After the New Deal, What? New York: Macmillan, 1936.
   America's Way Out. New York: Macmillan, 1931.
   As I See It. New York: Macmillan, 1932.
   The Challenge of War. New York: League for Industrial Democracy, 1924.
   The Choice Before Us. New York: Macmillan, 1934.
   Human Exploitation in the United States. New York: Frederick A. Stokes, 1934.
   The Socialist Cure for a Sick Society. New York: John Day, 1932.
   War: No Glory, No Profit, No Need. New York: Frederick A. Stokes, 1935.

   Harry W. Laidler:
   American Socialism — Its Aims and Practical Program. New York: Harper and Brothers, 1937.
   A History of Socialist Thought. New York: Thomas Y. Crowell, 1927.
   A Program for Modern America. New York: Thomas Y. Crowell, 1936.
   The Road Ahead. New York: Thomas Y. Crowell, 1932.
   Socialist Planning and a Socialist Program. New York: Falcon Press, 1932.
   Unemployment and Its Remedies. New York: League for Industrial Democracy, 1931.

   Kirby Page:
   Capitalism and Its Rivals. New York: Eddy and Page, 1936.
   Individualism and Socialism. New York: Farrar and Rinehart, 1933.
   Must We Go To War. New York: Farrar and Rinehart, 1937.
   National Defense. New York: Farrar and Rinehart, 1931.
   A New Economic Order. New York: Harcourt, Brace, 1930.
   War: Its Causes, Consequences and Cure. New York: George H. Doran, 1923.

3. The Socialist slate in 1910 in Milwaukee included Daniel W. Hoan, city attorney; Carl P. Dietz, comptroller; and Charles B. Whitnall, treasurer. Hoan later became mayor of Milwaukee for 24 years, from 1916 to 1940. Dietz was an alderman for many years until 1948. Whitnall became famous as a planner and park commissioner who helped establish Milwaukee County's park system.

4. Hoan defeated Mayor G.A. Bading by a vote of 33,863 to 32,306 on April 4, 1916.

5.   Hoan was re-elected in 1918 and again in 1920 when the terms were changed to four years. He was re-elected in 1924, 1928, 1932 and 1936, always in a hotly contested election and usually by a close vote. The newspapers roasted Hoan probably more than any other Milwaukee mayor, but he survived them in office until 1940. They never forgave him, although at the time of his death in 1961, a new generation of editors of the *Milwaukee Journal* had mellowed in their views about him.

6.   Julius Heil, a colorful Teutonic Milwaukee industrialist, was re-elected governor against Orland S. Loomis, the Progressive candidate. In the race for state treasurer, I received 382,237 votes—far more than I ever received again, but also far short of election. The winning candidate, Smith, a Republican, had 616,425 votes; Ringle, a Democrat, had 245,911 votes; and Schnarsky, Independent Socialist Labor, received 2,574.

7.   The newer Progressives with a Socialist background favored the principle "Production for Use." The ballots of the vote are preserved at the Milwaukee Public Library in its files of the Socialist Party.

8.   The Progressive Party voted to go out of existence in a convention at Portage in March, 1946. See "GOP Merger Approved at Portage Meet," *Milwaukee Journal*, March 18, 1946. Senator Robert M. LaFollette, Jr., apparently felt that his chances of re-election were better in the Republican column than in the Democratic column. His principal hurdle was the Republican primary, which he must have felt he could win.

9.   In my opinion the biggest personal force operating to pull the Progressives into the Democratic Party was Assemblyman Robert Tehan, later state senator and still later federal judge. His appealing personality and his recruiting ability were the biggest factors in attracting Progressives, former Socialists and liberals of all types into the Democratic Party to ultimately turn it into a winning organization.

10.   Alderman John L. Bohn was elected president of the Milwaukee Common Council in a dramatic public session at the Milwaukee Auditorium on April 16, 1940. The inauguration of Carl F. Zeidler was held in this large public building with thousands in attendance. The Federationists (members of the Farmer-Labor Progressive Federation) cast their votes for Alderman Carl Dietz on the first ballot, and then switched to Alderman Bohn, alderman of the 23rd Ward, a south side ward. The first ballot vote was Harry Devine, 12; John Bohn, 8; and Carl Dietz, 7. Fourteen votes were needed for election. These votes, added to the votes of other south side aldermen, were sufficient to defeat Alderman Harry J. Devine, alderman of the 16th Ward, Alderman Bohn's rival. Alderman Devine was a bitter foe of the Socialists and later the Federationists. Alderman Bohn had not incurred the enmity of the Federationists to this extent.

11.   The only existing evidence of this platform is a typewritten sheet I prepared. A copy of this sheet is in the Milwaukee Public Library. The party issued a campaign paper, but the distribution was poor.

12.   A good account of this amortization fund is contained in "Financing Local Government" in Daniel W. Hoan's *City Government* (New York: Harcourt, Brace, 1936).

13.   *Milwaukee Journal*, January 21, 1944, carried the information that Mayor Bohn included support of a debt-free program in his official position.

14.   "Zeidler Urges Housing Work," *Milwaukee Journal*, March 3, 1944.

15.   *Political Action*, October 8, 1910. *Political Action* was a Socialist newspaper published weekly at 344 Sixth Street, Milwaukee.

16.   The vote totals in the 1944 municipal primary for mayor were as follows: John L. Bohn, 31,837; John A. Seramur, 21,488; Herbert L. Mount, 20,636; Frank P. Zeidler, 20,374; George S. Mann, 2,275; and Arthur H. Schroeder, 1,504. Mayor Bohn, Mr. Seramur and Mr. Mount were all qualified men. I carried several wards, but was so heavily defeated in Milwaukee's east side Gold Coast wards that I could not catch up to the other candidates' vote totals.

17.   The totals: Bohn, 79,516; Seramur, 67,531.

18.   They were Supervisor Walter F. Hintz, Frederic Heath and George O. Strehlow. Other Socialists or Progressives were beaten. Heath was an early co-founder of the Socialist Party in about 1898 with Victor L. Berger, later Socialist congressman from Wisconsin.

19.   The vote in the primary for United States senator in Wisconsin in 1946 was as follows: McMurray, Democrat, 62,631; LaFollette, Republican, 202,557; McCarthy, Republican, 207,953; Stearns,

Republican, 29,608; Knappe, Socialist, 3,673. This was the election that brought Joseph McCarthy, a former Democrat, to office as United States senator and set off a string of political calamities for the nation. Liberals will always argue over this election in Wisconsin as to whether the defeat of LaFollette was due to his re-entry into the Republican Party instead of the Democratic Party, or to the vote taken from him by Stearns, the other Republican, or to the opposition of the Communist wing of the CIO, or to the opposition of the *Milwaukee Journal*. A factor more important than all of this is the fact that McCarthy gained more votes in the traditionally Democratic county of Milwaukee than LaFollette. In the city of Milwaukee alone, McCarthy led LaFollette by a vote of 35,037 to 28,176 as compared to the vote of McMurray, the Democratic candidate, which was only 25,848. In the general election, McCarthy led McMurray by a vote of 106,346 to 91,088 in the city. It was apparent that the right-wing Democrats had moved over into the Republican column to elect McCarthy, and this was the basic reason for his success.

20. In 1942, the Milwaukee Journal Company, in cooperation with the City Club of Milwaukee, published a program for the city entitled "How to Make Milwaukee a Better Community in Which to Live." The program advocated elimination of the city debt, no more bonds, permanent improvements to be financed by cash and a definite tax rate for permanent improvements.

21. Hoan, op cit, pages 156-173, "How a City May Completely Emancipate Itself from Banker Influence."

22. Samuil Nissenbaum died July 7, 1947.

23. "Tell Expenses in Bond Drive," *Milwaukee Journal*, April 5, 1947.

24. The vote totals of those elected to the Milwaukee Public School Board of Directors in 1947 were as follows: Frank P. Zeidler, 62,265; John F. Westphal, 61,093; Martin C. Baumann, 56,107; Margaret Conway, 51,983; George Hampel, Jr., 45,403.

25. See *Common Council, City of Milwaukee, Journal of Proceedings*, November 21, 1938, p. 1089, File Number 62907. This is a report by the Buildings-Grounds-Bridges Committee on Housing under the Wagner-Steagall Act. The report proposed that a housing authority be created only under the express conditions that the project would be occupied by families on relief and that the Milwaukee County Department of Outdoor Relief would guarantee necessary rentals. It also proposed a revolving fund under the building inspector to lend for improving substandard buildings and asked that the matter of cooperative housing be studied.

26. At the time of this writing in 1961, the dilapidated buildings with minor repairs to them are still standing. They are for the most part now in the path of a proposed expressway interchange.

27. The rejection took place on February 2, 1948, in the midst of the municipal campaign. See "Council Votes Death for Red Arrow Homes," *Milwaukee Journal*, February 3, 1948. The group proposing the development project was known as the Milwaukee Urban Redevelopment Corporation.

28. Victor L. Berger, 1860-1929, was the giant of the Milwaukee Socialist movement. His role as organizer, editor, teacher and dominant personality in the Socialist Party have been well chronicled. See Edward J. Muzik, "Victor Berger's Early Career," *Historical Messenger* of the Milwaukee County Historical Society, March, 1961, for an introduction to this greatest leader of the Socialist movement in Wisconsin. Subsequent Socialist leaders merely built on the organization that Berger had constructed. Most of us were not able to enlarge it and merely tried to hold it together. None of us who followed Berger possessed his organizing genius or his ability to inculcate his followers with an almost religious and fanatical devotion to the Socialist movement. None of us could or did try to become as dominant as he was.

29. Milton J. McGuire was elected as alderman of Milwaukee's Third Ward in 1936 and continued in this position until 1956 when he was a candidate for mayor and was defeated. It was thought that he did not stand for re-election as alderman of the Third Ward in 1956 because he did not want to challenge Alfred C. Hass, alderman of the First Ward. The Third Ward and First Wards had been redistricted and both aldermen found themselves in the same new ward, the new Third Ward. Alderman McGuire was president of the Milwaukee Common Council from 1942 to 1956 and was almost absolute boss. He was a principal spokesman for the large business interests in the community and had close ties with many business and corporation leaders. In 1960 he was appointed deputy city treasurer by City Treasurer Joseph Krueger for the purpose of establishing

liaison with the Common Council. In such a position McGuire was again able to dominate the trends of local government.

30. Copies of this call can be found at the Milwaukee Public Library. This call was mimeographed as was most of the literature of the Municipal Enterprise Committee and its successor, the Public Enterprise Committee. Printing had become almost too costly for so small a group. The call was signed by Stanley Budny, then manager of the Milwaukee Turners and a painter by trade. The call is entitled simply "A Call for a Meeting."

31. This statement is also in the files of the Public Enterprise Committee at the Milwaukee Public Library.

32. Penciled notes of the minutes of this meeting are in the files of the Public Enterprise Committee. William Buech, an insurance man, was chairman. Stanley Budny was secretary. Those attending included Wendelin Kraft, a tavern keeper; Arthur Urbanek, a city employees' union business agent; John Brodde, a machinist; Walter Uphoff, a sociologist and teacher in workers' education, but at this time a farm operator; John Schupp, an appliance store owner; John Ritter, a machinist; Milton Cohn, an attorney; Julius Drozewski, a machinist; Walter Bubbert, a landscape architect; Robert Gratz, an attorney; and Edward Guenther, occupation unknown to me.

33. "Reuss Asserts His Candidacy," *Milwaukee Journal*, November 30, 1947.

34. "City Socialists in New Move," *Milwaukee Journal*, November 30, 1947.

35. "Liberals Split in Mayoralty—Reuss, Zeidler Disagree on Policy, Coalition Attempt Choked Off," *Milwaukee Journal*, December 1, 1947.

36. "Reuss Begins Mayoralty Drive: Gives Program," *Milwaukee Sentinel*, December 2, 1947.

37. This part of the editorial really stung; I was 35 years of age and did not really consider myself a hackneyed public figure yet!

38. "New Milwaukee Group Opens Fiery Campaign," *Milwaukee Journal*, December 4, 1947.

39. "Liberal Group Meets: Talk of Zeidler Race," *Milwaukee Journal*, December 7, 1947. The subhead is "Former Socialists Play Big Part: Platform is Drafted; Seek to Gain Labor Support."

40. See "Mayor Bohn is Out of Race Officially," *Milwaukee Journal*, January 18, 1947. Also "Not Running Hoan Insists—Mayor Candidacy Papers Drawn Without His Permission," *Milwaukee Journal*, January 19, 1947. In this article Hoan said that a friend of his, Charles Boyd, had drawn nomination papers for him without his permission. See also *Milwaukee Sentinel*, February 8, 1947, reporting that Dan Hoan had consented to run after his friends called on him in a body.

41. The final decision for me to stand took place in a meeting of the Municipal Enterprise Committee on December 20, 1947. About 50 people attended this meeting.

42. "No Slate for Zeidler Group," *Milwaukee Sentinel*, January 4, 1948.

43. "Maier Argues with Zeidler," *Milwaukee Journal*, December 1947.

44. "Red Arrow Housing Stirs Bitter Wrangle," *Milwaukee Journal*, September 25, 1947.

45. "The Builders and the Wreckers," *Milwaukee Journal*, February 5, 1948, editorial.

46. "Red Arrow Housing Stirs Bitter Wrangle," *Milwaukee Journal*, September 25, 1947.

47. These minutes are in the files of the Public Enterprise Committee at the Milwaukee Public Library.

48. These were honorable men of tried and tested liberal persuasion. I had the pleasure of their association for many years before and after my terms in public office. Edward E. Matthes died November 22, 1954.

49. See "Reuss Flares at Charge of 'No Program,'" *Milwaukee Journal*, April 5, 1948. In an exchange in a debate, Mr. Reuss said he had a definite program. I claimed that Mr. Reuss in his own literature asserted that he did not have one.

50. A list of some of the endorsements is to be found in each of the two campaign newspapers that were printed and circulated by our committee in the campaigns. Both of these papers were named "The Voter's Digest." One appeared a week before the primary of 1948 municipal elections and one appeared a week before the election itself.

51. *Milwaukee Journal*, February 18, 1948.

52. *The Voter's Digest*, April, 1948. Copies of this campaign paper are at the Milwaukee Public Library.

53. "Fleming Club Won't Reveal Financing," *Milwaukee Journal*, February 2, 1948.

54. On February 29, 1948, the *Milwaukee Journal* published a table of items giving the candidates' views on the issues of the day. All agreed on the need for veterans' housing and all but one candidate agreed on the need for slum clearance.
55. The *Milwaukee Journal* of February 25, 1948, reported a series of campaign activities of the candidates and gave some idea of the tenor of their attacks on each other as well as some idea of the candidates' positive proposals.
56. "One of These Will Be Mayor: Here Are Closeups of Rivals," *Milwaukee Journal*, March 17, 1948. In this account there is a reference to the episode involving Mr. Hoan's candidacy.
57. See *Milwaukee Journal*, "Stalling on Redevelopment," January 27, 1948, editorial; "Hypocrisy, Housing and Blight," January 30, 1948, editorial; "Aldermen Who Prefer Blight," January 30, 1948, editorial.
58. "Council Votes Death for Red Arrow Homes," *Milwaukee Journal*, February 3, 1948.
59. "Deplore Death of Red Arrow," *Milwaukee Journal*, February 4, 1948.
60. "A Record Tax Rate," *Milwaukee Journal*, December 7, 1938. This was an editorial against municipal housing.
61. "Zeidler Defends Views," *Milwaukee Journal*, February 18, 1948.
62. "To Know Each Other's Problems," *Milwaukee Journal*, February 23, 1948, editorial.
63. "The One Question on Mayor," *Milwaukee Journal*, March 1, 1948.
64. The following *Journal* editorials were written in behalf of Mr. Reuss: "One Man Stands Out in the Race," March 3, 1948; "Qualifications of Henry Reuss," March 5, 1948; "What Henry Reuss Stands For," March 12, 1948; and "Henry Reuss and Leadership," March 15, 1948. It is interesting to note that when Mr. Reuss ran for mayor in 1960, after fine service in the United States House of Representatives, the paper did not give him one favorable editorial. It had changed its mind about him.
65. The paper was *The Voter's Digest*, March, 1948.
66. "Zeidler, Reuss Are Nominated for Mayor," *Milwaukee Journal*, March 17, 1948, signed by Lloyd Gladfelter.
67. One of the early articles with this type of reporting was "Zeidler, Reuss Give Views on Issuing Bonds," *Milwaukee Journal*, March 18, 1948. The headline used my name first but the article used the phrases "Henry S. Reuss, non-partisan" first and "Frank P. Zeidler, Socialist" second. I have no doubt that the editorial writers sincerely believed that the growth of a democratic socialist movement posed a great danger to the city, and this was one of their methods of arousing the public against that possibility.
68. Not only did this issue crop up in a *Journal* editorial on the day after the primary, but on March 19, 1948, Mr. Reuss stated that Milwaukee must not move backward by turning the City Hall back to Socialists. See *Milwaukee Journal*, March 19, 1948, "Prevent Old Wrangling at the City Hall—Reuss Sees Milwaukee Progress Stalemated If Socialist Wins: Zeidler Backs Merit System." I was talking on constructive issues and was not yet aware of what was in store for me on the issue of Socialism and liberalism.
69. A sample of my views and Mr. Reuss' views on the issue of borrowing and public indebtedness can be found in the following news accounts: "Policies Told by Candidates," *Milwaukee Journal*, February 20, 1948; "Issues on Bonds for Street Paving Raised," *Milwaukee Sentinel*, March 10, 1948; "Reuss, Zeidler, Give Take at Forum Event," *Milwaukee Journal*, March 25, 1948; "Rebuild, Reuss Plea; Zeidler Talks Cost," *Milwaukee Journal*, March 29, 1948.
70. "Here Are the Issues Between Mr. Zeidler and Mr. Reuss," *Milwaukee Journal*, March 17, 1948, editorial.
71. "Mayor Nominees Agree on Two Bond Issues," *Milwaukee Sentinel*, March 19, 1948.
72. "Zeidler Denies Reuss Charge," *Milwaukee Journal*, March 20, 1948.
73. "Reuss and Zeidler Argue on Socialism," *Milwaukee Journal*, March 22, 1948. See also "Reuss, Zeidler Voice Stand: Fire Pot Shots," *Milwaukee Sentinel*, March 22, 1948.
74. "Zeidler Raps Phony Issues—Assails Mayoral Rival for Making a Point of Socialism," *Milwaukee Journal*, March 22, 1948.
75. "Zeidler's Bugaboo About Plunging Into Debt Fades Away," *Milwaukee Journal*, March 23, 1948, editorial.

76. "Non-Partisan Vote Set-up is Outgrowth of Fusion—Old Parties Merged in City Elections While Socialist Continued to Act as a Unit," *Milwaukee Journal*, March 25, 1948.

77. "The Record Mr. Zeidler Made," *Milwaukee Journal*, March 25, 1948, editorial.

78. "Make Transport Company Pay for Street Use, Reuss Asks," *Milwaukee Sentinel*, March 26, 1948.

79. "Zeidler to Cost 5 Million a Year," *Milwaukee Sentinel*, March 28, 1948, front page story by William A. Norris.

80. "Why We Support Mr. Reuss," *Milwaukee Journal*, March 29, 1948, editorial.

81. "Zeidler Given CIO's Backing—Reuss and the Journal Raising False Issue of Socialism, Charge," *Milwaukee Journal*, March 29, 1948.

82. "Reuss, Zeidler Survive Foes' Sharp Queries," *Milwaukee Journal*, March 19, 1948.

83. "Raps 'Communism' Cry," *Milwaukee Journal*, April 1, 1948.

84. "Candidates Must Travel Fast in a Mad Whirl to Keep Dates," *Milwaukee Journal*, April 2, 1948.

85. *The Voter's Digest*, April, 1948.

86. "Zeidler Tells Stand on Reds," *Milwaukee Sentinel*, April 3, 1948.

87. "Here's the Choice Which the Voters Alone Can Make," *Milwaukee Journal*, April 4, 1948, editorial.

88. "Reuss Blast at Pamphlets—Hits Zeidler's Philosophy," *Milwaukee Journal*, April 4, 1948. See also "Reuss Rakes Collectivism," *Milwaukee Sentinel*, April 4, 1948.

89. "Frank Has Changed . . ." *Milwaukee Sentinel*, April 4, 1948.

90. "A Boost in Tax Rate to Hit Home Owner if Zeidler Wins," *Milwaukee Journal*, April 5, 1948.

91. "Tomorrow," *Milwaukee Journal*, April 5, 1948.

92. "Zeidler Talks About Bonds—Opposed 'Long Term,'" *Milwaukee Journal*, April 4, 1948.

93. "Where Now Milwaukee?" *Milwaukee Sentinel*, April 18-20, 1948.

Chapter 2
Serving as Mayor

When I became mayor in 1948, Milwaukee faced a number of serious problems that were common to many American cities toward the end of the 1940s and well into the 1950s. One of the most pressing problems arose from population expansion in the metropolitan areas.

The housing supply of the cities was seriously deficient because of the years of the Great Depression and because of war shortages. In the years following the war, the urban housing problem became a key issue in municipal elections. In the cities of the nation, liberal and progressive younger men were elected to the office of mayor because they promised to do something about the housing problem.[1] Across the country, there was strong interest in the issues of public housing and new national housing legislation.

Accompanying the housing shortage in the nation was a shortage of public works needed to cope with a population expansion. There was a great need for municipal public works such as water purification and street paving and widening. The veterans' families, doubled up in cramped housing quarters, could be accommodated in new areas only if there were new sewer and water lines, new roads, new schools, new fire stations, new electric and gas utilities and many other types of public construction needed to keep a city operating.

The veterans' housing problems were aggravated also by the fact that many of the veterans lived in temporary houses, quonsets, prefabs and other types of shelter that needed early replacement. In an effort to cushion the effects of the housing shortage, rent control existed in many places. Naturally, there was a concerted drive by landlords to eliminate rent control.

Inside American cities subtle changes in living patterns were taking place that required changes in public plans and policies. One of the most important changes was the flight to the suburbs by middle-income people as well as upper-income people. This flight was already evident in the 1940 census and it was greatly accelerated after World War II. This flight was promoted not only by the proliferation of the motor vehicle but by the hard-surfaced road and the electric power line. Many people found it more attractive to move to the open spaces of outlying areas than to live in the cities, which had become so congested during the streetcar era.

This outward movement left the lowest income families in the center of the cities. The population in the central cities therefore tended to become smaller and poorer. The core of the cities began to decay because many of the families could not pay enough for good shelter for themselves, nor could they supply the necessary purchasing power to keep the central business district thriving. As middle-income people moved out of the center of many cities, those people were often replaced by minority workers who had migrated from rural areas and who had only a precarious hold in the urban job market.

With the flight of many middle-income people from the central cities of metropolitan areas, the more upscale merchants departed also. Shopping centers appeared in outlying areas in such quantity, size and attractiveness as to hasten the decay of the central business district. As if this were not bad enough for the tax base of the central city, industries also moved out to newly incorporated suburbs where taxes were lower because school and municipal costs were lower.

School shortages became evident as the mounting birth rate resulted in more and more children presenting themselves to the schools for education. The need for the expansion of health, welfare and sanitation services increased with the increasing population and with the rising standard of living demanded by the citizens. An increase in prices and the demanded increase in public services brought a greater strain on the public treasury. These increases forced a rise in many types of taxes, but especially in property taxes, the mainstay of city government finances.

The continuous inflation also brought about a certain amount of labor unrest as the demands of labor increased with price increases, and as price increases occurred after labor settlements.

An enormous burden that attracted more attention than housing and redevelopment was the complex of urban problems caused by the rapid increase in ownership of private vehicles. The streets were too crowded and too narrow. There was not enough parking. The streetcars were impeded by automobiles. The central business districts were congested. A serious winter storm could completely tie up a city. The taxpayers, however, resisted paying for enough public improvements to meet the needs of the vehicle.

Not the least of the cities' problems was the fact that the cities had entered the age of the atom and we now faced the potential destruction of cities by atomic bombs.

These matters were among the issues I had to concern myself with in an inaugural message to the Milwaukee Common Council. But before writing a message I had to get a staff organized.

The staff of the mayor of Milwaukee was quite small. It consisted of an executive secretary, assistant secretary, an office secretary and a police officer. Folke R. Peterson, who had been an executive in show business, became my secretary. He was a Progressive. Stanley Budny, my long-time friend, consented to be assistant secretary. Mrs. Catherine Burgett, office secretary to Mayor John L. Bohn, continued in her position. Detective John F. Hanley, the only detective I knew on the police force, and one of the best, agreed to serve as police officer in the mayor's office. He replaced Eugene G. Einem, Mayor Bohn's police officer, who was elevated to detective for his faithful service.

Selecting a mayor's staff was not an easy task. The people chosen had to be suited for their tasks, and various civic and social groups had to feel satisfied with the selections. Many civic groups felt it necessary to have someone close to the mayor's office in order to feel that they were welcome with their problems or complaints. This situation produced a certain amount of pressure for the elected official, but it also provided benefits. The same individuals who came to the mayor's office transmitting the requests of social groups for recognition, legislation or protest also can make known the mayor's views to the group they represent. This is a system of personal communication which helps keep the mayor aware of what is happening outside of City Hall. A mayor who makes access to himself too difficult may fail to accurately gauge the state of public opinion. He courts political trouble because he is poorly informed. Fortunately the individuals who joined me in the work of the office represented a background that included small business, labor organizations and different geographic sections of the city, as well as many civic and fraternal organizations. It was as fine a team that I had to help me as any mayor ever had.

After the selection of a staff, several appointments to important boards and commissions were due immediately. I made every effort to keep my campaign pledge to see that all appointments were based on merit. As a result, some of the appointments went to individuals who had endorsed other candidates in this intense election but who had demonstrated their capacity to serve the public. Some of my own friends were dubious of such appointments. My opponents expected I would take revenge. Revenge was a common practice for those who won elections, but it was not a practice I would follow. The future problems were always more important to me than past grievances, which elections had a habit of making out of date.

Between April 6, 1948, and the date of the inaugural, April 20, 1948, I had to help wind up the affairs of the various campaign activities, make the necessary appointments and prepare an inaugural message. The tremendous fatigue of the campaign returned and I should have permitted myself a rest. Instead, I drove myself to meet the tasks because I faced a hostile press that I knew would look for any sign of deficiency and weakness on my part. Almost immediately the press was inquiring as to what I intended to do about the housing shortage now that I was elected. Driving myself in this way I now feel was a mistake, for I never really recovered from the initial fatigue of the election or from the spiritual beating I took from the editorial attacks of the press.

There were many congratulatory and other messages from citizens that needed replies. One of these letters was from a corner grocer. He wrote that he had voted for me but he really wanted to know what my position was on the subject of putting the city in the grocery business. He reminded me that Daniel W. Hoan, the former Milwaukee mayor and a Socialist, had engaged in selling produce after World War I in an effort to bring down high prices.

The sudden volume of correspondence forced me and my assistants to make adjustments at once. These matters were handled and I began to compose an inaugural address. I typed a rough draft and then cut down the verbiage to a compact and tightly worded message.[2]

The inaugural message called for coordination with county and regional plans. In housing I at once touched on the sore point of Milwaukee politics. I asked for money to start building two public housing projects, Northlawn and Southlawn, so that they could get underway by July of 1948. The planning had been curtailed by the previous administration. I asked for 600 new housing units for another project to be commenced shortly thereafter. This number of units was a relatively small amount, but even these small projects produced the greatest of all conflicts between the liberals and the conservatives in government. The issue of better housing was to be the central issue of my 12 years in office. It brought to the fore another issue, that of equal opportunity for various races in housing. This latter issue became the single most difficult problem I faced and continued after I left office.

In the inaugural message I asked local governments to build permanent housing instead of temporary housing. I requested that the city government give private builders every assistance in acquiring land and in getting utilities in place. This request was an indication that the city was about to begin a stepped up program of annexation of lands for new housing sites for private builders. This program also provoked much controversy in the succeeding decade.

My message offered support for the national Taft-Ellender-Wagner housing bill, which was enacted into law the following year and which became the basic law for all subsequent housing developments in urban areas.

In supporting redevelopment I suggested two methods by which the bond funds voted by the citizens could be used. One method was to assemble parcels of land in a blighted area for group sale, and the other was to use a lot-by-lot "infiltration" in neighborhoods that were only partially blighted.[3] I also asked for progress on a better building code.

For recommendations on traffic, I asked for the creation of a metropolitan transportation agency at the next session of the state Legislature. This subject also proved controversial during the entire period of my stay in office because it meant to many people public ownership of the transportation system. I also called for a transportation survey on the economic cost to the city of abandoning street railways, which paid taxes, for other types of transportation, which did not. My message also called for development of a rapid transit system—an idea that was later rejected by the Milwaukee Common Council. I also recommended the hiring of traffic engineering consultants to develop a coordinated transportation system. I asked also for the creation of an expressway system, segment by segment, so that each segment would be usable before the whole system could be completed.

On the subject of capital improvements, which was one of the major issues of the previous campaign, the message called for a revised six-year program of improvements that would fit the budget requirements. Coordination between city, county and school requests for public expenditures was recommended. Without such coordination, each legislative body asking for its own expenditures would produce a total that the property taxpayer would find too high. This coordination never really became effective during my entire time in office. As a result, over the succeeding decade each unit of government went deeper into debt trying to finance its own program of capital and physical improvements irrespective of what other units were asking.

The shortage of cultural projects in Milwaukee following the Depression and the war years had to be overcome. My inaugural message proposed to support a war memorial, a sports arena, a new main public library, a new museum, a new zoo and a new stadium. Some of these projects were being supported by civic groups in Milwaukee as projects for completion by county government. I proposed to lend the city's support to all projects, whether the construction was to be carried out by city government or by county government. All of these projects ultimately came into existence. The museum was commenced only after ten years of tedious community controversy with much opposition from property taxpayers.

On the controversial subject of labor, I pointed out that labor had reached a position of great responsibility in the community and I welcomed it to greater participation in public affairs. I also pledged that the city government stood ready to assist in the solution of industrial conflicts on a fair basis. There was later plenty of opportunity for city government to become interested in labor problems of many companies, as well as its own labor disputes.

In order to have a well-nourished industrial development, the inaugural message called for more land near rail tracks—the industrial park idea. It also called for a greater diversification of industry. Milwaukee was known as the city of brewing, but it had many other types of industry and it needed newer and more advanced types. In the message, I also expressed a need for efficiently trained and highly skilled artisans who were the basis of any great technological development and this meant encouragement of vocational and technical schools. This program was backed up later by my continuous support of the Milwaukee Vocational School (later the Milwaukee Area Technical College) in its building expansion, its assumption of the responsibility for educational television and in its curriculum expansion. I also gave encouragement to the universities in the area.

In two brief paragraphs in the message, I pledged support of the consumers' interests in public utility matters. To many hardcore conservatives, this brief statement rang an alarm bell in loud tones; privately owned utilities must not be mentioned at all except to support their demands. I also asked for a municipal food terminal, but this was never created because of opposition from certain cold storage warehousemen who dominated the state Republican Party and prevented favorable legislation from being enacted.

In regard to the tax problem, the message called for a special committee of public officials and citizens to prepare a comprehensive report on revenue sources and needs. Such a report was made shortly thereafter by a committee under Professor Harold Groves of the University of Wisconsin. The report provided the basis for confidence in the ability of the city to expand its territory as well as improve the quality and quantity of service. I called for larger portions of shared revenue from the state, but this situation never did materialize sufficiently to meet the city's annual deficits that resulted from borrowing.

I made a comment on city "housekeeping" in my inaugural message. I said I would conduct regular meetings with the major department and bureau heads. Such meetings were faithfully held every month for 12 years. The meetings were most productive in obtaining cooperation and a team spirit among the city's administrative officials.

My message asked for an administrative survey. This survey request was ultimately adopted. Out of 1,000 recommendations made by the survey a savings estimated at upwards of $2 million a year occurred in administrative organization and methods.

I supported the expansion of an existing interracial committee to include the broader field of all human rights. The committee's objectives were ultimately broadened. Unfortunately the Milwaukee Commission on Human Rights became a harassed committee despite its indispensable work in keeping community social relations moving in a progressive manner.

The inaugural message acknowledged the previous nationally recognized achievements in health, police, fire protection and public safety that stemmed from the Hoan administration. I promised to keep these levels of achievements and the record was kept. For several years Milwaukee had led the cities of its class in traffic safety. The Milwaukee Police Department was internationally known for its efficiency and integrity. The city had the best fire insurance record and the Milwaukee Health Department was a pioneer in public health service.

Milwaukee, once known as the "Athens of the West," had slipped culturally. Its wealthiest families, with but two exceptions, did not make any major contributions to the public in the form of libraries, museums, art galleries or other cultural buildings. I promised to give official encouragement to cultural objectives. The wealthiest families, however, kept to their pattern of not making grand contributions to major cultural improvements. They certainly would not change their ways for a liberal or Socialist mayor.

There was a brief comment in the inaugural address about the problem of city life in a troubled world where city-destroying weapons had lately come into existence. Shortly after this inaugural address, the Milwaukee Civil Defense and Disaster Committee was created at my call. I devoted much time over the next 12 years to studying the problem of how urban life could be more safely organized in the age of nuclear weapons.

The inaugural address offered specifics on implementing the Municipal Enterprise Committee platform. It has been said that the first effort of a public officeholder should not be to fulfill his platform pledges but to get re-elected. My first effort was to carry out what was in the Municipal Enterprise Committee platform and what I believed was good for the people of the city.

The position of mayor, important as it is, is often in the last analysis subordinate to the position of the city council or legislative body. In Milwaukee, the election of the Common Council was somewhat obscured by the struggle over the mayoralty. The more important of the two categories of elections was probably that of the Common Council. Unless it was progressively minded, the measures of progress would not get passed.

The Common Council that was elected chose for its president Alderman Milton J. McGuire, who represented the Third Ward.[4] Alderman McGuire had a philosophy most conservative in character and he was strongly in support of the large private enterprises, which in turn reciprocated with support of him. Although we were friendly personally, it was apparent from the beginning that there would be a division on philosophy of government between us. This division showed up many times over measures of progress such as in housing, education, utility regulation and other matters. Our differences finally culminated when Alderman McGuire and I made the race for mayor in 1956 in what proved to be a bitterly contested campaign, largely involving the race issue and political extremism. The corporation heads backed the alderman who appealed indirectly to racially prejudiced voters and to what I considered the McCarthyite element in Milwaukee politics.

Before the inauguration I called upon and paid my respects to the retiring mayor, the Honorable John L. Bohn. Ours was a simple talk as I recall it. We talked about housing, expressways, traffic, parking and a new stadium. Mayor Bohn pointed to the mayor's chair and said that was the "wired seat." He pointed to the walls and said, "Sometimes you think they have ears." He then stated that he controlled his own date book so that the pressure of office would not get out of hand, and he confessed some displeasure over editorial writers who had attacked him.[5]

Also before taking office, I made an appointment to see the editorial board of the *Milwaukee Journal* to tell them face-to-face what my objectives and policies would be. I went to call on this body of men in their conference room in the Milwaukee Journal building. I was accompanied by Harold Klitzke. The meeting was not particularly hostile, but neither was it especially friendly. It was a polite meeting and in it I repeated some of the objectives I had stated earlier in my campaign. What good this

50

meeting may have done, I do not know. The editors reserved their opinions, as they of course must until they can judge performance.

The inaugural on April 20, 1948, was a restrained one. The position of mayor looked too uncertain and the problems too great in view of my political isolation, but I nevertheless had greater confidence then in my ability to meet these problems than I had after some subsequent experiences with seemingly unsolvable social problems. After I took the oath of office at high noon, I went out to lunch with some of the campaign workers, and went back for afternoon inaugural ceremonies. The ceremonies were in the council chambers, which were small for the crowd of people to be admitted. I still felt fatigued from the campaign and I did not know if I had strength to get through the rather extended inaugural address, but it went along in good fashion.

The families of the other elected public officials were present including the city attorney, Walter J. Mattison, and the treasurer, Joseph J. Krueger. The elected comptroller, William Wendt was not present due to illness and his deputy Virgil H. Hurless was in his place.[6]

My family was also present. It took some doing for my wife to get our six children there. They ranged in age from eight to one year and I hoped they would keep very still. This part of the program worked out well. This family of six small children had been a factor in helping dispel the attempts by the newspapers to portray me as a kind of political demon. When one of the newspapers published a photograph of my wife and me with six small children in plain garb walking down the street, the charge of menace to democracy evaporated in the minds of those who saw the photograph.[7]

The inaugural day was memorable for one thing especially. It was the first time in Milwaukee that such a ceremony was televised. The glare of the television light still burns in my mind. The municipal campaign had been conducted by public meeting, by press release and by radio. Henceforth, the greatest opinion-forming medium for voters would be television. The candidate who could not afford it or who could not create a proper impression on television was lost. No longer would the bellowing voice in the large hall or the smooth radio presentation be the attributes of the winning candidate. It would be the television personality – not even his ideas or views – that would be the factor upon which people decided their votes. The sheer cost of television time practically doomed all third parties to defeat because they could not command the wealth of either business or labor for campaigning.

The situation that confronted me after inauguration was typical of the situation of most American mayors under a non-partisan system. The responsibility for failing to carry out a political program rests with the mayor, but not the credit for advancing it. The mayor can recommend, he can agitate and he can educate, but he cannot initiate legislation. If he is not a party boss, the mayor is dependent on the city council to initiate proper legislation for advancement, although the mayor may have large powers of recommendation. In this sense, the council is more important than the mayor. A liberal or progressive mayor cannot overcome an unprogressive council.

With this knowledge, I felt the only practical course was to encourage the Milwaukee Common Council to move along the path of liberalism without trying to force the aldermen to produce that which they deeply opposed. An early example of successful agreement with the Common Council involved two housing projects for veterans. It was not long before these projects, begun under Mayor Bohn's administration, were underway. Fortunately there was a community momentum at that time for public and veterans' housing with which a majority of the Common Council agreed. These two housing projects were financed by the City of Milwaukee without federal aid. The city contributed one-third of the cost and borrowed two-thirds from an insurance company. The two projects created a total of 580 units.

As I mentioned earlier, it is quite customary in party elections for the victors to exact revenge by ousting the political supporters of the losers. If these people cannot be fired outright, the trick often used by the political winners is to claim the need for reorganizing government and then to reorganize the departments or agencies in which opposition people can be found. I strictly eschewed any such tricks, and I determined to work with substantially the same department heads, appointive heads and boards and commissions as my predecessor to get on with the work. While I did not choose to reorganize departments, I still had many opportunities to remove full-time appointive heads. One of the reasons that I did not desire to change was that I knew most of these agency heads. They were decent and knowledgeable people who only needed encouragement to produce an effective program. Many of them, it is true, did not support me, but I decided to take the existing machinery that was in city government and move ahead with it. This was the speediest method to produce immediate benefits for the city. In this decision I was not mistaken. The existing machinery produced results as effectively as possible under the conditions the city found itself, especially as far as housing and urban renewal were concerned.

Moreover, it is highly important for an elected official that the top civil servants be utterly honest. An elected official can get into trouble very quickly with appointive heads who become involved in malfeasance in office or who engage in practices that, while not illegal, arouse the public dislike because they are considered on the borderline of dishonesty. I was very fortunate in that none of the major appointments I made to full-time public positions ever caused this embarrassment. Of the hundreds of appointments I made to boards and commissions, only one ever became involved, as far as I know, in public trouble, and this was minor.

Some of the major reappointments I made were originally made by my brother, Carl, when he was the mayor of the city. These appointments included Dr. E.R. Krumbiegel, the able health commissioner of Milwaukee, and Walter H. Swietlik, as honest a commissioner of public works as ever presided in any city in the nation.

I made it known to public employees that I would back them up in their duties and I avoided reprimanding them in public. If I had a difference with one of them, it was discussed in as friendly an atmosphere as possible. The differences were relatively few. One or two top civil servants had a kind of contempt for my views and background, but this was tolerable if they did not allow their contempt to interfere with the city's program.

As I promised in my inaugural address, I instituted a monthly meeting of departmental heads. These meetings gave each department head an idea of what I was thinking, and in turn I got an idea of what they were thinking. If an important program was being carried on, the department head in charge had a chance to explain it to the others with the beneficial results of better cooperation and better understanding. Not the least important was the fact that the heads of city departments felt they could come and discuss their problems with me for recommended courses of action. My door was always open to them.

The ordinances and customs of the City of Milwaukee demanded that the mayor sit as chairman of the Board of Estimates, which handled certain financial matters before the Common Council received them, such as the preparation of the budget. The mayor was also chairman of the Central Board of Purchases, which was a unified purchasing agency for all city departments. This board was created prior to my administration not only to save money, but to prevent graft. Milwaukee's Central Board of Purchases was never involved in any type of scandal during my entire 12 years in office. It was a strict and careful operation. It saved millions upon millions of dollars by its purchasing practices, which insured honest and competitive bidding under standards set by the board. Joseph Nicholson, another long-time civil servant, was a most scrupulous and efficient city purchasing agent.

I presided over these boards as well as the newly created Civil Defense Committee. This pattern was followed for my entire time in office. Some may state that the mayor sitting at such boards was a waste of time. Or some may state the contrary, but unless these matters of expenditure of city funds are carefully watched by the mayor, he will have much more trouble making explanations when things go wrong. The graft in purchases, the payroll padding and other similar matters that have involved the mayor's offices in other cities simply did not occur in my administration. This was not particularly appreciated by the hostile press, but I was glad of it for my own sake. During my time in office, there was some dishonesty and irregularity in government but it involved other elected officials over whom I had no administrative control.

In most city governments, there is usually a kind of strongman among the full-time civil servants. Such a man existed during most of my administration. He was George C. Saffran, the budget supervisor of the city. Mr. Saffran had been the deputy city comptroller under William Wendt, the comptroller, but a dispute arose in which Mr. Wendt discharged Mr. Saffran. Mr. Saffran claimed that another employee below him in rank had worked on the comptroller to make him dislike Mr. Saffran enough to get him discharged. Whatever the reason for the discharge, the members of the Common Council of the previous administration had found Mr. Saffran so valuable to them that they created the post of budget supervisor. In this post he was the advisor and guide to all councilmen. His advice was solid. He was capable. He could take issue without arousing too much animosity, and he had a great genius for effective organization. He and I had different political opinions—I am not sure if he ever voted for me—but he cooperated very well and was something of a liberal himself except with the city funds. These funds he required to be strictly handled, and he was a very effective team worker. A task given to him would be accomplished efficiently with a minimum of friction. He was in effect a kind of administrative manager much of his term, which was concluded by death shortly before I left office.[8]

The mayor is not only a chief administrative leader, but he also must serve as a political leader. There is an observation about local government that must be made here. At times in various cities of the nation, local government does not exist for the benefit of the people, but for the benefit of the political clique in power. The clique will dominate a party, and the party will dominate the city. Under such conditions, improvement in the city is not made because it ought to be done or because it is good for the people. It is done because the party boss of the ruling clique thinks it is good for him and his followers. A street is not paved because it needs paving. It is paved either because it gives work to party henchmen, or because it gives work to a grafting contractor who kicks back money into the party till, or because if the street is not paved it will become a political issue to be used against the party. This may also be true even of a health department, which in some cities is largely used to give employment to ward henchmen of the party who are quite unqualified as public health workers.

There would be none of this in my administration—not from myself and not from anyone I appointed to city government. No one should allow a city to be staffed with incompetent workers. During the campaign, when the newspapers were charging me with a Socialist machine, I said that the appointment of able and qualified people to positions in city government was "the cornerstone of good municipal administration." I stated, "If elected mayor, I shall base my appointments on ability, integrity and concern for the public welfare. Our citizens have the right to expect the best in our public officials, and I shall rigidly follow the merit system."[9]

In carrying out this pledge, I encountered people who chided me for not rewarding some campaign workers. I would point to this pledge, but this did not ease the hurt of those who struggled for liberalism in government and then saw conservatives and opponents of mine who could qualify under civil service get the jobs. I stayed with this pledge. Some have stated that this was the reason I never had a strong political organization. The Municipal Enterprise Committee (later the Public Enterprise Committee) never really was numerous or powerful in a machine sense. Certainly in the 1956 municipal election when I was running against the powerful Alderman McGuire, few of my appointees would come out and support me publicly. Some worked against me because they thought McGuire with his large financial backing and strong newspaper support would win. In this campaign I had a hard time getting six people together to help me initiate the campaign. Even the top civil service people, whose commission I had strengthened, and whom I had protected against the spoils system, I felt were somewhat hostile. I do not regret, however, having stayed with the merit system as a means of meeting my obligation to the people of the city, and in the long run it was better for the Public Enterprise Committee, for its members did not desert it after I was out of office.

The Socialist Party was very feeble during my administration. Not one single public employee that I know of asked to join the party. I continued to work with the party organization. In fact, I did much of the secretarial work personally, including typing letters, running the mimeograph machine and acting as office secretary. The members were mostly too advanced in years to do the work. I would not bring this work into City Hall but did it myself on Saturday afternoons and during vacations. Stanley Budny, the assistant secretary in the mayor's office, helped after hours and did as much of the work as I did.

Our main vehicle of reaching the people was the Municipal Enterprise Committee. This committee met every Saturday afternoon after the election until summer. After about July, 1948, it met in an open public meeting once a month. At each meeting there would be a public speaker on some city, county or state matter. At each meeting, too, I would report on my activities and on the problems that local government faced. Then I would be questioned by the members. They would make comments and criticisms and express their views. If they did not approve of what I did, they said so. This was a wholesome experience and is as valuable as any method for keeping an elected official's feet on the ground. When public officials start talking only to each other in a tight little clique, as so frequently happens, they move far away from what the public is thinking.

The newspapers never warmed up to the Municipal Enterprise Committee. This committee was a group of people who dared make public pronouncements independent of the newspapers, and the editors appeared not to like it. If the action of the committee was mentioned, the committee was derided as being composed of my personal camp followers. Actually if any of the editors had participated in the meeting, they would have discovered that the members, far from being dominated by me, had their own views and expressed them. The Municipal Enterprise Committee was a kind of public conscience. The committee later changed its name to the Public Enterprise Committee to encompass more opportunities to speak about county and state matters as well as about municipal matters.

The Public Enterprise Committee, as successor of the Municipal Enterprise Committee, published platforms in 1950 and 1951.[10] The 1951 platform was used in the 1952 municipal elections. It published a platform late in 1955 for the 1956 elections.[11] It also published a platform for the 1960 elections.[12]

In each case, except the latter, I declared my intention of running for election only after a platform was adopted. In 1960, my health was beginning to fail and I declined to stand for office before the 1960 platform was created. A platform was created nevertheless. Henry S. Reuss, our Democratic congressman at this time, who had become a candidate for mayor in 1960, approved the platform, which was similar to his own rather comprehensive and practical platform, and he received the endorsement of the committee.[13]

He was not elected, and the man who won, Democratic State Senator Henry W. Maier, naturally became a bitter opponent of the committee.

The Public Enterprise Committee also published platforms for Milwaukee County in 1955[14] and 1959.[15] These were the only comprehensive platforms that had ever been published for Milwaukee County. The committee also published platforms in two School Board elections—1959[16] and 1961.[17] How much effect these platforms had is difficult to say, but the committee was fulfilling its avowed function of preparing a comprehensive citizens' governmental program. The organization also published a monthly bulletin of comment called "The Public Enterprise Record."

One curious fact is that the committee published around 1955 an extended itemization of each plank of all the previous platforms and what happened to them— whether they were carried out or not.[18] This was the first detailed self-appraisal by a local political group that was put out into the open, as far as I know. The document, however, never was extensively used because the mass of detail was almost too much to digest, even for a scholar.

In making about 300 appointments to boards and commissions, I decided on several principles. One was that I would appoint an individual competent to do the job. It is not good for a publicly elected official to appoint a person who is a campaign supporter if that person cannot do the work and will get himself and his appointing officer into trouble. Further, appointees were encouraged to show initiative of their own. They were expected to be "self-starters," using their own abilities to meet problems and devise acceptable answers to difficulties the board encountered. I did not want to have to solve every problem for every individual on every board and commission—only the ones that seemed unsolvable. The appointed officials were expected to facilitate the work of their boards. This meant they had to have good judgment and originality. Such individuals also had to have demonstrated leadership in some organization where I could have had an opportunity to observe it.

I would not appoint members to boards and commissions who were fundamentally hostile to the work of the board or commission. I would not appoint any individuals to the Milwaukee Commission on Human Rights who believed in racial discrimination. Many organizations chided me for not giving them representation on housing and redevelopment authorities where they could impede progress. I would not set the fox to watching the geese.

Another principle I followed in making appointments was to avoid a conflict of interest. An individual may have been knowledgeable about a subject such as real estate practices, but I would not appoint him to a board such as the Planning Commission or the Board of Zoning Appeals if he wanted to get favors for himself and his friends. The same condition was true of appointing lawyers to the fire and police commission, or representatives of the tavern or brewing industry to that commission. I was on a constant watch for the possibility of conflict of interest. In a few appointments made by my predecessors where the conflict of interest developed after appointment, I did not make the reappointment. This brought recriminations.

Still another principle I followed was to try to get a spectrum of various types of knowledge on a board so that the members could reinforce each other's work. At one time on the Board of Public Land Commissioners, I appointed a lawyer, a realtor, an engineer, an architect, an investor, among others, to give a rounded-out "team."

Yet another principle was that of trying to get a cross-section of the community that represented economic groups, geographic location, civic and social groups, ethnic groups and political parties. It was my purpose to have as many people as possible feel that they and their groups were represented somewhere in government.

Urban life tends to stratify into various types and groups of people. An easily identified stratification is economic stratification. The rich tend to live near each other. The working people live in other neighborhoods. I could have made every single appointment to every board and commission out of one ward in Milwaukee, the 18th Ward, which includes the wealthiest families and also many people with the highest academic and professional training. There was always a tendency to look to this area for leadership in civic activity. This was a tendency that had to be resisted. I therefore looked into the working-class neighborhoods for leadership also. In some of the working-class wards it was almost impossible to find a community leader sufficiently qualified to serve on certain types of citywide boards due to the professional and technical stratification that had occurred in Milwaukee.

I appointed Republicans and Democrats and people of no party affiliation alike. Occasionally, if I made a Socialist appointment, the non-partisans in the Common Council would reject him solely because he was or had been a Socialist.[19]

The extreme conservatives in the Democratic Party and the Republican Party were my enemies as demonstrated in the 1956 election campaign, but there were enough liberal Democrats and liberal Republicans from which to choose community leaders. I believe that if a party wins, it is not in the interest of the social or political order to permit that party to engage in a Roman victory—the annihilation of all opposition. It strengthens democracy to allow minority representation in government, even if the minority finds it difficult to compromise on anything. There is a limit, however, to encouragement of opposition in government. I do not believe in encouraging extremists or absolutists.

I was satisfied with the way the appointees proved themselves when these principles were in operation. In making appointments I would review the composition of a board or commission and determine what was lacking in order to achieve well-rounded representation. Sometimes the boards were constituted very well and the person whose term was expiring was able and qualified. I would then make a reappointment. If not, I would get a list of names of individuals who might have the proper qualifications. After investigating the character and qualifications of any prospective appointee, I would make an appointment.

The replacement of an incumbent appointee was always difficult. It was the custom in my office not to summarily dismiss anyone, but to explain the problem the office was trying to meet, and to commend the previous appointee for his service. Sometimes such appointees were given other assignments. Sometimes the appointees were allowed to make their own decision as to the time in which they would want to retire. We tried to have all retire with honor. Stanley Budny, who later became the executive secretary, succeeding Folke R. Peterson, was a most tactful man who could discuss in a dignified yet friendly fashion the problems of new appointments and old appointments. I was most grateful to him.

The replacing of appointees is always somewhat painful, even though the replaced appointees had displaced someone else before them under similar circumstances and could also expect to be replaced. We tried to keep as many appointees as possible and to select new ones whose merits were so outstanding as not to have to be replaced in the middle of their term. Of the hundreds of appointments made, this problem of making a replacement within a term occurred only once and that was in connection with a major policy question on civil defense. The city and I were most fortunate to win the consent of such high caliber people to accept appointments.

The mayor has another task to perform. City Hall is the biggest single news source to the modern urban daily newspaper. The world may be on fire, war and strife may be occurring in remote parts of the globe, but to the people at home, the uncollected garbage in the alley, the collision on the next corner and the trouble on the school playground are more important facts of life. The people are interested in what the local authorities are doing about problems like these; hence every action at City Hall is followed closely by the press.

It was my policy to talk freely and openly with the press reporters, even those of the *Milwaukee Sentinel*, which was almost continuously hostile to me and whose stridency against me in the 1956 municipal election was unparalleled in Milwaukee's history. The reporters could reach me at any time. I accommodated them with such news as I had because I knew that they had deadlines to meet and also because the City Hall reporters were usually overloaded with assignments.[20] I never gave them a "no comment" on any subject as far as I can remember. I always tried to find something that I thought appropriate to say about all public issues, even if the only remark I made was that I did not think the subject they asked me to discuss was in my competence or field.

Usually I had opinions about things or I stated that I would certainly look into a subject to form a judgment about it one way or the other. The expression of "no comment" shows a lack of leadership and original thinking. I believe that citizens need and deserve a constant expression of leadership on municipal problems. The clearly expressed views of public officials are vital to good government. Many officials wait to see what public opinion is going to be so that they can gain a protective coloring by adopting it. A mayor should have the knowledge and experience to be able to pronounce a more informed judgment on municipal problems than the average citizen and should not wait to find out first what the people think in order to follow their lead.

Often I would read of some other municipal body or a study committee or the Legislature taking some action that I thought was hostile to the interests of the city. In the very next issue of the press I would make an extended comment expressing how the city's interest in the controversy appeared to me. Sometimes hostile views against the city would be advanced on Saturday morning when there was no staff at City Hall. I would not let such views get set in the minds of the citizens over the weekend without offering an alternative or a challenge. This sometimes meant that I would go to the newspaper's office myself and type out my own comments to appear in the Sunday morning editions.[21]

I also kept the newspapers fully informed of the progress of all major city activities, good or bad. No newspaper could ever say that they ferreted out information that the mayor's office was trying to conceal. This open policy was distastefully regarded by most other public officeholders. With some newspapermen, I was held in contempt because I made things so easy for the City Hall reporters. This was to them a mark of softness, not a sign of cooperation. However, I believed in the right of the public to know and I fought for this right, trying also to practice it myself.

The afternoon paper, the *Journal*, would call me for its stories early in the morning before I had gone to work; the morning paper, the *Sentinel*, would often reach me about eleven o'clock at night. This made for a long day.

I must say this for the City Hall reporters, they were almost all uniformly trying to be fair, not trying to wreck me or anyone else, but merely trying to do a good job for their papers, whatever their editorial directors thought. Hale Champion, Ed Bayley, Robert Houlihan, Lloyd Gladfelter, Norman Herington, Merrick S. Wing and John W. Kole were the principal City Hall reporters of the *Milwaukee Journal* whom I got to know quite well. Many others, men and women, were assigned to the City Hall run from time to time. Only one of the reporters from this paper I felt was hostile and skeptical because he did not believe that I was as above-board as he had heard. A fatal illness, unfortunately, seized this young man in the prime of life, and I never had the opportunity to change his impression.

Sentinel reporters on the City Hall run included Howard Bell, Trueman Farris, Joe Boyd and Roy Foley, who were honorable and decent men. One older *Sentinel* reporter, William A. Norris, who was given a broad range of propaganda assignments, became my implacable and bitter enemy. He was given leeway to write special articles to harpoon my program from time to time if he could. Needless to say, while he was a formidable antagonist, greatly feared by many public officials, he did not cow me. On one occasion, when he was attacking my annexation policies by writing editorials and columns, I invited him before a Common Council committee to explain his views and I read his own record of writings in which he had advocated annexation. He was most uncomfortable except behind his typewriter.[22]

Because of the open policy on press releases, and because most of the releases were accompanied by verbal comment instead of carefully slanted and formulated statements long agonized over, a full-time press secretary was not necessary. Instead, the job of assistant secretary was broadened to handle duties such as liaison with the Common Council, applications for appointments, cases of complaints, meetings with civic groups and the affairs of visiting dignitaries, among many other tasks.

It was not enough, however, to rely solely on day-to-day news developments to impart information on city policy to the people. I felt it necessary to speak to the various public and civic groups who were doing good work in the community, not only to explain my program, but also to encourage them in their work. This, I believe, is one of the most important functions of a city head.

Talk and ideas properly expressed in talk are vital to the world in which we live. The position of mayor is not just that of an administrator. It is a position of leadership expressed in words and in deeds consonant with those words. If the mayor does not furnish leadership, the vacuum of leadership in the community will be filled by a party boss, by an individual operating from the motives of self-interest or by some usually undesirable private or semi-secret agency.

I therefore for the first year as mayor accepted as many engagements as I reasonably could. I spoke to business organizations, to trade unions, to foreign language societies, to minority groups, to parent-teacher organizations, to street merchants' groups, to professional groups. Many requests had to be turned down because of lack of time, of course, but I managed to make many hundreds of talks ranging from a few words to speeches of some length. I had to reach the people for their own sake and to prevent the hostile editors from creating a negative impression of me.

After the election I was invited to a civic meeting of hundreds of representatives of the foremost industries of the city at a rather elaborate dinner. I was not uncomfortable in their presence, but I could see that these men moved in a stratum of society into which I had never entered. The affluence represented, the richness of garb and the mentality of competition were elements of a social milieu that was foreign to me as I had struggled most of my life to have enough work to keep going even for a short while. I did not envy this group, nor begrudge them their success or affluence. They were part of a different social sphere in which the organization of men to produce competitively for monetary returns was the prevailing objective and greatest value in life. As I remember it, the talk I made at the dinner on this occasion was complimentary of the companies being honored and quite brief.

Brief remarks, to the point and having some substance, were my objective in most public talks. When this information became known, the invitations increased in number.

I accepted many opportunities to speak to foreign language groups at their picnics or winter meetings and festivities. I felt this was necessary for the cause of democracy. If the mayor of the city comes to a foreign language organization, the people feel tied to the cause of democracy. They feel assured of themselves as being welcome additions to America because they have been told they are such by the mayor of the city. If they are turned down in their request, they feel snubbed or unworthy and may thus develop an attitude of hostility.

I was rewarded culturally by making such appearances. Not only did I get to know many fine men and women, but I also absorbed some knowledge of the culture and history of various nations and people. This was most fascinating. Folk dances, folk tunes and special music that I might never have had an opportunity to enjoy I found within the boundaries of my own city.

Among the groups whose cultural activities I learned to appreciate were people from Greece, Sicily, Italy, Croatia, Slovenia, Serbia, Slovakia, Bohemia, Swabia, Bavaria, Poland, Hungary, the Ukraine, Latvia, England, Scotland, Wales, Russia, Denmark, Norway, Sweden, Israel, Mexico, Canada, Lebanon and the Philippines. All of these lands had sent sizeable contingents to Milwaukee. Groups of people from these countries had formed to preserve the culture of their homeland or a particular region. To some of these groups I spoke many times. If I were to visit each of these lands, I would recognize something of my own city in them.

The lesson that I learned from this is that the American tradition is a fabric formed of many threads bound together by the ideals of equality of peoples and by brotherhood. This is a lesson the world needs to learn.

Some of these groups produced capable natural leaders who, in half a generation, had absorbed enough of American democracy to be able to serve well in elected offices and on appointed boards and commissions of local government.

The perpetuation of these groups, however, presented some difficulty for the older people because the public school system of America had a powerful effect on the children, often more than the family. The children, especially in the high schools, became so Americanized as to identify themselves not with the ancient homelands of their ancestors, but with their high school and its social environment. This was a good thing in many respects, but also it tended to diminish the value of some of the priceless cultural aspects of their heritage, particularly fluency in a language other than English.

The business of the mayor serving as chief ceremonial officer of the city was a most enjoyable one, but one which might tend to take away too much time from the other business. Street openings, groundbreaking ceremonies and ribbon cuttings were especially frequent in the construction season in Milwaukee from March to November. The beginning of a useful public project such as a bridge or a waterworks is always a source of satisfaction to those who fought for its creation and the groundbreaking ceremony is an appropriate way to note the victory and to inspire new achievements.

The mayor is official greeter to visiting dignitaries. In some of the nation's larger cities, this is a highly important and time-consuming task. In Milwaukee there was enough of this activity, but not so much as to distract from other vital business at hand. For example, it was a great privilege to be present at the opening of the various functions commemorating the creation of the St. Lawrence Seaway, including the occasion of the first ship of larger tonnage to enter the Milwaukee harbor.[23] The greetings of various young women such as Miss Hawaii, the Maid of Cotton and persons representing other promotional activities provided the City Hall press photographer with interesting photo shots of the young ladies.

One civic greeting I remember well involved a Milwaukee trade union that was playing host to a delegation of German trade union members about 1949. During this period, the United States government brought in many foreign visitors from Germany to Milwaukee, probably as a means of giving them a chance to see democracy in action. This delegation was taken by the Milwaukee union to one of the city's famous German restaurants, which featured an excellent, even sumptuous, cuisine. I sat next to a German worker from one of the banks.[24] He had fought with the German army in the Ukraine and had lived for many months among the Ukrainian people so that he learned to know their habits. I asked him what he thought about the United States. He said he felt more kinship with the Russians. "Why?" I asked. He pointed to the laden tables and said, "We and they do not have things like this. We are more poor." The wealth of America did not win a friend in this instance. I assured him that the American worker did not dine daily like this, nor in such plush surroundings.

Part of my task was also to speak to the citizens on patriotic occasions. For 12 years, with one exception, I made 10 to 17 public speeches at parks on each Fourth of July. Milwaukee held celebrations all day long in all of the major parks as a patriotic gesture and as a means of controlling destructive and injurious tendencies of children and adults alike on that day. This was a constructive activity initiated in 1910 by Socialist Mayor Emil Seidel who was horrified by reading in the papers on July 5 of that year of the injuries caused by unregulated fireworks use.

For 10 years I spoke as a representative of the city at the most solemn ceremonies honoring the dead at the Wood National Veterans Cemetery. Each time I spoke to the thousands of people I thought of my own brother, Carl, whose promising life the war with the Axis claimed, as with the lives of scores of millions of others.

In tending to official business of the city, I encountered a great deal of work. Several hundred ordinances and resolutions passed by the Common Council had to be studied and examined as they were submitted to me for my signature. Only a very small portion of these were vetoed. Many of these vetoes the Common Council overrode for various reasons, largely ideological and political. However, I made as certain as possible I would not sign something I did not know about and then have trouble explaining later what I did. I have been fortunate in that this type of experience of signing my name too hastily has not yet arisen to plague me.

In order to fix in my mind some of the voluminous transactions that filled these resolutions and ordinances, I kept an engineer's field book in my desk and noted the title and number of important resolutions and ordinances under an appropriate heading. This provided me with an index of references to check previous actions.

For the most part the resolutions and ordinances were signed because the consensus of the Common Council and myself was that these ordinances were desirable. Parking regulations, traffic regulations, real estate transactions and public works such as pavement, utility installations and public buildings constituted the largest part of the work. Nevertheless the job of being informed on all of the subject matter of the resolutions was a large task.

I did not make too frequent appearances in the committee rooms but instead sent one of my staff to observe proceedings and to keep me informed. Occasionally I would appear to urge a course of action on the committee or to take one side in a struggle over a basic issue. I would prepare myself as fully as possible.

My appearances before the Common Council itself were much more limited. I gave an annual message, I attended the adoption of the budget and public hearings on major issues and I occasionally gave testimony to the Common Council on important problems. I felt that a distinct separation, friendly if possible, between the mayor's office and the Common Council helped keep a system of appropriate checks and balances in local government. I would act as a watchdog, and the Common Council could also feel free to challenge and criticize my proposals without having me overshadow the free discussion of the aldermen. This concern of mine for an independent and strong Common Council was not appreciated. It was interpreted as a weakness. However, I had noted how the vigor of an honest and fair-minded legislative body can wither before the pressure of a powerful executive as had occurred in Germany, Italy and Russia under the dictators. Similarly, a decay of democracy in local government can occur if a mayor is also a party boss and can take reprisals on councilmen who express independent positions.

On the other hand a mayor should not appear weak before a council. I endeavored to strike a nice balance, according the Common Council dignity and respect, and expecting it in return.

There is always the temptation to develop a bitter animosity under such circumstances of attempting a balance. In politics, especially local government, the council or mayor may try to dominate each other. I did not try this, but sought by persuasion, education and force of public opinion to put over my views and I welcomed valid criticism and improvements. I did not in subsequent elections campaign to defeat any aldermen or other city officials when they stood for re-election.

At the end of 12 years, there was a small contingent of aldermen who pursued a policy of harassment because I had blocked them on handing out favors and because they were opposed to my views on housing and civil rights. If I had continued another term, the issue certainly would have been sharply joined with this group of men.

A mayor must rely heavily on his staff members. A mayor, just as a president or governor, is partly a team of people of which the elected official is the spokesman and the figure in the public eye. Fortunately again, I had a most excellent team of workers competent in every respect.

For 12 years continuously, I benefited from the faithful service of John F. Hanley, a lieutenant of the Milwaukee Police Department; Stanley Budny, originally assistant secretary and then executive secretary; and Mrs. Catherine Burgett, office secretary. We worked together with little friction. Folke R. Peterson served with me seven years as executive secretary. Even though he was in his own business in 1956, he helped organize my campaign for office that year. Albert M. Davis, a veteran and a trained social worker, was an assistant secretary for three years and a most delightful and able individual. Joseph M. Dries, a retired lieutenant colonel in the United States Army, a veteran of Omaha Beach and an information officer at the Panmunjom conferences in Korea, served for two years as assistant secretary.

Lieutenant Hanley was with me for practically every hour of the working day, except on his vacations, for 12 years. He was prompt and courteous, even under the most trying conditions, and never complaining. In my several illnesses during my term of office, he assisted me nobly. He created so many friends for the office by his courteous manner in dealing with visitors that he became one of our best assets in achieving popular support for our goals.

Mrs. Burgett had the task of turning out, with several splendid people sent to the office by civil service, a large amount of clerical and administrative work. It was promptly done, well done and cheerfully done. Some of the women who worked hard and faithfully were Elda Feldman, Shirley Ellinger, Shirley Kerwin, Florence Pelkowski, Ruth Revels, Audrey Eisch, Beverly Olson, Margaret Lynn and others.

As the work of the office grew, I acquired the aid of a most capable assistant city attorney, Arthur Saltzstein, to be administrative secretary. Mr. Saltzstein had extensive experience in legislative matters and local government. His help was invaluable.

Sol Ackerman became urban renewal coordinator as the program of urban renewal expanded.[25] He was the most informed of people on the progress and methods of advancing urban renewal. He could master federal procedures—no mean feat. He resigned for private employment in the housing development field in 1959 partly because of harassment and non-cooperation from public officials who were opposed to housing and civil rights.

Rolland Berger was the industrial development coordinator whose task it was to develop a program of encouraging the city to seek industry. He laid the foundations for an excellent industrial development program, but unfortunately my term of office came to an end shortly after he had initiated his major objectives, and he took a private position.

Another person who served the city and myself faithfully for 12 years was Ray Sheehan, housing and community services expediter. The expansion of the city limits was of such magnitude that the services could not always keep up with the expansion. This brought a lot of complaints about dusty roads, incorrect grading, sewer lines, water services, paving and so on. It was decided to create a special officer to expedite the solution of these complaints and they were handled with complete satisfaction by Mr. Sheehan. He was patient, courteous, tactful and firm when necessary.

The other types of complaints—neighbors' quarrels, landlord-tenant problems, unemployment problems, welfare problems, political issues and tax questions—were handled by the regular staff. Most people were given answers that satisfied them and most problems were solved eventually. Stanley Budny received most of the seemingly unsolvable problems and under the pressure of these complaints he expressed a philosophy: "and this too shall pass."

In many of the knotty problems involving public relations, strikes and other conflicts, I consulted with Manuel Meyers, who retained his detached viewpoint and judgment. He was in a position to gauge the public temper without being directly involved in the moment-to-moment developments. It was valuable and sound advice that he gave as often as he was called upon.

In any public office, the issues requiring the expression of a mayor's philosophy and viewpoint develop so fast and in so many ways that unless one has a consistent philosophy before coming into office there is likely to be a contradiction of conduct caused by the tugging and strains that develop on the mayor. I tried to be as consistent as possible. I supported public ownership, I defended civil rights, I favored housing and urban renewal, I favored a unified metropolitan government, I supported civil service, I supported public education and cultural development at the end of the 12 years even as I did in the beginning. I like to believe that there was a consistent tone which prevailed in each of my annual messages to the Common Council on these basic issues, and that these messages were consistent with the Public Enterprise Committee platforms.

There is a tendency when a man is placed in a position of prominence in any government for him to listen to the lobbyists and the special pleaders. The reason for this tendency is that these lobbyists and special pleaders hang around the seat of government and strike up friendships, whereas the average person never gets to City Hall except to pay taxes or take out some kind of permit. I tried to avoid doing what the special pleaders wanted. I tried to think in terms of the people of the city as a whole. It is this special pleading which leads many excellently motivated elected officials to stray from the principles they espoused as candidates.

The special pleaders and the lobbyists are powerful—make no mistake, they know their way around. I lost several battles to them on zoning changes, on land use, on franchises, on special projects for themselves, on special expenditures that they were able to get in the budget, on tavern and liquor control and on other issues. I won some battles, too, on each of these issues. Unfortunately, votes are sometimes influenced by small favors or gifts such as a meal, a couple of drinks, a holiday trip or a banquet. One never knows when the change occurs or how subtle and by what gradual stages the change takes place until voting time on the Common Council floor when the public interest suddenly is defeated.

One of the problems of the mayor is to be found in that he is taken shortly after election from the environment of his former friends and put into an environment where they can see him only with difficulty. Public officials and representatives of civic groups, commercial organizations and similar agencies now surround the head of the local government, especially in the larger city. The individual who supported the candidate to this situation may feel that he has been shunted aside and that he is no longer good enough to associate with the person he helped elect.

I tried to overcome this problem by keeping close to the organizations that elected me and reporting to the members in meetings, on a personal basis, so that the members could feel they had some input on the course of government.

Many times an individual would call me and say, "Look, Frank, I helped you in the last campaign, and I have not asked any favors of you, but now I want one. Our society, the such-and-such organization, is holding its annual meeting. They asked me to get you as speaker. Will you come?" As often as it was possible for me to say "yes" I did so. This was one way in which I could repay my friends for their support. The organization may have been big or small — I went anyway.

A mayor finds it necessary to be a member of civic organizations and fraternal groups, not to get votes particularly, for membership in such groups does not assure anyone of votes, but because the larger civic groups feel it necessary for their prestige to have the mayor officially on their roles as a member. Membership in such organizations cannot be pursued intensively because there simply is not time, but the membership brings with it the rewards of new friendships and of getting to know what people think and what is troubling them.

Among other organizations, I belonged to the Socialist Party, the Public Enterprise Committee, the Milwaukee Turners (whose organizational magazine I once edited), the Fraternal Order of Eagles, the Milwaukee Elks Lodge, the Knights of Pythias, the Technical Engineers Association (which was my union), the Engineering Society of Milwaukee, the South Division Civic Association, the South Side Old Settlers' Club, the Wisconsin Society of Land Surveyors and the Parent Teachers Association of Rufus King High School and the Center Street School. My attendance at meetings of course was infrequent, because I was usually speaking at other groups. Many groups conferred an honorary membership upon me, partly out of friendship and partly because they wanted to have the mayor of the city associated with their program. Many advancement associations in certain districts of the city conferred honorary memberships; these included the Sixteenth Street-Muskego Avenue Businessmen's Association and the Burleigh Street Advancement Association. Attendance at meetings of these groups was a means of learning about the various facets of life in a city.

Later on I received honorary membership from several cultural or civic groups such as Alpha Kappa Delta, a sociological fraternity at Marquette University; Alpha Phi Omega, a service fraternity at the University of Wisconsin-Milwaukee; the Layton Park Lions Club; a great number of unions; South Division High School; the Milwaukee Junior Association of Commerce and other groups. I had the privilege of honorary membership in the Schwaben Maennerchor and the Milwaukee Liederkranz, two singing societies with a long history in Milwaukee.

When a person is elected to the position of public office or reaches a higher level of civil service status, he finds professional organizations helpful for his work and objectives. I took an active part in the League of Wisconsin Municipalities, the United States Conference of Mayors, the American Municipal Association, the United States Civil Defense Council and several other professional organizations. I had occasion to give formal addresses before national conventions of finance officers, planners, public administrators, civil defense organizers, as well as to the United States Conference of Mayors and the American Municipal Association on subjects of municipal concern.

I took a great interest in the American Municipal Association, which was an organization composed of over 40 state leagues of cities and most of the major cities of the nation. I served for six consecutive years on the executive committee. This was an honor in that usually the terms are rotated each two years. During this period of time I helped strengthen the organization to become one of the largest municipal organizations of its kind.[26]

Through the American Municipal Association I came to rejoice in the friendship of Carl Chatters who was its executive secretary, a foremost student of municipal finance, and later, almost to the time of his death in 1960, the comptroller of the City of Chicago. When Carl Chatters was stricken by a heart attack about 1951, Frederick McMillan of the League of Wisconsin Municipalities and I wrote the whole municipal policy of the organization at its convention in Washington that year. This convention was presided over by Mayor Quigg Newton of Denver, a most progressive mayor. Later, within a decade, municipal affairs became so complicated that the policy had to be prepared by special committees. At this time I presided over the civil defense committee of the organization and drafted much of the civil defense policy, which was made the official policy of the organization.

It was my privilege to serve on the committee to select a director for the association to succeed Carl Chatters when he resigned. Patrick Healy, Jr., a businessman from Utah who had been secretary of the North Carolina Municipal League became the executive director. Mr. Healy proved to be a competent administrator and the organization grew under his guidance.

I also worked closely with the United States Conference of Mayors under Paul Betters and later his brother Harry Betters who served as executive directors. At several of the conferences of this organization I helped prepare the official municipal policy, which was similar to but shorter than the American Municipal Association policy. For both organizations, I made numerous appearances before congressional committees on various matters. These matters included housing and urban renewal, civil defense, intergovernmental relations, transportation and other matters.

The American Municipal Association honored me by making me its representative for six years to the United States National Commission for the United Nations Educational, Scientific and Cultural Organization (UNESCO). This was a most enjoyable assignment and one in which I felt I was making some contribution to the future safety and protection of cities from the devastation of war.

I was also a member of the Great Lakes-St. Lawrence Association, an organization that lobbied for the St. Lawrence Seaway. I was a member of the Great Lakes Harbor Association and was active in the controversy with the City of Chicago over the diversion of Lake Michigan water.

Belonging to these national organizations required attending conferences and making public appearances from time to time in other cities. At the conferences, I usually was drafted onto some committee and I would work the whole period of the conference. In speaking in other cities, I traveled almost always by train, and this sometimes meant I came into the city early in the morning and left late at night after discharging my business, so that the travel was somewhat fatiguing and I began to hate it for its wearying qualities.

Besides belonging to organizations, the office of mayor required that contact be maintained with people by correspondence. A great many letters came into the office daily on all kinds of subjects. Every letter was answered by my staff or mostly by myself. Even crank letters that were signed were acknowledged. Some letters were threatening, but by far the majority of letters were friendly, constructive and were sent for a good reason. Some of the crank letters were the work of people whom we soon came to identify; these persons had borderline mental problems that were evident from the letters themselves. They did not cause us much fear, but one did worry about the fate of such persons, for unfortunately there was little that could be done to help them. Mental illness is a sorrowing physical phenomenon that presents itself almost daily to the public office holder in some form or another.

At Christmastime, Mrs. Zeidler and I would send out about 3,000 to 3,500 simple Christmas cards to friends and campaign workers. The expense and work was borne by ourselves and our children as soon as they were old enough to help. The cards bore a simple Christmas greeting from "Agnes and Frank Zeidler and Family." This was to remind ourselves and our friends that someday my term of office and title would come to an end, and we must resume our status as citizens without title.

The foregoing description of some of the duties of the mayor administratively, politically, socially and otherwise is a relatively brief resume of the job. It is therefore no wonder that this type of office inflicts a great physical and mental strain that may cause an officeholder to lose a sense of balance or judgment. Under such strains a person may make utterances or perform actions that bring about ultimate disrepute and defeat.

The position of mayor required an immense amount of work. One had to be up early in the morning, and after the close of the working day the mayor had to attend the ceremonial functions of the community. In addition, Saturdays and Sundays are the days of the festivities of the working people, and the mayor turns down invitations to these events only at his political peril.

The decisions arriving at the mayor's desk are the problems that no one else down the line can solve. This requires intense cogitation. The mayor must have time to reflect, but in the larger cities this is not always given him. He must go to official breakfasts, luncheons and dinners, and sometimes is expected to stay around after the evening meeting.

The excessive opportunities to eat and drink are great dangers of all public life. I found it necessary to attend many evening dinner meetings. Consequently I gained weight, going from 145 to about 173 pounds. This weight gain I now believe was the single most injurious factor in my years in office. Carrying around excess weight, sitting much of the time, lack of proper exercise, being cooped up in an office into which the sun shone for only a few morning hours — all these conditions were physically and psychologically unhealthy.

In October of 1949, a series of three gas utility strikes that I helped negotiate to a successful conclusion — once all night — weakened my resistance and I came down with hepatitis. I was speaking at Pulaski High School in Milwaukee on Columbus Day when my mind blanked out. I recovered and kept on speaking, but the warning sign was there. I was unable to return again to work until late in December of that year. I never did get the full strength back that I had enjoyed before my first successful mayoral campaign, a campaign that in itself gave me a nervous exhaustion just before its end.

In 1951, a tumor was removed from inside my left ribs. This kept me out of office for over a month. It was difficult to recover from because it was a major operation. The mental strain was also severe after these two prolonged illnesses.

When problems became acute enough, and when there was great tension over an issue, which occurred many times, my mind would not shut off at night. This was a sign of anxiety. Another disturbing problem occurred. If I had had to speak too much during a day—and this was true many days—I would find myself making speeches in my dreams at night and this was more exhausting than being awake. One discovered in public office that there were not only physical limits to one's endurance but also mental limits that were often reached without the warning signs that physical limits put forth.

Ethical problems also confront the policy-making officeholder. The question of civil rights, the war on alcoholism and crime, the war on slums, the struggle for traffic safety, were among those that produced some mental strains. How far should one go in fighting the liquor lobby? How far should one press civil rights? How far should one go in providing housing for low-income people? These ethical problems required expenditures of much mental energy to arrive at a solution, and usually then only a partial solution.

A public officeholder is also affected by the tragedies, disasters and calamities that daily befall some people in the city.

The deaths of citizens—by accidents on the streets, by fire in slum houses, by explosions or other disasters—occur frequently and often involve the life of leading public officials, especially the mayor. The officials must think, "How much are we responsible for fire deaths? Did our inspection fail? How much are we responsible for traffic deaths? Did our enforcement of laws fail?" It is true that some public officials hold themselves not a whit responsible for such conditions and seek to change them only if they can get credit for personally introducing favorable legislation. This attitude always seemed to me morally inadequate.

The death of friends is a matter that seems to recur daily in the larger cities. A major public officeholder gets to know thousands of people and is quite friendly with them. Almost every night, as he reads the press, there is the notice of the death of a friend. This should mean attendance either at the funeral or at the funeral home. Each event is something of a personal shock. "What did the struggle for life avail the departed friend?" one thinks. To the conscientious public servant, there is usually more of mourning than of rejoicing in public life, for the ultimate tragedy of death is always intruding.

Another condition hard to bear emotionally is the public attack in the newspapers either by charges from another public official or from the editorialists.

This produces a kind of shock unless one develops a philosophy of absolute opposition to the newspapers and attacks them at every possible opportunity.

I did not adopt this attitude. Nor did I go to any effort especially to win the support of the editorial writers of the newspapers. If they wrote an editorial critical of me, I would try to answer it by a deed that proved them wrong. If their editorial required a statement of policy, I took the next opportunity afforded me at a public meeting to explain my position and to see that my explanation was reported in the press. I tried not to attack the press directly at any time, but I was finally forced into taking issue with the *Milwaukee Sentinel* for its attempt to portray me as a Stalin Communist in the 1956 campaign. Nevertheless every editorial had a sting that left its bite on one's spirit, and most editorials I received were critical. Fortunately the editors, while not wanting to praise a liberal administration, could not find many issues on which to pick a fight.

The strain of the burdens of office had become quite heavy in 1955 and I fully intended not to stand for office again in 1956. I prepared and published a lengthy statement of policies I thought Milwaukee should follow after that year.[27] However, right-wing elements had begun circulating racially charged rumors designed to promote prejudice and I was determined to fight them on it. I was re-elected. By 1959, however, the strain was too great and I told my friends early in the summer of that year that I would not run again and that they should look around for another liberal to support. This was unacceptable to them. It was not until October of that year that I could make the decision stick and in this I was aided by the firm advice of Dr. Einar R. Daniels who told me another term might prove fatal. I had gone through surgery in 1959 and I had not recovered from it as well as I had wanted.

The issue of whether or not I was "too friendly" to minorities was again going to be raised and I should have liked to have fought it out once more, but enough was enough. As it was, the issue was circulated sub rosa and according to some accounts, the winning candidate, Henry W. Maier, made use of this issue in the 1960 municipal elections to seek votes by disassociating himself from my administration.

It was not only the physical strain that determined me not to stand again. I think that 12 years in one publicly elected office of major importance is enough for an individual, and it is wholesome for the public to have a change so as to have more people exercised in the functions of democracy. Moreover I felt myself spoiling for a fight with the liquor and tavern industry over the social disorders they created, with the suburbs over planning, with the realtors over creating a ghetto in the center of Milwaukee, with the state government for not taking cognizance of the need for the civil protection of the great urban clusters, and with the motor vehicle owners over taxation. Above all I felt a need to work for world peace on a level and plane higher than city government. It was to spare the people of the city some of these fights and to better reform my own ideas that I stepped aside.

There were certain problems of philosophy in government that arose and presented dilemmas. Some of these problems consisted of a whole complex of problems related to how a person believing in public ownership of basic industries and monopolies administers a government where those industries and monopolies are privately owned. Should private industry be encouraged to come to a city? In order to get it, should it be given tax inducements and special offers for reducing wage costs? If one does not believe in public ownership, should the purpose of government be primarily to serve private industry because private industry is the taxpayer that keeps government going? Should one spend any time worrying about the non-productive people, the low-income people and the community misfits because they eat up taxes and community services and cannot compete with more productive people in other cities? Should the government be administered primarily to make it easier for industry and for the private enterprisers since, after all, the rest of the people and the government itself depend on the earnings of the private enterprisers for wages and the income of the city? Is not the first concern of the city, even under a "Socialist" mayor, to compete with the industries of other cities, and is not this concern best manifested by helping the rich and successful grow richer?

It seemed to me that there were two ways to answer this group of questions. One is the usual answer—help the rich enterprisers grow richer and hope that the crumbs that fall off their tables can nourish their employees and the rest of the people in the city. The primary purpose of an American city now is to serve as a place to make money more easily than in some other place. This is why cities have grown larger in the postwar era. Under such a philosophy, the true government of the city consists of the big businesses and their owners. City officials exist to enact laws and ordinances that create the pattern of urban conduct required by such owners and businesses. The mayor of many an American city is fearful of the big businesses and rich families of his city.

The other way to answer this question is to reason that the purpose of a city is solely to advance human progress. The primary purpose of a city should be to help as many of its inhabitants as possible. Business can be helped, of course, but not business alone. The aged, the ill, the social outcasts, the unfortunate and all those broken down in life must be helped by the local government even if it means taxation of the successful people. The successful people can generally take care of themselves, but the others cannot and they have few spokesmen or defenders. I felt that the social programs advancing the condition of the low-income people and the unfortunate were not in the long run costly to government or the rich, but brought prosperity by bringing new consumers into the market where the capacity to produce often now exceeded the demand. Also, the disturbances of a social order racked by the necessities of competition, forcing workers to a minimum standard in order that the rich could grow richer, will ultimately destroy the laissez-faire society. Therefore, my philosophy on social and welfare problems was that the successful business people, in order to keep being successful, must show a responsibility for the unfortunate and less successful, even to the point of being substantially taxed. Without such a program, capitalism must eventually be supplanted by some economic order that concerns itself with the needs of more people than does capitalism.

In a sense, I was protecting the capitalist system by fighting for amelioration of conditions under it, rather than by pursuing the "Verelendstheorie" of the Communists—namely, to make things so bad that people revolt. My position of course was not appreciated by the Mark Hanna capitalists of Milwaukee. The continual scheming of many people in their own interest, coupled with a resentment toward being forced to pay for anything, especially government services for other people, is too often an ingrained habit so that it becomes difficult to see the larger interrelationship of things. However, under the American system the drive for one's own self-interest is the primary motive of the social order, and this drive must now be modified by a system of taxation that takes care of the welfare problems created by the system and by the natural hardships of life itself as life matures.

I have described some of the strains and duties placed on a mayor in a city of some 750,000 people. Multiply these strains many times and one has some idea of the pressure of forces focused on the president of the United States. Is it possible that one person can fulfill this enormous task and do it justice? I have often wondered.

What is needed for the top administrative job in the larger cities is a division of the work. The mayor is a ceremonial officer, a political officer and administrative officer. It might be better for the American system to adopt some of the British municipal practices. The mayor may be a ceremonial officer and a political leader. The administrative officer should be a full-time civil service assistant. In every larger city the mayor should be reinforced by a manager to reduce the burden of the job.

NOTES FOR CHAPTER 2

1. Among the more prominent of such persons so elected were De Lesseps Morrison in New Orleans, Quigg Newton in Denver, and somewhat later, Richard Lee in New Haven, Joseph Dillon in St. Paul and Ben West in Nashville. Some of the older men in public office such as David Lawrence of Pittsburgh, Joseph Darst of St. Louis, William Hartsfield of Atlanta, William Devin of Seattle and Fletcher Bowron of Los Angeles also were active in meeting the housing needs of their cities.
2. "Inaugural Address of Mayor Frank P. Zeidler," *Common Council Proceedings*, City of Milwaukee, April 20, 1948.
3. See the discussion on infiltration of decaying areas with public housing in the inaugural address, ibid.
4. Some labor leaders tried to get Alderman Raymond W. Fleming to oppose Alderman McGuire. Fleming refused this support but received some votes anyway. See "Labor Aims to Block McGuire as President of New Council," *Milwaukee Journal*, April 16, 1948, and "McGuire Gets Council's Nod for President," *Milwaukee Journal*, April 21, 1948.
5. For a report of this meeting, see the *Milwaukee Journal*, April 16, 1948.
6. For a further account of this event, see "Zeidler Takes Oath as City's Executive," *Milwaukee Journal*, April 20, 1948, and "Zeidler Holds Housing Talk," *Milwaukee Journal*, April 21, 1948. This paper made no editorial comment on my message. For this I was grateful, as I had expected an attack of some kind.
7. See the *Milwaukee Journal*, March 18, 1948.
8. George C. Saffran died June 21, 1958. He had a good influence on the Common Council and on Milwaukee.
9. See *The Voter's Digest*, April, 1948. This was the campaign paper of my supporters.
10. The titles of the Public Enterprise Committee platforms in 1950 and 1951 were "Tentative Draft of Public Enterprise Committee Platform, March 4, 1950," and "A Civic Program for Metropolitan Milwaukee, Public Enterprise Committee, December, 1951."
11. *Continue Progress in Good Government*, Public Enterprise Committee, December, 1955.
12. *Public Enterprise Committee Program for the City of Milwaukee*, December, 1959.
13. "Zeidler Unit Hears Reuss," *Milwaukee Journal*, November 20, 1959.
14. Copies of this county platform are rare and the author has not been able to locate one.
15. *Public Enterprise Committee Program for the County of Milwaukee*, December, 1959.
16. *Proposed Program for Voter Guidance in the 1959 Election of Board of Public School Directors*. Public Enterprise Committee of Milwaukee.
17. *Public Enterprise Committee Program for Voter Guidance in the Election of the City of Milwaukee Board of Public School Directors*, March, 1961.
18. *Platforms and Planks of the Public Enterprise Committee*, circa 1955.
19. This happened to Mr. Arthur Urbanek whom I nominated to the Board of Appeals. "Ban Zeidler Choice for Job," *Milwaukee Journal*, June 15, 1948.
20. I worked in the office of the *Milwaukee Leader*, a Socialist daily, whose successor paper, the *Milwaukee Post* died about 1941. I did some "rewrite" work and an occasional editorial.
21. There is a picture of one such event in *The Little Journal*, a house organ of the Milwaukee Journal Company, in 1949.
22. The exchange between Norris and myself on annexation occurred in 1957. Norris continued to attack me on annexation, but later diversified his attack to all kinds of subjects—expressways especially.
23. "Dutch Ship Wins Race to Harbor," *Milwaukee Sentinel*, April 30, 1959.
24. If my memory serves me correctly the name of this German worker was Georg Ammon of Frankfurt am Main. He was a bank worker.
25. It was Mr. Ackerman, I believe, who suggested to Mr. Henry S. Reuss the use of Wisconsin housing statutes to begin the famous Red Arrow project, which became a point of fierce contention between the forces for better housing and those opposed.

26. Among the members of a committee that expanded the organization were Joseph Clark, mayor of Philadelphia, later United States senator; Allen Thompson, mayor of Jackson, Mississippi; Robertson Smith of the Idaho Municipal League; Herbert Bingham of the Tennessee Municipal League; and Clarence C. Ludwig of the League of Minnesota Municipalities and distinguished professor of the University of Minnesota.

27. *A Course of Action for the City of Milwaukee for 1956 and the Following Years*, 1955, Frank P. Zeidler.

Frank and Agnes Zeidler walk near their home with their six children in the spring of 1948. This photo helped convince voters that the mayoral candidate was not the villain he had been made out to be. The children (left to right, front to back): Anita, Michael, Dorothy, Clara, Jeannette and Mary.

Photos from the Milwaukee Journal, © 2005 Journal Sentinel Inc., reproduced with permission

The two contenders for Milwaukee mayor in 1948 were Frank P. Zeidler and Henry S. Reuss. When Reuss ran again for mayor in 1960, the *Milwaukee Journal* and the *Milwaukee Sentinel* gave editorial support to Henry W. Maier. Reuss served in Congress from 1954 to 1983.

Frank Zeidler accepts congratulations from Walter H. Uphoff, one of the founding members of the Municipal Enterprise Committee, in the mayor's office on inauguration day, April 20, 1948. A photo of Frank's brother Carl is visible in the background.

Frank Zeidler studies the United Nations Universal Declaration on Human Rights, adopted by the General Assembly on December 10, 1948. At the left is Alderman Milton McGuire. The document begins by stating that "recognition of the inherent dignity and of the equal and inalienable rights of all members of the human family is the foundation of freedom, justice and peace in the world."

Photo from the Milwaukee Journal, © 2005 Journal Sentinel Inc., reproduced with permission

Frank Zeidler speaks at a Fourth of July celebration in Red Arrow Park in 1949. Standing next to Zeidler is newly elected County Supervisor William F. O'Donnell, who would later serve as county executive from 1976 to 1988.

Frank Zeidler attends a Milwaukee Press Club birthday celebration for the city on January 31, 1950. Seated next to him is Daniel Hoan who served as Milwaukee's mayor from 1916 to 1940, when he was defeated by Carl Zeidler. Seated at the right is John Bohn who became Milwaukee's mayor after Carl left for the war in 1942. Alderman Valentine V. Kujawa stands at the left.

A delegation of Wisconsin officials meets with United States Senator Alexander Wiley to discuss natural gas rates and consumer protection on May 10, 1951. Left to right: Stewart Honeck, deputy attorney general of Wisconsin; Vernon Thomson, attorney general and later governor of Wisconsin; Harry Slater, assistant city attorney of Milwaukee; Governor Walter Kohler, Jr.; Senator Wiley; Philip Drotning, assistant to the governor; John Doerfer, chairman of the Wisconsin Public Service Commission; and Mayor Frank Zeidler.

Photo from the Milwaukee Journal, © 2005 Journal Sentinel Inc., reproduced with permission

Agnes and Frank Zeidler discuss the election returns at WTMJ in April of 1952. Zeidler defeated State Senator Leonard Fons by a final tally of 152,658 to 58,599.

The 1956 Milwaukee Common Council. Standing, left to right: Ralph F. Kelly (9th Ward), Valentine V. Kujawa (11), Ralph J. Landowski (18), George W. Whittow (10), Bernard B. Kroenke (13), Charles H. Quirk (4), Fred P. Meyers (6), James J. Mortier (1), John H. Budzien (19), Mathias F. Schimenz (12), Martin E. Schreiber (7), and Clarence A. Heiden (15). Seated, left to right: Vincent A. Schmit (20), James H. Collins (16), Alfred C. Hass (3), Joseph Schmidt (17), Vel R. Phillips (2), Irving G. Rahn (5), Peter H. Hoffman (8) and Richard B. Nowakowski (14).

Frank Zeidler takes time to enjoy one of Milwaukee's favorite pastimes.

Historic Photo Collection of Milwaukee Public Library - Chicago Photo Press Photographer

Frank Zeidler takes in a Braves game with Lou Perini, owner of the team. In 1957, the Milwaukee Braves won the World Series by defeating the New York Yankees. Agnes Zeidler is visible between the two men. Detective John (Jack) Hanley is seated at the right wearing a dark suit.

The City Hall annex was completed in 1959 during Frank Zeidler's third term as mayor. On May 16, 1995, it was designated the Frank P. Zeidler Municipal Building.

Zeidler Union Square Park, named in honor of Carl Zeidler, is located in downtown Milwaukee between Michigan and Clybourn Streets.

The Milwaukee Public Library's Frank P. Zeidler Humanities Room was dedicated on June 18, 1997. The dedication plaque quotes Zeidler: "The Milwaukee Public Library was a main source of my education, ideals and civic policy, and its riches in information have been invaluable to the people of Milwaukee and the state."

Frank Zeidler today keeps a busy schedule and enjoys exchanging ideas and stories with the many people he meets.

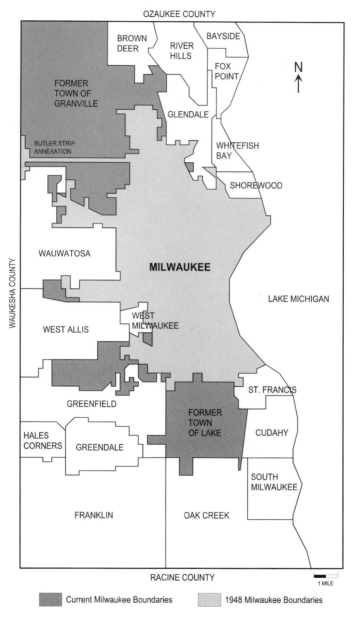

In 1948 the boundaries of the City of Milwaukee were in a state of flux due to continuing annexation efforts and court cases. A 1951 Wisconsin Supreme Court ruling nullified several Milwaukee annexations including the Butler strip annexation.

Chapter 3

Growing Milwaukee

An issue of major proportions in my three terms as mayor of Milwaukee arose out of the expansion of the city's boundaries. This issue grew in magnitude and vehemence right to the end of my tenure of office, and it subsided somewhat when my successor adopted a softer position vis-à-vis the suburbs.[1]

By the time I left office in 1960, the suburban influences on city government had grown to a clearly dominant position, even though the suburbs had been rebuffed somewhat in the 1956 municipal election in which their candidate, Alderman Milton J. McGuire, the president of the Common Council, was defeated.

The fact that this issue of city expansion was to become so intense was not fully indicated at the time of my election to a first term of office in 1948. A principal issue in that campaign was housing. The platform of the Municipal Enterprise Committee of 1947 and my inaugural address of 1948 featured the issues of housing and city planning, with an emphasis on internal planning, more than the issue of city expansion.[2]

However, it was not entirely a surprise when the subject of expansion arose and developed into a sharp conflict as time went on because the City of Milwaukee had struggled with surrounding governments for many decades preceding my election to office. The nature of this struggle I understood somewhat from hearing older men talk when I was entering political life in the 1930s.

The early battle of the City of Milwaukee to expand against hostile suburban and township officials was rather well known in the community and has been chronicled in an interesting booklet entitled "Making Milwaukee Mightier," which was prepared for the Board of Public Land Commissioners in 1929 by Arthur M. Werba, the annexation supervisor, and John L. Grunwald, an assistant secretary of Mayor Daniel W. Hoan.[3] The city's struggle to expand from about 26 square miles in 1922 to nearly 42 square miles in 1929, as related by these men, was later repeated in essence after 1946 to the final closing of the "Iron Ring," as the ring of suburbs around Milwaukee was described.

Werba and Grunwald reported in their booklet that prior to the 1890s annexations to the city were made by the state Legislature, with no control over the annexation by the people being annexed or by the annexing city. This law was changed to one requiring annexation by petition of the majority of electors and owners of half of the real estate involved. The authors of the booklet regarded this procedure as more satisfactory, but this method proved too cumbrous to meet the growth of the community and left too much to individual self-interest. Because of the defects of this law, Milwaukee County ultimately became a county of 19 communities with conflicting and competing interests. The ideal of one local government for the metropolitan area, which Werba and Grunwald had envisioned, was thus disastrously defeated.

The annexation law, which called for a petition from people to be annexed, was not in itself satisfactory to the City of Milwaukee, so that the city government in 1920 created the position of annexation director to supervise the work of annexation to the city and to encourage it. The principal work of the annexation director was to secure petitions from people outside of the city with sufficient signatures of electors and land owners in order to annex a piece of land. This work resulted in much competitive activity between the city and nearby suburbs or townships. With more than half of the electors and half of the land owners, the city could force some unwilling people to be annexed. The annexations often had a strange shape to them, and of necessity the process could not be neat and tidy as far as annexing total tracts of land with a common characteristic.

Nevertheless, the annexation laws were of some use, in that Milwaukee grew as a city to encompass about 44 square miles by 1946, with the majority of annexations occurring during the 1920s. Some of the annexations resulted in highly irregular boundaries such as that which occurred along W. Bluemound Road in Milwaukee about 1925, when Milwaukee and Wauwatosa raced each other in annexing territory. After a bitter six-year fight, the City of North Milwaukee consolidated with Milwaukee in 1929. Other significant land additions were made to the city around this time, including some of its nicest residential areas and most important industrial areas.

However, Milwaukee's annexation program incurred the hostility of the officials of existing suburbs and townships. Their jobs were threatened and they proceeded to fight court and legislative battles that significantly impeded and ultimately overcame Milwaukee's ability to annex. The annexation battles of the 1920s gave rise to an organization of suburban officials and attorneys known as the Milwaukee County League of Municipalities, which was dubbed the "Iron Ring." The expression "Iron

Ring" was also used to describe the actual suburbs themselves around the city. The term was used interchangeably with these two meanings.

During the Depression years, Milwaukee stopped annexation because it could not afford the outlay of money required. In addition, the city had suffered the misfortune of working with subdividers who had the city install utilities in new subdivisions only to have those subdivisions lie idle from 1929 to 1947 because of the Depression and the Second World War.[4]

After the war, however, the city planner, Elmer Krieger, and Arthur M. Werba, who had directed annexation in the 1920s, deemed it a good idea to again institute a program of annexation. They persuaded the Common Council and Mayor John L. Bohn to reinstitute the program of growth. Many of the outlying areas in Milwaukee County were experiencing rapid development following the war and annexation was an effective means of providing residents of these areas with necessary municipal services such as water, sewers and schools. Approval of the annexation program came in September of 1946, when the Department of Abstracting and Annexation was re-established.[5] This department was placed under the supervision of Arthur M. Werba, the veteran of the annexation struggles. He was thoroughly familiar with annexation procedures and knew the legal tricks and patterns of suburban officials in fighting Milwaukee's expansion. Mr. Werba ultimately held the position of annexation supervisor until 1954, when he was succeeded by Mr. Joseph R. Lamping.

The initial rate of progress in annexation was slow. In 1947 the city had 11 annexations, amounting to 0.794 square miles. In 1948 the momentum picked up and the city increased 2.246 square miles in 23 annexations. In 1949 there were 16 annexations bringing in only .546 square miles. In 1950, 38 annexations brought in 1.840 square miles, and in 1951, 36 annexations brought in .914 square miles. Because these annexations were fiercely contested, only relatively small tracts of land could be annexed. By 1951, the annexation struggles between Milwaukee and its suburbs were in full contest.

During this period of 1948 to 1951, there was much opposition to annexing by some people including, of course, township officials. Opposition frequently came from residents in areas to be annexed. Some of the residents in these areas, particularly in the Town of Lake, went to the area because of low taxes. According to the law of that time, Wisconsin returned half of the state income taxes collected from individuals and corporations to the community in which the taxpayer was located. The return of half of the state income taxes from the Lakeside power plant in the Town of Lake was so great as to bring a considerable reduction in property taxes. People seeking easy tax payments moved into the township. In other areas adjacent to Milwaukee, many low-income workers moved outside of the city to build small homes with their own labor and to enjoy the low taxes of a rural area.

For the first newcomers from the city in these rural areas, this pattern of living was relatively satisfactory. It was made even more satisfactory by the improvement of highways and motor vehicles. However, other people, forced out of the city by lot shortages and land speculation, also moved into the rural areas adjacent to the city and the problems of those areas mounted. The most serious problem was a shortage of water caused by the dropping of water tables from private wells. Another serious problem was sewage disposal, although this was relieved in some measure by the Metropolitan Sewerage Commission building sanitary sewers outside of the incorporated city limits. Another problem was the lack of a sufficient tax base from residences to pay for schools. The need for water, which the Milwaukee government would not supply beyond its boundaries, forced many annexations to the city. Later this practice became an issue of bitter contention as suburbs sought to get city water without joining the city.

The philosophy of the city government during this period of annexation may be summarized as follows:

1. The city recognized the need to expand urban organization in order to meet the needs of a growing metropolitan population.

2. The city felt that it had the special powers to organize this growth effectively and to engage in modern planning.

3. The city leaders were imbued with the idea of a planned urban growth that had been fostered by earlier civic leaders such as Charles B. Whitnall, a former member of the city and county planning committees, who favored introducing green spaces into the city and reducing density of occupation of land.

4. The city was opposed to fragmented governments and suburban communities as an impedance to planning and regarded them as parasitic growths on the central city of the metropolitan area.

5. The city was prepared to accept the financial cost of expansion for its long-range benefits to the city.

6. The city was opposed to extending its services, particularly water service, beyond its boundaries because this encouraged the formation of uncooperative suburbs.

7. The city felt that it could render services better, more cheaply and more efficiently than the suburbs.

8. The city needed land for residential and industrial expansion.

These basic principles, derived from the decades of the 1910s and 1920s, strongly permeated the thinking of Milwaukee officials in the 1940s and 1950s until the Iron Ring closed on the city.[6]

Underlying the city's desire for growth were the even more fundamental issues of land planning and land use to improve the city as a place in which to live. In fact, one of the primary goals of the Socialist movement in Milwaukee, and generally throughout the world, had been to improve cities by eliminating slums, introducing parks and recreation and keeping a clean city.[7]

The vision of a beautifully planned city that many Milwaukeeans held no doubt came from their recent contacts with their European homeland. People chose to remember not the slums of European cities but their magnificent centers, such as in Vienna.[8]

The dreams of Charles B. Whitnall were still strongly in the minds of Milwaukee officials as to the possibilities of making a city attractive. His pamphleteering had a pronounced effect on the park system and on city growth and planning.[9]

The attempt to put this dream into a reality was, however, an entirely different matter. The Municipal Enterprise Committee platform of December, 1947, featured the subject of planning. In its opening statement, it asserted:

> The key to Milwaukee's future as the foremost large city of America lies in city planning and in an efficient, intelligent and progressive administration.
>
> Large cities are essentially large workshops where vast numbers of people congregate together in order to produce efficiently the world's goods and to raise the standards of human life and enjoyment. Unless cities are intelligently planned, they may become overcrowded and congested workshops, places in which the workers and producers are neither efficiently employed nor adequately fed and housed.
>
> Because of the great changes occurring in the technical world, Milwaukee as a large city must be an attractive place for both workers and enterprisers, or the city will lose its place in competition with other cities of America.
>
> Planning, free from the influence of private pressures, must extend to all phases of city life—not only to construction and layout, but also to finances, to health and safety, and to human welfare.

The ugliness, the dirt, the blight, the overcrowding of the city were to be removed by good planning, but the emphasis on the outward movement of the city boundaries did not come until later. The platform of the Municipal Enterprise Committee and official statements of the city government did not focus on the subject of growth. Even my inaugural address in April of 1948 did not dwell on this most lively of all issues—city expansion.

The city government, in my administration, continued the slow pace of city expansion, while the actual population spread of the central city to the suburbs continued at a much more rapid pace. This phenomenon had been occurring in cities since the 1920s and Milwaukee was no exception. As a result, when the city boundaries slowly approached some new territory, that territory was likely filled with a number of hostile residents who typically wanted city water, but did not want to join the city.

Milwaukee's position on its water service was simple—no water service would
be extended beyond the city boundaries and those who wanted such service would
have to join the city. The issue was raised in the case of the Ampco Metal plant in the
Town of Greenfield during the Second World War. This plant wanted water service,
and ultimately it was given such service, but the Common Council's Public Utilities
Committee warned that plants outside the city limits must be prepared to be annexed
to the city.[10]

By 1946, a number of plants outside of the city had received water service and
this alarmed the editors of the *Milwaukee Journal*. In an editorial of June 25, 1946, "City
Cannot Endure If This Sort of Thing Continues," the *Journal* noted that someone in the
city government had permitted the extension of watermains to numerous industrial
plants outside of city boundaries. The editorial said, "The arrangement that has been
entered into . . . deprives the city of the income taxes, not to mention the real estate
taxes, that would accrue to it if these plants were annexed to Milwaukee." The
editorial continued,

> Milwaukee does not want to adopt a dog in the manger
> attitude. Its tendency is to be helpful. But if the withholding of
> essential services is the only way to break the anti-annexation iron
> ring, then the city will have to protect itself. These plants, when
> they asked for water, should have been invited to become a part of
> the city.
>
> There is some talk about a metropolitan water district which
> would take over the Milwaukee water facilities. Such a district
> would further extend the income tax loss, further enrich the
> townships and villages and impoverish Milwaukee.
>
> The central city has got to be maintained. Every industrialist
> and most other citizens know it. It will stagnate or be further
> impoverished if the tax base is additionally destroyed. Apparently
> there must be annexations, a complete countywide consolidation or
> a change in income tax distributions if this is not to happen.

This editorial precisely defined the city's position. In subsequent years, however,
the *Journal* made a complete change in judgment and became the leading instrument
in demanding that water service be sent out of the city's boundaries, that consolidation
was impossible and that income tax distribution changes were politically impossible as
well.

By 1946, Werba and the city were busily engaged in annexation and stories on
annexation troubles appeared with some frequency in the press. The city was engaged
in a major attempt to expand its boundaries in the townships of Wauwatosa, Lake,
Milwaukee and Granville especially, and to some extent in Greenfield. The town
officials fought back. On one occasion, a panoply of city officials was marshaled for an
annexation meeting in 1946 at Custer High School. Mayor John L. Bohn appeared

with other Milwaukee officials including Fire Chief Edward Wischer and Health Commissioner E.R. Krumbiegel to explain the benefits of annexation to Granville citizens. The meeting featured a clash between Werba and Granville citizens led by C.R. Dineen, the dean of the Iron Ring attorneys.[11]

The attempt by Werba and the city to annex lands in the Town of Milwaukee, along N. Green Bay Avenue and N. Port Washington Road, stirred town leaders to action to form a city beginning in 1946.[12] These actions eventually led to the formation of the City of Glendale.

One of the most important activities of Mr. Werba at this time in 1946 was the attempt to annex near the Village of Butler in Waukesha County in order to gain industrial lands for Milwaukee. At N. 124th Street, the county line, there was a piece of land about two miles long and about a quarter of a mile in width along the Chicago and Northwestern Railway property, adjacent to Butler. This north-south strip of land was connected to another strip of land, extending east and west along Hampton Avenue from about N. 47th Street to N. 124th Street. This piece of land was about four miles long and 330 feet wide. Half of it was in the Town of Wauwatosa and half in the Town of Granville. The peculiar shape of this annexation, which came to be known as the "Butler strip annexation," was made possible by the eastern end, which had enough electors and property owners to comprise more than 50 percent of the total. These electors and owners could therefore compel the annexation of the rest of the territory.

The Village of Butler had requested approval from the Wisconsin Public Service Commission for a waterworks but some citizens opposed the $300,000 expenditure as unnecessary if Milwaukee annexed Butler. In joining with those who opposed the expenditure, Mr. Werba offered the hope of water service with annexation.[13]

Werba subsequently filed a petition with the Milwaukee Common Council for the Butler strip annexation. This petition was fought by Alderman R.A. Steinhagen, who was thought to be a civil engineer for some of the towns and therefore opposed to the diminishing of their territory through absorption by the city. In the dispute over this issue in one of the Common Council's committees, Werba told Alderman Steinhagen and the others present that annexation was needed for city expansion and warned that the suburbs were planning a fight over the Milwaukee waterworks to force the city into a metropolitan system which would cost city taxpayers millions of dollars. Werba pointed out that a bill was to be introduced into the 1947 state Legislature to create such a system.[14] Thus the issue of the suburbs gaining control of the waterworks as a means of countering the city's annexation efforts appeared in the open and was to become a major issue of contention between the city and suburbs.

The ultimate failure of the Butler strip annexation led to further fragmentation of government in the area and would have far-reaching consequences not only for Milwaukee but for the region.

Milwaukee's attempts at annexation typically met with stiff resistance. Township officials fought back by lawsuit, by political pressure on people who might consider annexation and through the Legislature.[15]

In the 1947 state Legislature, Senator Edward F. Hilker of Racine introduced a bill giving cities the power to annex neighboring territory if it received some city service other than fire protection, but the towns mustered enough strength to stop the bill.[16]

A typical annexation problem occurred in the Lake and Greenfield townships when the city began annexation of 100 acres in the vicinity of what became the Southgate shopping center at S. 27th Street and W. Morgan Avenue. The towns disputed this plot, and both the City of Milwaukee and the Town of Lake attempted to administer part of it for a time.[17]

In August of 1947, the Milwaukee Common Council weighed in on the annexation battles by issuing a declaration of policy encouraging annexation for the purpose of providing sites for home building. The Common Council at that time gave support to the mayor and the Department of Public Works to pursue a course of further annexation.[18]

The issues of annexation had caught the attention of the Legislature, not only from the bills presented and argued, but also from the frequent news items in the press. In February of 1948, a subcommittee of the Wisconsin Legislative Council held a meeting on the issues between the city and suburbs, with leading officials speaking for both groups. Mayor Bohn headed the city delegation and C.R. Dineen led the suburban opposition.[19] This was the first of many meetings of its type held between legislative sessions.

Werba's efforts, despite the intense opposition, resulted in 3.9 square miles being added to the city in the period from 1946 to August of 1948.[20]

The suburbs again countered the city in the 1949 Legislature. Democratic Assemblyman Leland S. (Packy) McParland of Cudahy introduced a series of bills to prevent the city from circulating annexation petitions or from using municipally owned property to support petitions. He also proposed requiring 75 percent of the owners of an area to sign the petition, along with other provisions the city considered onerous. These bills persisted in the Legislature until late in the session and required all the efforts of the city to defeat them.[21]

At one of several hearings on annexation in this session of the Legislature, I appeared before an Assembly committee and stated that McParland's bills were "designed to harass annexation or stop it completely." I asked the Legislature to "make a broad decision as to whether annexation is desirable or not. Who is right and wrong on this question?" I also stated that the town attorneys were working for "indescribable municipal confusion in a metropolitan area." As usual, the towns were well represented, but the principal attack came from attorneys for suburbs that were at the time not interested in annexing their own urban fringes.[22] I asserted that attempts to block annexation were in effect attempts to block housing for those who needed it, since there was a housing shortage at this time.

One of McParland's bills, which would have stopped all annexation whenever a lawsuit was pending, was considered by the state Assembly. McParland was a popular legislator and this was probably done as a kind of courtesy. The bill did not pass, much to the relief of Milwaukee officials.[23]

Annexing was also spurred by a lack of industrial sites,[24] and the city sought to put funds in the budget for the acquisition of large areas of raw land outside of the city.[25] This attempt, however, never materialized in additional annexation.

Another problem was the effect of annexation on the Milwaukee School Board budget. The newly annexed lands were swiftly built up and the houses were filled with families whose children required entrance into the Milwaukee school system. School officials complained of the burden but succeeded in meeting the challenges brought by annexation.[26]

A corollary problem was that new territories brought into the city took away pupils and tax support from individual school districts in the towns. This problem eventually grew to a furious uproar that would later reach its climax in the Granville area.

In 1950, the City of Milwaukee was heartened by a favorable decision by Circuit Court Judge Clarence E. Rinehard upholding the Butler strip annexation. The Town of Wauwatosa had contended that the annexation was not contiguous to Milwaukee and was defective in regard to electors, among other charges.[27]

This victory, and the assumption that the ruling of Judge Rinehard would be sustained by the Supreme Court of Wisconsin, led some Milwaukee people to advocate that the city annex into Waukesha County and take in an additional area of 10 square miles to form a new satellite city, which would offer several advantages, such as from the perspective of civil defense.[28] This idea was supported by some city officials and by William A. Norris, an influential columnist for the *Milwaukee Sentinel* and a frequent commentator on annexation. A proposal of this type was embodied in a 1951 report by Elmer Krieger, city planner and secretary of the Board of Land Commissioners. The proposal was to create a new part of the city at the end of the Butler strip annexation, with a new design and fed by express highways.[29]

Earlier in the year I had made a similar proposal at a birthday luncheon for the City of Milwaukee held annually by the Milwaukee Press Club. I proposed a dispersal of the Milwaukee population into Waukesha County and the replanning of the metropolitan area to include satellite cities under a single planning control. I also proposed the introduction of green spaces. Part of the reason behind the proposal for dispersal was to reduce the vulnerability of the city to atomic destruction, for I did a great deal of thinking about the defense of cities from the time of the first explosion of an atomic bomb.[30] As nearly as I can recall, this proposal received a hostile comment from the suburban press, and a strained silence from the Milwaukee press.

All of these ideas about city expansion, however, were nullified in April of 1951 when the Wisconsin Supreme Court handed down a decision on annexation with an opinion by Justice Edward J. Gehl. The decision invalidated Milwaukee's annexation of the Butler strip as well as 205 acres in the unincorporated township of Greenfield. The court's decision hinged on the point that a referendum of the persons in the annexed territories, as required by the laws of 1898, had not been held. The city had not held such votes, having deemed it sufficient to have the majority of the electors sign a petition. The city's annexation procedure of 52 years was thus knocked out and for a while it appeared that all recent annexations were jeopardized.[31] This decision was released on April 3, 1951, the same day that the advocates of low-rent public housing in the city lost a referendum question that required each public housing project to be approved by Milwaukee voters. I regarded it as a "black day" in the history of the city.

Prior to the decision of the state Supreme Court on the Butler strip annexation, the city had fought another crucial annexation battle. Southwest of the city, in the township of Greenfield, near S. 43rd Street and W. Lincoln Avenue, there were industrial companies paying relatively nominal town taxes. The Greenfield township, however, began to fill up with population, and the population demanded services, particularly school services. This meant a rise in town taxes and therefore the taxes of the companies. Two companies were especially involved — the Froedtert Grain and Malting Company and the Globe Steel Tube Company. The companies sought to be annexed to the nearby Village of West Milwaukee, which had much heavy industry, only about 5,000 people and very low property taxes because of the large return on state income taxes to the village. Milwaukee sought to forestall this move and was ultimately defeated in a Circuit Court decision rendered in favor of West Milwaukee, which was already swollen with industrial property.[32] Subsequently other nearby industrial property also went into West Milwaukee, while Milwaukee annexed the nearby residential areas with a heavy cost for schools and other services.

Parts of the Wauwatosa township were annexed by Milwaukee during the year of 1950, and the town began to disappear.[33] The largest part of the Wauwatosa township, however, was taken in by the City of Wauwatosa in February of 1953 when about eight square miles were annexed.

Despite the annexation activity of the City of Milwaukee, it was apparent in 1950 that the rate of city annexation was not keeping up with the spread of population, which was dispersing in a wide circular pattern. According to a report made by Werba and the Annexation Department, the 1950 census had shown this population distribution and without the annexation of new lands Milwaukee would have posted a net loss in population.[34]

The suburban influence was again evident in the 1951 Legislature. A bill was proposed to block Milwaukee's annexation efforts, before the state Supreme Court achieved the same result by issuing its ruling.[35] In response to the Supreme Court decision, the city immediately sought to introduce new legislation to again have a workable annexation procedure.[36]

Again the city engaged in a bitter struggle with the Iron Ring of suburbs and their numerous attorneys. In one of the hearings, a town attorney, William Bowman, stated the basic concept of the suburbs in their opposition to Milwaukee. "What's so good about the City of Milwaukee?" he shouted, and I was compelled to remind him that it was reputed to have the finest record of municipal administration in the nation.[37]

The city, in order to show the members of the Legislature exactly what was going on, invited them to visit the city, which they did late in April of 1951. This action was immediately countered by the suburbs, which brought them back to the area early in May.[38]

The result of all this activity was somewhat helpful for the city in terms of annexation legislation. A law was passed in the Legislature that killed the 1898 law and enacted substantially the same type of procedure in getting signatures of electors and property owners that the city had been following. In addition, the new law required the posting of notices in the territory to be annexed. However, in larger terms of metropolitan planning, this law was still grossly inadequate and was one of the reasons for numerous incorporations. But the law was better than nothing for the city.[39]

Some of the suburban fringes that had been opposing Milwaukee's plans to annex succeeded in incorporating. Glendale formed an incorporation that included the heavily industrialized area known as the "Schlitz terminal" along N. Port Washington Road. This incorporation defeated Milwaukee's attempt to annex directly northward. Subsequently Glendale sought to annex all of the remaining parts of the Town of Milwaukee but did not succeed in annexing the area known as Bayside, which formed a village of its own.[40] Thus the Town of Milwaukee went out of existence, but the residents who were annexed by Glendale gained a sizeable tax base for themselves.

This example encouraged people in the eastern end of the Town of Lake to incorporate as St. Francis in July of 1951. The City of Milwaukee could not stop this action, which left the rest of the rural and residential areas of the town in a difficult position. This led to discussions of annexing the remaining portion of the Town of Lake to Milwaukee.[41]

Closing of the annexation routes to the direct north, southeast and south still left Milwaukee with the opportunity to annex to the southwest, south of West Allis, to the direct west, between West Allis and Wauwatosa, and to the northwest. The opportunity to annex to the west and south led to a spectacular proposal by private citizens to annex land along the Milwaukee-Waukesha rapid transit electric line. This line was in a precarious position, having passed from corporation to corporation, each one weaker than its predecessor in its ability to keep the line going. By 1951 it was in serious danger. It had corporate owners who had very few financial resources and almost no experience in operating such a line. A move was made to annex 38 square miles along this line in Waukesha County and southwestern Milwaukee County by a group of five men who posted annexation notices in the territory and who had received the encouragement and advice of William A. Norris. This annexation ultimately failed because of suburban opposition, because Milwaukee officials thought it was too bold and because the rapid transit line failed before action on annexation could be taken.[42]

While these plans for annexing large territories to the west and southwest were under consideration, a second proposal to annex about 27 square miles of the Town of

Granville to Milwaukee was presented. This plan seemed to me to be more feasible because of the contiguous and compact character of all parcels of this tract. The City of Milwaukee considered the Granville annexation at the same time as the proposed transit line annexation, thus giving the city the potential to acquire a total of 65 square miles of land. There was naturally much suburban opposition.[43]

The size of these actions brought from Werba the comment that piecemeal annexation in small tracts was not working and that a master plan for the area was needed. Werba was concerned that people living in these relatively open areas would be disturbed by having their land taxed as city land and by carrying the financial burden of improvements such as paved streets, curbs, gutters and sidewalks. As I recall, he was also uneasy about the size of the 38-square-mile annexation but welcomed the Granville annexation.[44]

A different kind of reaction came from the City of West Allis. It changed its attitude from opposing annexation of itself to seeking annexation. It targeted 12 square miles for annexation to counter Milwaukee's annexations. Ultimately, the area north of West Allis, including the Wisconsin State Fair Park, which Milwaukee desired to annex, went into West Allis, as did about six other square miles in 1954.[45]

The Iron Ring continued to close around Milwaukee. The majority of the remaining Town of Wauwatosa was claimed by an annexation to the City of Wauwatosa in 1953. The Town of Greendale was the subject of attempts by the City of Milwaukee in the early 1950s to expand its territory, first through the encouragement of a private housing corporation formed by some veterans, including city employees, and then by annexation, but these efforts ultimately proved unsuccessful. The Greenfield and Granville townships were among the few areas left for Milwaukee to annex through some break in the Iron Ring. Here the struggles to annex and consolidate caused situations that had numerous and complex ramifications. The issues of school district boundaries, water service extension, metropolitan area studies and many other matters evolved out of the city's attempt to annex Granville.

The entire process of annexation proved to be cumbersome and difficult. First, the City of Milwaukee would send out solicitors into territory of the townships contiguous with the city to seek signatures on annexation petitions. After sufficient signatures were obtained and the boundaries of the territory to be annexed were described, a petition for annexation would be filed with the Common Council. Notices would be posted on utility poles in the territory to be annexed. A hearing would be held before the Common Council and an ordinance would be passed making the annexation effective within a certain number of days.

The question of securing signatures was a delicate one and the solicitors encountered many experiences, not quite of the cloak-and-dagger kind, but certainly within the realm of political salesmanship, as those for annexation and those opposed each sought the numerical advantage in persuading people to sign their petitions. The struggle for signatures at times would come to a situation in which an individual would sign an annexation petition, then those opposed to the annexation would get the individual to withdraw the signature, and then those for the petition would get the individual to withdraw his signature from the withdrawal. This made for some fine points in court cases.

In the territory brought into the city, some owners and electors favored annexation and others did not, but were forced in. This led to disputes and litigation. The shape of the annexations were of such configuration that they were often difficult to describe, and because they were usually rather small in later years they became known as "piecemeal annexations." This became a phrase to contend with as some Milwaukee officials said they were opposed to this type of annexation and urged the city to include large tracts. This latter course was impossible except by consolidation, and so piecemeal annexation continued. The phrase was also used to thwart Milwaukee's growth; in the 1955 fight over the incorporation of Oak Creek, Governor Walter Kohler supported special anti-Milwaukee legislation by saying he was against piecemeal annexation.

Piecemeal annexation often caused a school district to be diminished in size and it proved troublesome for the extension of services such as water, sewers and trash collection, but this was what the Legislature had decreed as the method of growth for the City of Milwaukee, while giving large tracts of lands to newly incorporated areas under special laws.

Annexation problems were rapidly mounting in the Granville area. The members of the Annexation Department staff showed me a map of the Town of Granville that detailed the postings and overpostings of Milwaukee and Brown Deer. The conglomeration of overlapping procedures was such as to be almost verbally indescribable. The area was a patch of legal plasters and all semblance of adequate planning was lost in the legal complexities. When I saw this map of annexation postings, I felt that the only course of action was to appeal to the governor to get some legislative action to straighten out the mess. The legislative enactments governing city growth had broken down in a maze of legal red tape and only the attorneys specializing in township incorporations would profit by it. The map of Milwaukee County municipalities was not being made by planners or students of scientific land use, but by town and village attorneys who were paid fees for the amount of litigation they conducted.[46]

The Wisconsin Legislative Council agreed to take up the city expansion issue—the postings, the litigation, the unworkable procedures and the need for legislative action to keep the corridors of growth open.

Representatives from the Legislature held a meeting in Milwaukee on June 16, 1952. The meeting showcased the whole panoply of complaints of the cities against the suburbs and the suburbs against the cities.[47]

Legislative action was of course necessarily slow—too slow to meet the rapidly changing situation—and the struggle of the city to grow against the suburbs' desire to form new communities simply continued. Each time the Legislature was deliberating with a problem, events had moved beyond the situation the Legislature was contemplating. Thus, in 1952, the city was still compelled to engage in piecemeal annexations because there was no alternative. In 38 annexations, the city gained 1.800

square miles, so that in 1952 its area was 50.699 as compared with 44.174 square miles in 1944. By 1952, the estimated population had grown to 650,000.

I continued to demand improved master plans for reconstruction of metropolitan areas and typically expressed my views in a speech to the American Society of Planning Officials in Boston in October, 1952, entitled "Don't Fence Me In." I called for new laws of metropolitan areas, new planning powers, freezing of rural areas near cities and so on, with the thought in the back of my mind of introducing green spaces.[48]

The problems of urban expansion, however, did not come without a cost to the city. There was a school of thought that the city should not expand because it would cost upward of $22 million to put in all city services in a square mile of new development with a population of 12,000 to 15,000 persons, which meant a density of about five homes to the acre. While there was some sentiment not to engage in expansion because of the cost, this view was outweighed by the feeling that if the city did not incorporate new urban areas within its own boundaries, new suburbs would form that would find a method to force the city to pay its expansion costs anyway without the city getting the benefit of a new tax base.

The costs of expansion showed up on each succeeding budget, chiefly in the form of new sewers, watermains, streets, alleys and schools. The bonded indebtedness of the city also increased as these new facilities were put in to help the subdividers, builders and new homeowners. Because of the increased costs and because of the constantly rising tax load, the city government decided to make a case for financial aid from the state. A delegation from Milwaukee called upon Governor Kohler on January 9, 1953, to request funds for the city to serve its growing and expanding population.[49]

About this same time, the struggle for reapportionment in the state Legislature was underway, and there was an attempt to reduce the influence of Milwaukee by basing representation on area rather than population. The full story of this reapportionment battle is an account all in itself, but it is mentioned here because it was beginning to be apparent that the Legislature was not too sympathetic with the problems of the central city in metropolitan growth, or even with the whole metropolitan area itself. The dominance of the Milwaukee area and its problems, whether urban or suburban, was an annoyance to legislators from rural areas and small towns, whose legislative problems could be solved by fish and game laws or by highway grants.

In a speech at a Milwaukee Press Club birthday luncheon for the city on January 31, 1953, I expressed a favorable view about the creation of a federal department of municipal affairs to help cities if their needs were not met by their state legislatures. I said that the attitude of the Wisconsin Assembly in voting 67 to 31 to change the state Constitution so that state Senate districts could be represented on the basis of area was an indication that the cities could not look to the state for help. If the states were going to punish the cities, the cities would bypass them and go to the federal government. I opined that the state legislatures were not listening to city problems.[50]

The area fight on reapportionment and the urban expansion of Milwaukee had by this time made the suburbs hypersensitive and swift to react to any Milwaukee position of planned expansion. It was, therefore, no surprise to read in the press on February 5, 1953, that a delegation from West Allis had called on Governor Kohler to oppose the views of Milwaukee as expressed in its recent conference with the governor. The original meeting of the City of Milwaukee was only indirectly concerned with the problem of annexation, but the suburban leaders interpreted this meeting of city officials with the governor as a propaganda meeting to get the governor's help in annexation. They accused me of being unwilling to meet with them to carry on searching discussions, and they presented a 15-page statement with their own principles and purposes in existing as independent fragments in the metropolitan complex.[51]

It is of importance to repeat what this position was because it was a kind of basic ideological statement of the suburban reason for their separate existence. As reported in the press, the document stated,

> To declare the suburban position: that the suburbs will cooperate in the solution of mutual problems and share in the expense of those projects which are truly of community-wide concern, if their rights of political integrity and self-determination are respected.
>
> To offer a suggestion (which has been ignored by Mayor Zeidler in the past), that there be established a municipalities council for Milwaukee County made up of representatives of the several towns, cities and villages, to implement proper co-operation and sharing among the local governments.
>
> To correct certain manifest inaccuracies and misstatements in Milwaukee's memorandum, to give a more balanced picture of conditions as they really exist in Milwaukee County, and to dispel the impression attempted in Milwaukee's memorandum that all of Milwaukee's troubles are caused by the suburbs.

Having stated a desire to cooperate without yielding the right to form new suburbs or keep the old ones, the statement continued:

> Milwaukee County today contains 230,000 people who live in the suburbs, 670,000 who live in the city of Milwaukee. Shortly after Mayor Zeidler took office in 1948, Milwaukee embarked upon an aggressive and determined annexation program, based on the widely publicized premise that Milwaukee's destiny lies in unlimited growth. A corrolary (sic) to this premise has been another: that all existing units of government in Milwaukee County should be supplanted by one, the City of Milwaukee.

The 230,000 people of the suburbs do not contest Milwaukee's right to grow, provided that such growth is secured with the full consent and that Milwaukee respect the integrity of other municipalities. The suburbs believe that there is a place, even in a large metropolitan area, for small, efficient municipal government, offering a high degree of participation by citizens, strong civic and community spirit, low crime rates, and other 'small town' virtues. They feel it is unimportant whether any given unit of government grow, just so the Milwaukee area grows and prospers.

The suburbs believe that there should not be created in Milwaukee County a huge municipal creation to spawn the big city evils so repugnant to the traditions of Wisconsin.

The suburbs feel that a great stride forward could be made in Milwaukee County by the establishment of a municipalities council, composed of representatives from the town, cities, and villages to explore and define areas of cooperation, to decide upon projects of community-wide concern and to devise and set up methods of cooperation and cost sharing. We believe that the Milwaukee community has never had fair opportunity to solve its own problems and that Milwaukee should agree to participate in such an effort.

The statement further said that in the past 10 years the suburbs had provided space for 55,000 new residents while Milwaukee had added only 50,000. The suburbs further argued that Milwaukee's annexation and public housing were detrimental because they brought a higher property tax. The suburbs also objected to participating in a proposed $7 million museum.

In the statement the suburbs objected to the city's claim that it was losing taxes because high-income residents had moved to the suburbs. The suburbs said that the city's fiscal difficulties were due to grandiose, unplanned, subsidized annexation.

This statement is worth quoting in some length because it was so revealing of the suburban position. The suburbs in effect expressed the fundamental belief that many small units of government in the metropolitan area were desirable as compared to one unit. They did not object to the city expanding if it was not at the expense of the suburbs. They knew that Milwaukee could not expand by taking in incorporated places, but only by taking in territory from the unincorporated townships, and thus the suburbs seemed to ask for veto power over the city expanding into the townships.

The suburban statement seemed utterly reasonable in asking for a council of municipalities, but it did not say that there was already such a council—the Milwaukee County League of Municipalities—which was known as the Iron Ring and which was formed chiefly to fight Milwaukee's expansion. Neither did the suburbs want to yield the tax advantages that came about as a result of the incorporation of areas with a large industrial base and few people; the suburbs wanted to continue taking advantage of the state income tax return of 50 percent from their large industries and thus relieve the few residents of property taxes.

The idea of reasonable discussion of common problems was another idea that seemed sound, but did not work out in practice. Most of the suburbs that were formed were deficient in some major respect, such as being unable or unwilling to supply water to their residents. Thus a meeting with them would result in their proposals to have Milwaukee use its tax base to supply their deficiencies whatever they were.

Illustrations of the first of the above two conditions were found in the incorporation of Glendale in December of 1950 in the area just north of Capitol Drive, including the Schlitz terminal and other industries along N. Port Washington Road. This incorporation was designed to provide a tax island for residents north of W. Silver Spring Road and N. Green Bay Avenue by having the industries carry the tax load for them. Incidentally, this work, as I remember it, was the product of a legal expert, C.R. Dineen, an attorney who specialized in annexation matters, and a county planner, Roland Hertel. C.R. Dineen was a doughty fighter for the suburbs and a worthy opponent.

Another incorporation with a similar intent took place within the Town of Lake. The residents of the eastern portion of this township discovered that the western portion was filling in with population and that the advantage from having a large electric power generating plant was diminishing because no other industry was coming in. The residents of the eastern area, which was known as St. Francis because of a seminary located there, proceeded to incorporate as the City of St. Francis in July of 1951. The newly formed city included the power plant, thus leaving the remaining residents of the Town of Lake facing a large increase in taxes due to a weakened tax base.

When the press asked me to comment on the statement of West Allis officials, which was a kind of masterpiece of theology supporting suburban "apartheid," I stated that it was a waste of time to sit down with suburban officials because there was "no area of compromise. Our meetings usually wind up in a discussion of the Milwaukee water system. They cast covetous eyes on it."[52]

I further stated that I had not been elected mayor to preside at the liquidation of Milwaukee's assets, and that the tax differential between Milwaukee and its suburbs was a major problem because the suburbs had made themselves into tax-free pockets, thereby taking away big sources of taxes from the towns, which were in financial straits as a result. I also chided the suburbs for supporting the system of area representation in the legislature against population representation.

The leadership that the City of West Allis furnished against Milwaukee in annexation and other matters always used to puzzle me, and I have still not found the answer for it. The leadership was fortified in its position by a weekly newspaper, the *West Allis Star*, which ran editorials in almost every issue attacking Milwaukee and myself. It attacked me editorially in the issue of February 12, 1953, for not yielding to the suburbs' position and asked the villages to gird for a fight to the finish against Milwaukee's annexation.[53]

Some clue to the conduct of these suburban papers is to be found in the work of Werba and Grunwald,[54] who claimed that a reason for the fight against consolidation and annexation was the fact that the suburban press enjoyed revenue from official printing. Further, appeals were made to suburban consumers to shop with the advertisers in the suburban press, and in essence, therefore, a basic reason for the existence of the suburbs was to be found in the desire of the suburban press to stay in business in opposition to the huge metropolitan dailies.

In 1953, the city annexed 2.509 square miles in 44 annexations, which brought the area up to 54.978 square miles. This increased growth also had its effect on the school system, which was trying to keep up with the load of new pupils from the brand new subdivisions, and on the sewer budget, and on the waterworks, which had need to expand. The expansion of the waterworks soon became a central issue in the city's struggle for outward growth and in the internal problems, physical and political, of the city. The demands of the subdividers who were building houses under the terms of easy credit began to outstrip the abilities of the sewerage system and waterworks to meet their needs and this ultimately led to the most serious consequences in these areas, both inside the city and in the suburbs.

The increasing restrictions imposed by the Iron Ring and the inability of the City of Milwaukee or any other entity to plan for land use in the metropolitan area became more disturbing and was reflected in my speeches from that time to the end of my service as mayor. In the inaugural address of my second term of office beginning on April 6, 1952, I said that the city's most important problems involved the relationships of the city to its urban fringe and to the state government. The hotly debated issues of equality of taxation, equality of representation and equality of services were directly tied to urban-suburban relationships. The question of how to permit the orderly growth and planned expansion of the city, I stated, was a legislative problem. The Wisconsin Legislature, however, had not met its responsibility in dealing with this urban issue because it had allowed the formation of governments in Milwaukee County that were tiny in size but with such large tax bases that they did not have local taxes. I noted that the St. Francis incorporation had taken away the tax advantage of a large power plant from the Town of Lake and I predicted that the town might have no choice but to join with Milwaukee because of the loss.[55]

In a speech to a meeting of the American Society of Planning Officials, I said:

> The central American city is the production of America, and under the right kind of federal and state government it can be the arsenal of democracy and of free people the world over. But the central city is highly vulnerable and it needs to be redesigned and replanned from the point of view of preserving human values and the point of view of national defense.

A people living in the constant threat of destruction cannot act intelligently or peacefully; a people living in a bad environment will find it difficult to rise to the heights of good citizenship; a people whose main stimulus for production comes from military reasons cannot act as good neighbors. In the United States we can overcome all three of these difficulties by setting about on a master plan to reconstruct our metropolitan centers. Such a plan will put a basic floor under our economy in peacetime, if it is combined with a broader plan for similar rehabilitation of rural areas and regions. The program will reduce the effects of blight on the human being, and it will remove a great deal of fear on the part of the modern city dweller in this age of global conflict. [56]

Having thus stated the problem I offered some suggestions. I said that the primary responsibility for urban improvement rested with state legislatures, and if they failed, then the metropolitan target areas would have to obtain relief from the Congress. I said it was incumbent on every state legislature to recognize under the law critical metropolitan areas of the state. The multiplicity of governments should be reduced by use of the borough system or by consolidation into a single unit of government. New powers of planning and zoning into unsettled regions should be given to these governments and the objective should be to reduce population densities to 5,000 people per square mile or fewer, to freeze rural areas close to the city and to judiciously disperse industry.

I advocated fireproof construction and new sources of revenues to take out slums. I also advocated that the Housing and Home Finance Agency, the National Security Resources Board and the federal Bureau of Roads jointly compose their policies so that they did not work at cross purposes to each other, with one building the cities ever more densely and the others urging decentralization.

I said that "the Congress should provide incentives to state governments to get busy on this problem of metropolitan planning and development, or face the loss of jurisdiction over these areas." It was this policy that I continued to pursue for the next eight years until my retirement from public office.

The need for a metropolitan area to be free from tortuous, involved and multitudinous forms of government I again stressed in a talk before the National Institute of Municipal Clerks in Omaha in May of 1953. Here I coupled the demand for a single planned government in the metropolitan area with certain other demands as constituting a "bill of rights" for cities. Further demands included equal representation in legislatures based on population, full measure of home rule, a just system of taxation that did not bear down disproportionately on city people and free access by cities to the federal government for relief from problems created by federal policies or by unjust forms of state government. Other demands included special consideration by state and federal governments of the problems of traffic congestion, population density and industrial development as well as consideration for the special social problems created by congested living, insecurity of employment and large shifts in population. Most of the solutions to these problems were hindered by fragmented governments in the metropolitan areas.[57]

During the period of 1953 and 1954, serious discussions took place between officials of the Town of Lake and the City of Milwaukee. Lake officials headed by Town Chairman John Budzien were considering joining the City of Milwaukee because the cost of development of their area appeared too high after the Lakeside power plant was removed from the tax base of the town and included in the incorporation of St. Francis. A consolidation agreement was ultimately worked out to deal with matters of assets, pension systems, methods of rendering services and similar matters. Much of the agreement was worked out by the city attorneys and town attorneys, with the special aid of the city comptroller, Virgil H. Hurless, and a Common Council committee. Chairman Budzien ably steered the discussions to a fruitful conclusion. The city was interested in the consolidation because it needed additional raw land for builders and for potential industrial sites.

On April 6, 1954, the consolidation ordinance was submitted to the voters of the township and the city and was approved in both cases. In the city, the vote was overwhelmingly in favor: 78,060 to 19,415. The principal objection in the city I judged to come from a fear of increased city taxes because of the need to provide additional municipal services to the town.

Because of the town chairman's able leadership, it was only natural that the Common Council should elect him to be the alderman from the new ward, the 19th. Alderman Budzien continued to serve after I left office, having won a narrow election victory in 1960. He was commonly conceded to be one of the ablest aldermen. He was not particularly friendly to many of my objectives, and certainly not to my political philosophy, but he was a good conservative balance in the Milwaukee Common Council.

After the consolidation of the Town of Lake with Milwaukee, the city spent much time arranging the smooth integration of both governments. The addition of the township added 9.351 square miles and 13,000 inhabitants to the city. A total of about 1,750 acres of the area was deemed suitable for industrial sites.

There were 66 other annexations during the year of 1954 adding more than three square miles to the city so that with consolidation the total growth during this year amounted to 12.612 square miles. The total area of the city was now 67.590 square miles.

Early in 1954, the Wisconsin Supreme Court handed down a ruling on an annexation case of 314 acres in the Town of Wauwatosa, near N. 92nd Street and W. Capitol Drive. This case was contested by the town and affected about 50 annexations made by Milwaukee between 1951 and 1953. The case concerned whether the procedure used by the city met the requirements of the annexation law of 1952, which had replaced the law of 1898. The town had claimed, among other things, that the city had not passed a charter ordinance to elect to use the 1952 law as its legal basis for annexation. A Milwaukee County Circuit Court had ruled that the city did not need to pass such an ordinance but merely a simple annexation ordinance.[58] In February of 1954, the state Supreme Court issued a decision in favor of the City of Milwaukee. This was a great victory, but it also meant heavy fiscal burdens and problems of community service in the newly annexed areas. A few weeks earlier, I had expressed some doubts about the ability of the city to keep up with the annexations because of the costs and I had hoped that a sewer service charge might be instituted to help carry the sewer costs of new areas.[59]

In 1954, the City of Milwaukee was also confronted by a problem arising from an attempt to incorporate the entire Town of Granville. In January of that year, Richard W. Cutler, another able attorney working on town and suburban matters, announced an effort to incorporate the town as a fourth-class city. I immediately stated that this would mean Milwaukee would be ringed by suburbs and I indicated city opposition, therefore, to this attempt. Having posted the area for annexation, the city was not as helpless in the matter of determining the future of this unincorporated area as it was in the case of the Glendale and St. Francis incorporations.[60]

In the areawide discussion that was going on about annexation and city and suburban rivalry, I had written a letter to the *West Allis Star*, pointing out that there must be a yielding of "sovereignty" to solve metropolitan problems, and that communities were not absolutely independent. Even now, West Allis itself was dependent on Milwaukee for water and on the Sewerage Commission for sewer service.[61] The *Star* replied that cooperation with Zeidler was impossible because he wanted a single unit of government in the area.[62] This was the inflexible suburban position.

Several times that year I repeated my position that the federal government and the states should take more interest in the cities. On one occasion I said that the state and federal governments would inevitably weaken themselves if they did not recognize that their own future success was tightly bound up with the solution of the problems of local government, and that unless local governments were healthy, national governments would not be successful.[63]

On another occasion at a regional meeting of the Council of State Governments in French Lick, Indiana, I criticized the state legislatures for being "unresponsive" to cities. I said that the state legislatures were responsible for the way cities flourished and if the legislatures were unwilling to give urban areas proper representation or unwilling to hear their problems, the urban-rural conflict would continue. I said that the states needed a different attitude now that 60 percent of the people were living in cities as compared to 150 years ago when only 5 percent of the people lived in cities.[64]

The Community Development Department, formerly known as the Annexation Department, worked on the annexation of lands in the Town of Oak Creek, which had become adjacent to Milwaukee by virtue of its consolidation with the Town of Lake. One tract of land near S. 20th Street and W. College Avenue was annexed. The city also continued to try annexations in the Granville area where it had made a considerable number of postings.

By this time it had become apparent that a factor of social culture was working against the city in obtaining support from people for annexing their lands. Some people appeared to want to be annexed to other communities because they had personal ties to neighborhoods nearest them, as in the case of people near West Allis. Another important reason for opposition to Milwaukee annexation was that people wanted a more socially acceptable address which they could get from a suburb rather than from Milwaukee.[65]

In February of 1955, Richard Cutler, as the attorney for a citizens' committee desiring to incorporate Granville, asked for a halt to annexation in order to investigate a proposed City of Granville and its probable costs. I did not favor a halt to the process because I feared that during any truce Granville would be incorporated and another link forged in the Iron Ring.[66]

The year 1955 brought another legislative session and this was to be a most unhappy year for Milwaukee in terms of its planned growth. Among the problems presented to the city was a proposed bill to give a statutory standing to a countywide study committee known as the "Committee of 21." Created by the Milwaukee County Board for the purpose of discussing metropolitan problems, the Committee of 21 was comprised of seven county officials, seven city officials and seven suburban officials. The proposed bill to give the committee statutory authority was supported by a group of local business leaders called the Greater Milwaukee Committee (the successors of the 1948 Corporation, which had fought to have the city leave its debt-free status) and also by the City Club. I opposed this proposal and the Common Council was divided on it. I was opposed because the proposal was, in my opinion, an attempt to preclude any investigation by the state into metropolitan problems. I had not objected to the Committee of 21 when it was formed on a voluntary basis following the failure of the 1953 state Legislature to create a state commission to study the metropolitan area, but I was opposed to the creation of a statutory committee of any type that would be dominated by suburban interests.

I said on the occasion of the proposal of this bill that it was originated by outside organizations and suburbs that wanted to control some of the city's major policies but had been unable to do so directly. Through this committee a minority could control a majority. I reiterated that I had favored a state study of metropolitan problems but the suburbs had defeated such a bill. Edward Gerhardy, president of the Greater Milwaukee Committee, said that the nature of the Committee of 21 was not as important as a start on studying metropolitan problems. This position failed to take notice of the fact that the suburbs would not compromise in any way on the issue of tax differentials in their favor, and so the composition of a study committee was very important.[67]

This issue is worthy of notice because it indicated that the suburbs were becoming strong enough to slow the city's growth. The suburbs were moving into a position by means of study committees to get recommendations from such committees, packed in their favor, to have the City of Milwaukee render to the suburbs vital services that they could not or would not furnish to themselves. This issue was to become increasingly contentious.

The Judiciary Committee of the Common Council voted to oppose legal status for the Committee of 21, although two leading councilmen, Alderman Milton J. McGuire, president of the Common Council and Alderman Matt Schimenz, a well-informed attorney, supported it. These two men supported this bill as the next best thing to a legislative study.

I again declared my opposition to a statutory standing for the Committee of 21 because of the likelihood that the suburbs would then use the committee as their means of conducting and controlling a local study of metropolitan problems, thereby avoiding a more objective statewide study. I said that the suburbs did not want to help with the problems of the central city, and each suburb was interested only in a particular problem that it wanted solved for itself. I repeated that the suburbs wanted the Iron Ring closed around Milwaukee. "Once the ring is closed," I said, "the suburbs will press the city for services which they can't supply themselves." I warned that once they acquired city water, they would pull industry away from the city.

I also stated that there were no indications the suburbs were willing to give anything towards making genuine cooperation work. I was afraid that if this bill passed, "inequities would be permanently saddled on the people of Milwaukee."

It was interesting that this bill was introduced by State Senator Allen Busby of West Milwaukee. He represented the most favored community of the Iron Ring — West Milwaukee had an enormous tax base, few residents and low taxes. His brother, County Supervisor Bert B. Busby, was chairman of the Committee of 21. If I could judge any position that these two gentlemen would take, it would be to preserve the extraordinary discriminatory advantages that their home community and other wealthy suburbs received.[68]

I addressed the full Common Council when it considered the bill. I pointed out that the Committee of 21 would become a new governmental agency with powers superior to local government, that it could not be disbanded and that it would be a policy-making body not directly responsible to the people, besides being unrepresentative of the population. This was not what I considered the answer for a metropolitan government. The Common Council voted to support the principle of favoring a statewide study of the urban area instead of giving statutory powers to the Committee of 21.[69]

I had judged that the suburbs did not want a statewide study because they could not control it, and because a local "study" of the Milwaukee County area could be packed with suburban people who would make findings in their favor.

When the Committee of 21 later considered Senator Allen Busby's bill, the chairman of the committee, Supervisor Bert Busby, said his committee would go ahead and support the bill because 19 units of government in the county favored it even though the Milwaukee Common Council had voted 24 to 3 against it.[70]

The Busby bill, however, was a minor threat compared to the major one in the proposed piece of legislation known as the "Oak Creek bill." This was a bill proposed by a group in the township of Oak Creek with the help of a Milwaukee attorney, Anthony X. Basile, who sought special legislation to incorporate the whole township of Oak Creek as a fourth-class city in order to prevent Milwaukee from expanding into the township. Another important factor was the existence of a new power plant built by the Wisconsin Electric Power Company in Oak Creek at the junction of the lakeshore and the county line. The income tax return from the plant swelled the treasury of the township and this enabled it to pay an enormous legal fee to lobby the proposed bill through the Legislature.[71]

Basile was a lobbying genius. He put the bill through the state Senate with a whopping 24-to-9 vote and then had it carried in the Assembly with a 44-to-42 vote when he persuaded a south side Democratic assemblyman, George Sokolowski, to vote with him. If Sokolowski had not voted for Basile's bill, it would have lost on a tie. Sokolowski claimed he had voted with the majority for the bill to be able to vote for reconsideration.[72]

Not only did the Legislature pass the Oak Creek bill at the behest of the suburbs, but it also passed a bill preventing Milwaukee from providing water service to any area that had formed its own water district. The Legislature passed another bill permitting the sale of housing projects and requiring referendum approval on new public housing.[73]

The passage of these bills was dismaying. It was my opinion that the Republicans of the Milwaukee suburbs, who held the purse strings of the Republican Party, were the real force behind these anti-city bills. I did not have much hope that Governor Walter Kohler, a conservative Republican, would veto any of these bills. Nevertheless, I stated publicly that I would ask the governor to veto the Oak Creek bill and the water district bill.[74]

Meanwhile there were developments on other fronts of the urban fringe. In Granville especially there was a flurry of activity by citizens who favored annexation to Milwaukee and others who favored incorporation. Vincent A. Schmit, a leading attorney of the town who favored annexation, protested that small annexations of "180 acres or so" hurt Milwaukee because of the accompanying construction of low-cost homes and prefabricated homes, which were resented by people with expensive homes. However, these small annexations were all the city could achieve and usually it could annex only a few acres at a time.[75]

In July of 1955, after a meeting in Granville in which 400 residents voted to fight Milwaukee, I spoke out against the policies of C.R. Dineen and Richard W. Cutler in their attempt at incorporation. I expressed opposition to the two attorneys because they were seeking to create multiple governments in the metropolitan area and hence to constrict Milwaukee, which was already overcrowded within its boundaries.[76]

Along with Assistant City Attorney Harry G. Slater, I traveled to Madison to speak to the governor's legal counsel to urge a veto of the Oak Creek bill, but the governor signed it into law. The new law allowed townships with a population of 5,000, spread over many square miles and with an equalized valuation of $20 million, to incorporate as a city when they could not qualify as a village as far as urban characteristics were concerned. I said that the signing of this bill was a cruel blow to the City of Milwaukee, and that it would tend to make Milwaukee a vast slum because towns such as Granville, Greenfield and Franklin could also qualify under the law to become cities.

The governor was quoted as saying that piecemeal annexation of surrounding areas caused serious dislocations and worked serious hardships on communities. He said the bill would prevent such annexations while the problem was studied. The governor also pointed out that the new law faced court action as the attorney general had questioned its constitutionality. He said he had signed the bill in the belief that its merits for the time being exceeded the harm that conceivably might be done under its provisions.

I felt it necessary to comment on the governor's statements. I said that piecemeal annexation was the only kind of annexation allowed under present state laws, and that as far as testing the validity of the new law, the City of Milwaukee could not start court action. I warned that the law would have the gravest financial consequences for Milwaukee because expanding industry would leave and cause us to lose our tax base, with no chance for the city to recover. The new law, I said, in effect told builders to go elsewhere because the city could no longer supply them with new lands. The law would also force the 700,000 people of the city to build up vertically instead of expanding horizontally.

I also remarked that the theories of the governor's legal staff in advising him to sign the Oak Creek bill were truly amazing. If they believed that small city government was better for people than big city government, then Milwaukee should be broken up into 100 units of 7,000 people each. I also pointed out that in one fell swoop the Legislature had given a rural government more territory than the City of Milwaukee had been able to gain by annexation in 10 years, and this I said was discrimination against the 700,000 people in Milwaukee.

Milwaukee was thus deemed an undesirable community that should not be allowed to grow, and so Milwaukee became a Cinderella of the state's cities.

Anthony X. Basile, the attorney who promoted the bill, discounted the idea that it was unconstitutional because it was special legislation. He said there were all types of special laws affecting Milwaukee.[77]

The monstrous character of the Oak Creek bill aroused even a lethargic *Milwaukee Journal*, which, while it bore the name "Milwaukee," had not been active lately in the struggles of the city to find lands for its growing population. The newspaper editorialized on the bill after it became law and criticized the governor for abetting the Legislature in its bias against cities.[78]

The formation of Oak Creek did not proceed as smoothly as Anthony Basile and town officials had hoped. In November of 1955, Attorney General Vernon W. Thomson ordered the secretary of state not to issue a certificate of incorporation until the state Supreme Court tested the validity of the case. This order brought a cry of outrage from Basile, who said, "The town of Oak Creek is the victim of one of the greatest conspiracies in the history of the state." He charged that the governor and the attorney general were setting a dangerous precedent by interfering with the process of incorporation. Basile also charged that the governor had been pressured by me because Milwaukee had appealed the case to the Wisconsin Supreme Court. Basile told his clients in the town to start acting as a fourth-class city despite the blocking of the incorporation.[79]

Basile based his charges on the fact that Governor Kohler had told me he signed the Oak Creek bill in the full conviction that it would be tested in the courts; the attorney general had questioned the constitutionality of allowing any township adjoining Milwaukee to incorporate even if the township did not have the characteristics of a city. The governor also said that if he had not signed the bill it would have come up at every session of the Legislature.[80]

Oak Creek officials met in November of 1955 and declared their town a city. They scheduled an election of municipal officers for December 27, 1955. The meeting was an occasion for the denunciation of the City of Milwaukee, its mayor and the *Milwaukee Journal*. The principal assailants were Basile and William H. Bowman. Basile said he was proud to have lobbied the bill through the Legislature and he charged that Milwaukee officials had not acted responsibly in their work of representing the city before the Legislature. The press reported that the crowd shouted to send Zeidler back to Russia.[81]

The matter of Basile's denunciation of the governor, however, was not concluded until some weeks later in November. Basile and town officials held a meeting with Governor Kohler, who had given them just about everything they had wanted by signing their bill. Naturally the governor was incensed by their charges that he had conspired against them in secret meetings with Milwaukee officials. The governor pounded the table in assailing what he termed was a misrepresentation. He said his meeting with Milwaukee officials concerned the anti-public housing bill passed by the same Legislature and that he, the governor, had opened the conversation of the Oak Creek bill. He said that the Oak Creek officials could not say he was unfriendly to them because he had signed their bill. Unabashed by this, Basile told the governor to let them have their incorporation and then they would consent to have the case tested, and Kohler agreed to let them have the best advantage they could against the City of Milwaukee.[82]

Oak Creek ultimately won all its tests because the City of Milwaukee was ruled ineligible to bring suit. Additional incorporations of townships took place, such as Franklin and Greenfield in Milwaukee County, New Berlin in Waukesha County and Mequon in Ozaukee County, either under this new law or under the impetus given by the law. Thus the Legislature, under the influence of suburban attorneys armed with plenty of funds for lobbying, deliberately set out to provide for an other than orderly growth of the City of Milwaukee and the Milwaukee metropolitan area.

While city officials were busy fighting the Oak Creek case, Milwaukee was trying to annex additional lands. In 1955, Milwaukee added 4.57 square miles, which brought an increase in the city's population by 8,817. A major annexation occurred in

Wauwatosa near N. 76th and Congress Streets. This annexation brought in 1.24 square miles and eliminated an irregular boundary.[83]

Milwaukee's Community Development Department also outlined plans for additional annexation in 1956 to include four more square miles.

While the city was trying to induce the governor to veto the Oak Creek bill and the anti-public housing bill, a dispute arose between the Kohler Company, located near Sheboygan, and the United Auto Workers over the unloading of a cargo of clay aboard a Norwegian vessel. The harbors of Sheboygan and Milwaukee were both disrupted. The nature of this dispute and all its ramifications is a story in itself. A bitter division took place in both cities and throughout the state over this strike at the harbors. Before Milwaukee city officials could negotiate a peaceful solution, the vessel went to Montreal to unload.[85]

The net result of this strike in the port was a further strain on city-suburban relations. Legislation was introduced to attempt to take the publicly owned Port of Milwaukee away from the city's control and give it to private interests. The official publication of the Public Enterprise Committee of Milwaukee, the *Public Enterprise Record*, in the issue of September, 1959, protested against the growing suburban influence in Milwaukee city affairs, and stated that the suburban and out-of-city leaders were interested in taking over the Port of Milwaukee, using the Kohler affair as a pretext. The publication further charged that they were also interested in trying to take over the waterworks. The *Record* said,

> The ability of Milwaukee to resist the suburban leaders and to prevent the parceling out of its powers is not very great. The chief papers, daily and weekly, are written, edited and controlled by suburban leaders. Many of the influential societies and civic groups have large contingents of suburban people on them, who help form judgments on the city of Milwaukee. The big dailies seldom scold suburban officials—the scoldings seem reserved for Milwaukee officials.[86]

This tendency was reinforced as the Iron Ring grew tighter.

The writhings of Laocoon were duplicated by Milwaukee as it strove this way and that to escape the enclosing ring of incorporations. From time to time some comment would appear from a suburban leader in an attempt to portray great reasonableness against Milwaukee's unreasonableness. At the annual dinner of the Greater Milwaukee Committee in honor of such civic progress as had been made up to 1955, Hubert O. Wolfe, president of the Milwaukee County League of Municipalities and attorney for the Village of Shorewood, devoted his time on the program to discussing city-suburban relations. He stated that the suburbs would meet with the city any time, but that they did not want to be dictated to or treated as poor relations. He asked for discussion of mutual problems openly and thoroughly, and mentioned water supply, sewage and sanitation problems. He said the suburbs were willing to cooperate but wanted no free rides.[87]

What this statement meant, as I interpreted it, was that the suburbs were willing to sit down with the City of Milwaukee to see how the city could furnish the suburbs with water, sewers and incinerators, but they would not talk about unequal tax burdens, slum clearance or problems the city had. As for the willingness of the suburbs to pay their own way, this I never believed because the basic reason that suburbs wanted discussions with the city was to have the city pay for the capital expansion of services they needed. When it came time for the city to charge rates to the suburbs, they would fight the rates before the Wisconsin Public Service Commission, or the courts, so that the city would end up losing money on services furnished outside of its borders.

It should be noted that the expansion of the City of Milwaukee was part of an effort to address the problem of blight clearance. City officials felt that if new lands could be developed for housing, this would relieve housing pressure in the center of the city, thereby making clearance less costly and allowing better enforcement of building laws. Thus city expansion was necessary for the best success in blight clearance efforts.[88]

My successor in office, Henry W. Maier, later expressed shock at the cost of annexation and claimed that little urban renewal had been done. He should have appreciated that his problem of urban renewal had been made easier by Milwaukee's expansion, which had reduced housing pressure in the center of the city and had made better code enforcement possible, so that the blighted conditions in Milwaukee were not as extensive or as severe as in other cities.

The expansion of the city that took place from 1946 to 1955 resulted in a considerable expenditure of funds for capital improvements in the outer wards. At a meeting of the Sertoma Service Club on December 8, 1955, I commented on this need for expansion. "Pushing our living areas outward gives the city more room for clearance of blighted areas, although slum clearance work in Milwaukee has advanced at a lamentable pace." I reported that during 1950 to 1953 the seven interior wards received about $10.2 million for capital improvements, the 12 intermediate wards received $6.9 million and the eight outer wards $26.8 million. Expansion enabled the city to upgrade its housing. The slowness of federal urban renewal programs alluded to in this speech is another subject in itself.[89]

The relatively rapid assimilation of urbanized lands in the Granville area by annexation and the prospect that much of the town would be built up in residences without an industrial tax base seemed to tip the scales with many people of the township of Granville in favor of consolidation with Milwaukee. Matters came to a head quickly. A report had been issued regarding Granville's future for growth. After this report, favoring the attachment of the remaining portion of the town to Milwaukee, I invited Granville people to talk over the matter of consolidation with Milwaukee, just as consolidation had occurred with the Town of Lake.[90]

Granville at this time had about 22 square miles out of an original 36 square miles remaining in unincorporated territory, and George C. Saffran, the city budget supervisor, had estimated it would cost about $100 million to improve this town to city standards.[91]

The problem of bringing this area into the city in a consolidation was not only a financial one but also a political and legal one. A referendum would have to be held on April 3, 1956. This meant that a consolidation agreement would have to be reached and introduced in the Milwaukee Common Council by February 21, and passed by March 7, in order to be on the ballot on April 3. Some doubt was expressed that this could be done.[92]

In the middle of January of 1956, the town held a meeting at which a merger with the city was favored and later in the month the town board asked the City of Milwaukee to appoint a committee to negotiate a consolidation agreement between the two municipalities. The town board asked that six conditions be met by the city. The board requested a 25 percent reduction in property tax assessment below city levels, representation on the Common Council, an advisory board to represent the town area, a formal schedule on municipal service to be rendered, a mutually acceptable planning of public improvements in the town and employment by the city of town employees and school teachers.[93]

The request for a tax assessment 25 percent below the regular city assessment apparently arose out of a practice instituted by Arthur M. Werba in conjunction with the tax commissioner, Thomas A. Byrne, to assess properties in newly annexed areas at only 75 percent of the current city assessment. This was done on the theory that the new areas did not have full city services such as paved streets, street lighting and fire alarm boxes, and therefore for a period of five years the areas would enjoy a lower assessment. This practice resulted in difficulties for the people and the assessors when the five-year period was up. Nevertheless, it eased the transition from town lands to urban lands for the owners because town assessors had a tendency to make soft assessments in areas where people might be thinking of joining the city.

In the midst of this activity, the harbingers of future legal storms appeared. The Village of Brown Deer filed a petition to annex 1.5 square miles of Granville in January of 1956. Brown Deer had incorporated in 1955, in a kind of anti-Milwaukee movement, and it appeared that anti-Milwaukee forces in Granville had joined with Brown Deer officials. The petition had 1,700 signatures and the Granville town attorney said this proposed annexation by Brown Deer would jeopardize the proposed consolidation with Milwaukee.[94]

Early in February of 1956, City of Milwaukee officials and Granville town officials began their initial talks that resulted in the formulation of a consolidation agreement in time to be put on the ballot in both jurisdictions for April 3, 1956. The work of making the agreement rested in Milwaukee with the Common Council's Judiciary Committee and with many city officials, including George C. Saffran, the budget supervisor; Virgil H. Hurless, the city comptroller; Walter J. Mattison, the city attorney; Harry G. Slater, his deputy; Richard F. Maruszewski, an assistant city

116

attorney; Thomas A. Byrne, the tax commissioner; and Joseph R. Lamping, director of the Community Development Department.

It must be said here that despite fundamental differences about the philosophy of government, practically all elected officials of the city favored annexation and consolidation and vigorously supported it. Even Alderman John Budzien was helpful because of his experience in the Town of Lake and he, too, played an important role in the Granville consolidation.

It should be stated, too, that although I spoke often about annexation and urban expansion, and pressed hard for it as a public policy for Milwaukee, the actual work of getting petitions, processing the new areas and planning their expansion was, of course, done by many others, without whose efforts the expansion of the city could not have taken place.

The above named persons, along with the members of the council's annexation committees, usually headed by Alderman Fred P. Meyers, and the members of the council's judiciary committees, each had vital roles to play. If they were so minded to make an account of their roles as I am, they could tell many interesting critical situations in which their own activity meant the difference between successful annexation or defeat. The legal twists and turns are beyond my capacity to relate.

Lawsuits to prevent the consolidation were initiated, but in March I extended a public invitation to the residents of Granville to join "the finest city in the world." I also expressed my belief that the people of Milwaukee would favor consolidation with Granville because of the opportunities for developing fine residential and industrial areas.[95]

The referendum for consolidation carried in both jurisdictions on April 3, 1956. In commenting on this, William A. Norris, columnist for the *Milwaukee Sentinel*, wrote,

> A few years from now, Milwaukeeans looking back at the election of April 3, 1956, may decide that the most important thing that happened on that date was the vote for the consolidation of the Town of Granville with the City of Milwaukee.
>
> I am assuming in this column that the consolidation will be upheld in the courts.
>
> Granville gives Milwaukee a chance, for the first time in its history, to make long-range, large-scale plans for healthy growth.[96]

The process of obtaining a consolidation between Milwaukee and Granville with its 22 square miles was all the more remarkable because it was carried out against the background of one of the most bitter municipal campaigns in Milwaukee history—the race for mayor between Alderman Milton J. McGuire and myself.

This campaign involved two issues of interest here. One was my charge that McGuire's campaign was heavily backed by non-residents of Milwaukee as shown by his filed campaign receipts and disbursements. These listed a high proportion of suburbanites backing McGuire. This was a serious charge which the *Milwaukee*

Sentinel, completely opposed to me, felt necessary to answer. In an editorial entitled "Outsiders," on February 15, 1956, the *Sentinel* supported the participation of outsiders in Milwaukee municipal elections and attacked me for raising the cry. The *Sentinel* asserted that my forces believed that non-residence should bar any kind of interest or participation in a city election or a city problem. The newspaper stated that employees and owners of businesses who made their money in Milwaukee and spent it there had a right to be interested in the city government. This statement from the newspaper was an open invitation to suburban people to take over the policies of Milwaukee city government.

In the municipal campaign of 1956, Alderman McGuire and I also exchanged blows on annexation policies. In his campaign platform, McGuire had expressed doubts about annexation although he had supported the whole program up to that time. His platform bore many striking similarities to the writings of William A. Norris.

In a debate before the Milwaukee Young Democrats in February of 1956, I charged that McGuire's platform displayed a dangerous indecision as to whether he was for or against annexation. I said his program contained implied criticism of the Community Development Department, and that department, I said, was directly responsible to the Common Council and not to me. McGuire's criticism of the Community Development Department was therefore a criticism of himself and the Common Council.

Later in the campaign, I sent a long letter to the Common Council saying that Norris in his columns had done an about-face on the question of annexation. I quoted from 12 of his columns starting in August of 1951 in which he favored annexation, and I said that I was sending this information to the Common Council because the city's Community Development Department was responsible to the council, and that an attack on the department's policies was an attack on the council.

Norris called this "buck passing" and then asked what had happened to certain of his plans to annex along the railroad lines and to annex lands to create a self-contained community in the Granville area. He said that I had changed my mind about these proposals of his.[97] Circumstances had made his proposals impossible and he was disappointed over the fact that they had not come to fruition.

During the period of this heated campaign, the state Supreme Court upheld in March of 1956 a ruling by Circuit Judge Francis X. Swietlik that a two-square-mile annexation in the Town of Greenfield was valid. This area lying west and south of S. 68th Street and W. Oklahoma Avenue had been annexed in July of 1954.[98]

During this same period a study by the city itself revealed that providing permanent improvements and municipal services to the annexed areas had increased the city's debt between $30 million and $40 million in the last six years and would in the future result in a $10 million deficit annually. During this time, $92 million had been spent for permanent improvement, of which 60 percent had gone into the outer wards. Assessments in these wards had jumped 100 percent. In terms of city expenditures, the outer wards received $235 per capita more than they paid in taxes per capita. The middle wards had $2.70 less spent on them than they paid in taxes per capita, and the inner wards received $69.62 more per capita than they paid in taxes. The middle wards were financing the outer "cambium layer" of urban growth as well as the rehabilitation of the inner wards.[99] It was thought, however, that the outer wards would soon pay for themselves in tax revenues.

Given the prospect of a merger with Granville, the City of Milwaukee was left with the Town of Greenfield as the only area remaining for annexation. Thereafter, if the city were to expand and gain some unity in the metropolitan area it would have to be by consolidation or some form of metropolitan government.

In January, I went to a hearing during the 1956 Legislature in Madison with Richard Maruszewski, the assistant city attorney who specialized in annexation cases. I expressed a hope that the difficulties between Milwaukee and its suburbs could be lessened. I stated that Milwaukee was intensely concerned lest it become another Boston ringed by suburbs four deep. I described to the Legislature's Urban Development Committee how current methods of annexation made for resistance in townships by cutting into the tax base available for school financing. I also described how industries moved into the suburbs outside of the city to benefit from lower property taxes. I pointed out the need for redeveloping the city, but noted that the cost of such development was falling on people with the lowest income because the higher-income groups were able to move to the suburbs with tax advantages. Mr. Maruszewski told of the troubles he had with petitions, annexation notice postings, withdrawals of names on petitions, withdrawals of withdrawals and withdrawals of withdrawals of withdrawals.[100]

The prospect of ending outmoded methods of annexation by creating a new form of unified government in metropolitan areas was beginning to emerge in the discussion of municipal theory, policy and objectives. In May of 1956, I told the annual meeting of the Wisconsin League of Women Voters at Lake Delton that the state governments should develop a new form of metropolitan area government. I charged that the state governments had systematically sought to make the residents of the metropolitan area second-class citizens. I noted once again how the central cities were burdened by difficult problems that the cities themselves could not solve and that the state governments had failed to solve or refused to address. The people of the central cities, I claimed, had found that their state governments were often politically hostile toward the cities, that the state taxed them heavily and disproportionately, that the state did not return sufficient benefits and that the state tended to ignore metropolitan problems in favor of rural problems. I said that the cities went to the federal government for highway, welfare, social, sewage, housing and traffic problem solutions because the states had failed to meet their needs. I noted how the Wisconsin Supreme Court had saved the metropolitan areas of the state from unequal representation in the Legislature, which had befallen Cook County, Illinois, and Wayne County, Michigan. I also charged that the philosophy of states' rights would sever connections between metropolitan areas and the federal government.[101]

A few days later, Alderman Martin E. Schreiber, who had been elected Common Council president after Alderman McGuire left the council to run for mayor, joined with me in making a public statement on the city's policy toward the suburbs. (Alderman Martin E. Schreiber was the father of Martin J. Schreiber who would later become Wisconsin's governor.) Alderman Schreiber and I said that the city would continue to follow the pattern of recent years. Milwaukee favored the establishment of a single government for the metropolitan area based on the extension of the government of the central city. If one government could not be established through cooperative or legislative action, the city would invite individual suburbs, incorporated or unincorporated, to merge with it. Milwaukee strongly opposed the incorporation of new suburbs to form "tax-free" cities or villages that did not bear their equal share of the area tax burden. The city would be extremely reluctant to consider the transfer of any governmental functions to the county unless the county strengthened its administrative machinery to carry out such functions.

In another statement, we pointed out that the problems of metropolitan areas were not coterminous with the boundaries of the county. The urban area extended into several counties, so an enlarged metropolitan concept of government was needed. We also could see no logic in dismantling our city and giving our powers to others when we already had the necessary municipal powers, the basic system of government and the facilities needed to serve new urban areas.[102]

An expression of policy such as this was not one for the spokesmen of the suburbs to let pass. The *West Allis Star* came out with a blast in its editorial columns of May 24, 1956. This editorial—entitled "Mr. Zeidler's 'One World'"—said that my view of the value of the county was wrong because the county had taken the building of expressways out of the city's hands when the cost had grown too high. The city's reluctance to transfer other functions to the county was interpreted as part of an attempt to enlist the county's help in dissolving suburbs. The editorial criticized Milwaukee for its consolidations with Granville and the Town of Lake and for having to raise $60 million for schools because of expansion. The editorial said that the suburbs should tell Milwaukee where to go because Milwaukee had a vicious plan hatched to liquidate its neighbors.

> Except for the omission of such names as Khruschev (sic), Malenkov and others of their ilk, the plan to gobble up the suburbs sounds like something that might have been nurtured in the Kremlin. It's that stupid and that un-American.
>
> Suburban officials, particularly those representing West Allis, have waged a bitter fight against Milwaukee's attempts at complete domination. We are at the threshold of an even bigger fight. It will demand the whole-hearted support of every person in the suburbs who believes that our freedom of speech, religion and press also includes the determination to live under the kind of government which we choose.

That idea of Americanism and Democracy seems foreign to Mr. Zeidler's way of thinking. But his viewpoint is understandable when you consider his political background.[103]

Two matters are of interest in this editorial. The first and most important is the statement that the people can determine to live under the kind of government they choose. This was the basic statement of the suburbs, and it was hard to answer because it was and is the foundation of all nationalism, including American nationalism. This idea when applied in its naked form to metropolitan areas was taken to mean that any fragment of people could form their own government of any size whatsoever for local purposes and choose to cooperate or not in the solutions of urban problems. This idea pressed to its fullest extent, of course, would mean administrative and governmental chaos in metropolitan areas. Later spokesmen for the suburbs were to modify this idea somewhat.

The lesser matter of interest was the attack on me because of my party affiliation as a democratic Socialist. Whenever my opponents got angry enough against me in debate on a public issue, they sought to demolish any appeal of my arguments and reasoning by attacking my party affiliations. This is, no doubt, a legitimate political trick or device, but when my opponents went so far as to link me with totalitarians and dictators, at this I balked. Accordingly, I wrote a letter to the *Star* asking for a retraction of several statements made in the editorial. The *Star* published the letter, in which I objected to being likened to Khrushchev and to the statement on "foreign" thinking. I said,

> These statements, in my opinion, are attempts to imply that I am a Russian Communist and one given to Communist methods of procedure. I consider this libelous matter and I herewith demand a retraction of these statements as is my right under Section 331.05 of the Wisconsin Statutes.
>
> My defense of the City of Milwaukee from being stripped of its functions and powers to act on behalf of its people must not be termed Communist either directly or by implication.

The *Star* replied that Zeidler was not a Communist nor did the editorial label him as such; any implication he placed in the editorial was placed by himself and not by the publisher of the paper. Then the editorial went in for another attack. It said,

> The point which we made was that Zeidler's training in Socialism seems to have little concern for the individual. Certainly his continued insistence that the suburbs must disappear is contrary to American ideals. It substitutes force of law for human dignity. It is repugnant to the nth degree.

121

> Mr. Zeidler has never made it a secret that he was and is now a Socialist. Socialism in its purest sense is a political and economical theory of social organization based on the collective or governmental ownership and management of the essential means for production and distribution of goods. In short, it is not in complete sympathy with our present way of life based on freedom of economic existence.

In short, I was not a Communist, but I still was un-American. Then to finish off, the editorial said that I wanted to bail out my people by saddling some of their problems on the suburbs. I let this latest sally go, because other problems loomed ahead.[104]

Several interrelated problems on urban-suburban relations were developing at the same time. The city was like a juggler with several balls in the air, and some of the sentiment was beginning to follow that of Alderman Matt Schimenz. He thought annexation ought to be reviewed because the city had added more than 30 square miles, and if the city were to pursue an extensive program of slum clearance, blight elimination and urban renewal in its old areas, an annexation slowdown might be necessary.[105] The desire for urban redevelopment was getting stronger and this program appeared to be hostile to annexation when, as a matter of fact, annexation helped reduce the need for costly redevelopment, if codes of housing and building were properly enforced.

The first major issue occurred in the area of the former Town of Lake, the 19th Ward. People in the area protested that the 1956 assessments were higher than their 1954 and 1955 assessments. The city assessors were raising assessments in the ward to the same level as the rest of the city. Thomas A. Byrne, the tax commissioner, defended the assessments by saying that the people had been told that their assessments were 35 to 40 percent below city levels, that a flat 10 percent increase would occur when the areas came into the city and that assessors would then use the city's methods of assessing the property. City assessments at that time were 50 percent of the true market value. The alderman of the ward, John H. Budzien, complained that the assessors followed the "book and conceded nothing."[106]

Petitions containing 1,500 signatures of property owners protesting increased assessments were soon filed with the tax commissioner, who promised a full review from the Board of Assessors.[107]

It was not a surprise to the city to see that William Bowman, its old enemy, was announcing that he would press a taxpayer suit to the state Supreme Court demanding that the 1954 consolidation be declared "void because of a background of fraud." He said he would make a strong effort to have the Legislature pass a law canceling out the consolidation and restoring the old Town of Lake. He had discussed with irate property owners in the 19th Ward the possibility of detaching from Milwaukee and joining another municipality, perhaps the new city of Oak Creek. Bowman also charged that the city had secretly financed the 1952 and 1954 campaigns of Town Chairman John H. Budzien and Town Supervisor Ray Conell, and that these men had agreed to further the ambitions of the city to gain control of the territory.

The Town of Lake always had sharply contending factions, and it appeared to me that Bowman had picked up one of these factions to support him in an attack on the city. In the same news story as Bowman's announcement of bringing suit, some gloom was expressed by Milwaukee officials because of the passage of the anti-Milwaukee "Oak Creek bill." I said that the city would fight to the end every effort to detach its territory or to overcome the consolidation. I said that a group of suburban attorneys, of which Bowman was a member, would leave no stone unturned in fighting the city because that was their livelihood. This group, I said, had done irreparable harm to the growth of the city and it had induced the Legislature to pass the Oak Creek bill to strangle the city. This latest suit was another harassing technique.[108]

During the month of August, 1956, I asked George C. Saffran, the budget director, to ascertain how much were the expenditures by the city in the former Town of Lake area in the time since it came into Milwaukee in 1954, and how much was received in taxes from this territory. This was to answer the criticism that the city took high taxes but put nothing into the town. Saffran reported that $2,671,171 had been spent on operations and maintenance in the town, and $1,117,821 for improvements, which did not include school costs, nor paying of debts. In addition, $500,000 had been spent in constructing water lines. Only $1,400,000 had been received in taxes.[109]

This brought forth a heated response from Alderman Budzien, who said that this statement, comparing taxes collected in the former Town of Lake with expenditures, is "slanted to slap down property owners who objected to increased assessments." Budzien claimed that this statement prejudiced their appeals pending before the Board of Review.[110]

In September of 1956, William H. Bowman continued to push his charges against the city. He claimed that the city had spent $2,500 to influence the old Town of Lake to join the city and had violated the Corrupt Practices Act because the city had not reported the expenditure. Bowman challenged me to a debate. I told him to put his charges into writing and then come to City Hall to discuss them. I said publicly, "It is unfortunate that a man of Mr. Bowman's caliber has gotten into this situation. It can only do injury, not good. Relief cannot be attained by the abuse of public officials. It can be attained only through the exercise of the due process of law." I asked the tax commissioner to patiently explain how assessments were made to Bowman.

My response to Bowman was in the form of a letter in which I also charged that he had an "unlawyerlike manner" in handling the tax complaints of his clients. I said that it seemed that he was trying to lead them into a misdirected mass movement. I told him it was a mistake to think that what was an administrative decision in tax procedure could be considered a political issue and solved by political means.[111]

Bowman's response was to serve me with a subpoena to appear before a court commissioner in order to answer five questions: How much money was spent by the City of Milwaukee to influence Town of Lake elections? Were the expenditures reported under the Corrupt Practices Act? What secret deals were made with Town of Lake officials that were not included in the consolidation contract? Has the city violated its consolidation contract by overassessing Town of Lake property? How can you justify the deficits you publicly attribute to the Town of Lake?

I did not wait for a hearing before the court commissioner to reply to the charges. I said that Bowman did not want to answer my letter nor give evidence to support his charges, so he was going on a fishing expedition since he had no proof. I defended Alderman Budzien from Bowman's charges, although I did not know whether the alderman would be comfortable about my defending him since we were poles apart on political philosophy.

In answer to the first two questions, in which Bowman asked about expenditures, I told him to look at the budget of the Community Development Department. It was not responsible to me, but to the Common Council, and that department could answer his questions. I absolutely denied any secret deals because there were none, and as to the question of violating the consolidation contract by overassessing, I said this was like the old question, "Have you stopped beating your wife?" There was no proof of unfair assessment and Bowman's charge was another example of his unlawyerlike conduct. As to the excess of city expenditures in the former town over receipts, I said I would be glad to furnish him with the statistics. I then charged Bowman with harassing tactics, which he was also using in the Town of Greenfield, and I told him he could be of more use to his clients by taking their case to the tax commissioner since the commissioner made the assessments under the statutes and not the mayor.[112]

Later in the month I appeared before Circuit Court Commissioner Roland Mietus in his office to be examined by Bowman in a suit brought by Edmund Toman to nullify the city-town merger. Bowman opined that he had spent several months on a Circuit Court order examining city records but found no pertinent one. He said these existed but that he had been given a "snow job." I said that I knew of no such records, and the examination ended inconclusively. My attorney, Assistant City Attorney Alan Steinmetz, kept replying to Bowman that there were no records of the type he wanted.[113]

The issue of the tax complaints became dormant and was ultimately settled by a procedure set up in the law in which some adjustments were made based on evidence shown.

This flurry with Bowman in the Town of Lake ran simultaneously with a more serious and involved problem in the Granville consolidation. In July of 1956, Circuit Court Judge Harvey L. Neelen, an able judge, nullified the April 3, 1956, consolidation of the 22-square-mile Town of Granville by the City of Milwaukee. He ruled that the consolidation ordinances passed by the Milwaukee Common Council and the Granville Board were invalid because annexation moves by the Village of Brown Deer took precedence.

The immediate effect of this decision was to remove Milwaukee's jurisdiction over the area, restore the Town of Granville as a governmental unit, cause the Village of Brown Deer to expand about 11 square miles and restore the Granville-Brown Deer Union High School district boundaries. This situation caused consternation for the City of Milwaukee, which had proceeded very carefully to introduce its administrative services in the area immediately after the consolidation.[114]

Brown Deer had claimed that its annexation proceedings taking place in October preceded the city's efforts at consolidation and that its annexation proceedings were not nullified by consolidation. Harold Fuhrman, the village attorney, delivered a typical suburban comment on this occasion. He said of Judge Neelen's decision, "This turn of events delivers the town of Granville from the treachery and tyranny which befell the Town of Lake." He praised the court and said it was a vindication of an independent judiciary because many people had warned him that it would be impossible to obtain justice from a local court in a struggle with the great and powerful City of Milwaukee.[115]

The city had to react immediately. I began action at once to reopen the case involving its merger with Granville. The city claimed that Judge Neelen in making his ruling had gone beyond the scope of legal issues in a demurrer filed by the city to a Brown Deer complaint, and the ultimate facts of the alleged annexation to the Village of Brown Deer would have to be tried and determined.

I objected to Fuhrman's statement and protested his intemperate and abusive language. I said it was unworthy of a person trained in judicial procedure. "The continual stream of abuse directed at the city by some suburban attorneys has been bad enough, but this expression goes far beyond the grounds of propriety." I said that Fuhrman ought to retract the entire expression, and that "the use of the words 'treachery and tyranny' in connection with the city and the fulfilling of its obligations is untrue and uncalled for." Fuhrman said he would not retract his statements. He said he would defend them in detail, that the choice of words was fair comment and that he would show the misrepresentations made to the people of both the Lake and Granville townships prior to voting on a consolidation referendum.[116]

The city's problems in the two consolidation cases were prominently played up in the press and naturally drew the attention of the state legislators and suburban officials and sympathizers, in addition to those who openly fought the city. The city greatly feared the power of the Iron Ring in the Legislature, especially when that power was backed by the opinion-forming media.

In July of 1956, Milwaukee officials discussed a series of countermeasures to combat the continuing attacks on the city by its suburban neighbors. Three resolutions were introduced into the Common Council to help implement this policy.

One resolution proposed to establish a citizens' advisory committee on community development to help formulate municipal policy on annexation, consolidation and related problems and to help lobby the Legislature. The purpose of this effort was to counter suburban representatives who would swarm on the Legislature and impress it by sheer numbers. It was thought that if advancement associations and civic groups could make an appearance for the city before the Legislature, these appearances would help counter the illusion of numbers that the suburbs presented, since they represented fewer people than lived in the city itself.

In a second resolution, the city attorney's office was to be given the general power to contest annexations by other municipalities in areas adjoining Milwaukee. A third resolution called for the creation of a special committee of city officials to find out what city services each suburb wanted that the city could supply. As nearly as I can recall none of these programs came to be implemented because subsequent events moved too swiftly.[117]

As the opportunity afforded itself, I spoke on the subject of city-suburban relations. In August of 1956, I addressed the American Federation of State, County and Municipal Employees and charged the Wisconsin Legislature and certain suburban attorneys with promoting the fragmentation of local governments. I criticized the Oak Creek law and pointed with concern to the impending referendum in the Town of Greenfield to incorporate that town as a city. I said that if the ring of suburbs were to close, it would be impossible to overcome blighted conditions in the city because the physical facilities of municipal engineering could not overcome the too intensive land use. I felt that redevelopment would be limited if the city had to put back into already overcrowded communities even more people than were there when redevelopment began. I suggested that "it may even become necessary to limit the population of Milwaukee in order to avoid an unmanageable population and traffic situation."[118]

I also decided to visit Toronto to inspect the recently formed Municipality of Metropolitan Toronto, which had been created in response to the problem of a fragmented metropolitan area. After meeting with numerous officials, I concluded that this metropolitan system worked yet created "duplication and injustice." The tax base of Toronto was being used to help the suburbs meet their needs and only a shell of city government was left. A complete consolidation would have been better.

I took the occasion of reporting on this visit to oppose any privately made study of the problems of Milwaukee County, which was then being suggested. I stated,

> What we need is an impartial study by the state government —
> a study that will recognize that the greatest inequity in the
> Milwaukee area is brought about by the incorporation of new
> municipalities to capture a large tax base to benefit a relatively few
> people. I cannot see how any responsible official of government can
> advocate further fragmentation of local government when all the
> experts say there are too many fragments now.[119]

The issue of the city-suburban problem in Milwaukee had drawn the attention of the governor and the Legislature. By now, everyone was agreed that a study of the problem should be made and the question was: "By whom?" The city took the position that it wanted a statewide study on urban-suburban problems conducted by the Legislature, not only for and in Milwaukee County, but wherever such problems existed. In this way the city hoped to gain the support of other major municipalities such as Madison, Green Bay and Racine, which had similar troubles from their suburbs. The suburbs took the view that only Milwaukee County should be studied, and this they did because they wanted to dominate the study and direct its findings to their own ends.

The Committee of 21, which had been created by the County Board at the instigation of suburban leaders, debated the issue of what kind of bill should be sponsored or favored in the Legislature. City officials on the committee took the view that only a statewide study of metropolitan problems should be considered.[120] Suburban members of the committee wanted an independent agency to study metropolitan problems. Meetings grew acrimonious and there was talk of the city quitting and the committee disbanding.[121]

The proposed incorporation of the Town of Greenfield was actively pursued by the town during this period of the late summer and fall of 1956. The town was contesting city annexations and William Bowman was a leader in the attempt to incorporate.[122]

A master move of the suburban lobby was about to unfold against the city. Early in September of 1956, on a Friday afternoon, as I recall it, I received a telephone call from Governor Walter Kohler, Jr., about a committee he intended to appoint. He said he was under great pressure to appoint a committee to look at Milwaukee's problems, and he asked whether I would give him my opinion of some individuals he had under consideration. He then gave some names of suburban people, most of whom were hostile to Milwaukee, and the names of some people who were sympathetic. I gave the governor my opinion and in addition asked him not to make a decision to appoint any committee on Milwaukee metropolitan problems until we in Milwaukee had a chance to present our case. I said that I would mail some documents on the subject immediately. As I recall our conversation, I was distinctly left with the impression that the governor would await our documents. He asked me not to make any announcement of this matter.

However, on the next day, a Saturday, I learned from a *Milwaukee Journal* reporter that the governor had already appointed the committee. It seemed to me that his decision had been made shortly after he talked to me and that his call to me was mostly a matter of "touching bases" politically. My reaction was one of indignation, and I immediately charged that this was a committee to see how the Milwaukee waterworks could be taken over. I said that the seven-member committee that the governor had appointed was weighted against the city and I wanted to know who had secretly pressured the governor to appoint this committee. It was my concern that this stacked committee would obviously produce a report to take away the waterworks without giving the city tax equality, and I did not want the foes of the city to cite such a report as "authority" for proposing legislation to take the waterworks.

The reaction of the governor was featured in the press. "Some people always cry before they're even hurt," he said and he asserted that the committee was not "stacked for or against anyone." He said it was "ridiculous to prejudge the committee since no one has any idea what it will come up with." I felt I had a very good idea of what the committee would come up with. The governor said the members of the committee were "men of high character and integrity" who should come forth with "an impartial and objective study" of the metropolitan area and its problems. And then, to give his whole position away, the governor said that the study committee would not interfere with the plans of Whitefish Bay, Glendale and Fox Point to consider building a new waterworks to serve their communities. The north shore suburbs could have their own water system carved out of Milwaukee's system, but Milwaukee would have to give up control of its own waterworks to the other suburbs.[123]

My next response was to say that I would continue to fight for a statewide study of metropolitan problems by the Legislature in spite of a special governor's committee to make such an investigation for the Milwaukee area. I said that I saw "the same portents in the committee appointed by Governor Kohler as were present in the Oak Creek bill. We were told this bill wouldn't hurt Milwaukee, but it did."

I added that I was disappointed that the official weight of the Common Council had not been enough to get a statewide study of metropolitan problems from the Legislature, and that an unofficial group of major businessmen appeared to have more influence on the affairs of the city than an officially constituted body. I foresaw terrific pressure to take away the waterworks and I noted the fiscal dangers the city would face as a result. I expressed the hope that the governor's committee would not meet in secret (which it subsequently did) and I expressed confidence that the appointees of the committee who lived in the city would not permit the stripping of the city's waterworks without protection against loss in industry.[124]

The committee appointed by the governor was headed by Robert E. Dineen, an executive of the Northwestern Mutual Life Insurance Company. (Robert Dineen was not related to C.R. Dineen, the prominent Iron Ring attorney). The committee was supposed to study metropolitan problems, but curiously enough—or rather not curiously at all—it decided to concentrate on studying the sewerage system and waterworks first. At this time, as I recall it, there was some agitation to expand the powers of the Metropolitan Sewerage Commission to supply services, and I fully expected that this would be the answer given by this committee to solve the suburban water problem, without having the suburbs assume their share of the burden of metropolitan problems.

Mr. Dineen, the committee chairman, said that a "lack of time" would prevent his committee from studying matters other than water and sewer problems. When I was informed of Mr. Dineen's statement, I said that the city would continue to press for a statewide study of metropolitan problems by the Legislature. I said, "It is obvious that the governor's committee does not intend to do a complete job. I think we will find that getting Milwaukee water to the suburbs is its only interest."[125]

The committee held its first meeting behind closed doors at Milwaukee's top social club, the Milwaukee Club. The chairman said that a report had to be made by December 15, 1956, and this was the reason for only taking up the matters of sewers and water supply. It proposed to borrow a staff from local businesses and from the

Citizens' Governmental Research Bureau. The Greater Milwaukee Committee would pay the expenses.[126]

The committee, to answer my charges, said that it did not want to get in a battle of words with anyone and that none of the members arrived with any preconceived ideas or with ties to any individual unit of government. I have often wondered how men who knew beforehand what recommendations they would make could flatly say that they had no preconceived ideas or biases.

The *Milwaukee Sentinel* was quick to join the fight against the city. On September 12, 1956, it came out with an editorial entitled "Provincialism," in which it called my reaction alarming. It criticized me for branding the governor's action as an attempt to "steal" the waterworks and turn it over to the suburbs. It asserted that my charges that the committee was stacked against Milwaukee and that secret forces had worked on the governor were "faintly ridiculous because the governor had been openly urged by the Greater Milwaukee Committee to appoint such a committee." The editorial said that "Mayor Zeidler's attitudes in this matter strike us as being unnecessarily provincial. . . . He appears to be piqued that he was not consulted before an appeal was made to the state's chief executive. He seems oblivious to the fact that there are good Milwaukeeans living in the suburbs as well as inside the artificial lines that we call our city limits." This last sentence was a proposal by the *Sentinel* for suburban control of the city government. According to the *Sentinel*, suburban Milwaukeeans were also good city people and should have a say in the city government, but city people should stay out of suburban affairs.[127] A dangerous stratification of population was taking place and this editorial was a sign of it.

William A. Norris, of the *Sentinel*, also took the occasion to write another in his long series of attacks on me, and sought to defend the committee's decision not to study the matter of tax inequality by saying that another committee was studying this problem.[128]

I rejoiced, however, in getting some support from the *Capital Times* in Madison. In an editorial in this paper of September 13, 1956, it noted my charges that the study committee was weighted in favor of the suburbs and would recommend legislative action to force Milwaukee to supply water to the suburbs while placing the burden of development of such a system on Milwaukee users. It noted also the big business complexion of the committee and said that the pressure from big business helped to explain why the *Sentinel* wrote a critical editorial. The *Capital Times* editorial stated, "As mayor of Milwaukee, Mayor Zeidler's first responsibility is to see to it that the city is not given away to the suburbs."[129]

My charge of a surprise being sprung on the city did not sit well with the governor or his office. Some weeks later the governor's executive secretary, Phil Drotning, a very able man, said that he had sat in the governor's office when the governor had discussed over the telephone with me his plans to appoint the committee to study Milwaukee water and sewer problems. He said that at least five and perhaps seven of 14 names submitted by the governor were individuals acceptable to me and that I regarded them as persons who considered the problems with fairness, intelligence and impartiality. Drotning said that I was aware of what the governor intended to do, but noted, "This is not to say that the mayor indicated his approval of the idea."[130]

In my reply I said that the governor had informed me of his plans but had asked me not to tell anybody. I said, "The governor called me when he already had made up his mind. He said he was under heavy pressure and I pleaded with him to give the people of Milwaukee consideration on the committee, because they are so much more numerous and ought to have proportionate representation." I also pleaded with the governor to make the committee statewide and to include in its field of study all metropolitan problems instead of only water and sewer problems in the Milwaukee metropolitan area. I told the governor that he was being pressured as part of an attempt to take away Milwaukee's waterworks and that the rest was merely window dressing. I also said that it could not be considered official information when the governor gave me information and told me not to tell anybody about it.[131]

In September of 1956, an issue of the *Public Enterprise Record* roasted the press by asserting that there were "few editorial champions of the city government or its officials." The *Record* said that the opinion-formers of the community — the owners of the newspapers, the editorial writers and the owners of businesses — lived in the suburbs and that they naturally were more sympathetic to the place of their residences than they were to the city. The article said that only a courageous public official could stand up to the continuous stream of suburban abuse and adverse editorial criticism from papers that bore the label "Milwaukee."[132]

The *Sentinel* and the *Journal* both felt it necessary to respond to this criticism of their suburban partiality. In an editorial of September 28, 1956, the *Sentinel* objected to the assumption in the *Public Enterprise Record* that it was almost inevitable that the governor's study committee would recommend taking the waterworks away from Milwaukee without forcing an equal sharing of the tax burden throughout the area. The *Sentinel* said this assumption was totally unwarranted and appeared to be an attempt to destroy confidence in the committee before it had a chance to gather data on which to base its decision.[133] Again I wondered how the editors of this paper could have written this article with a straight face.

The next day the *Sentinel* followed with an editorial attacking the Public Enterprise Committee for saying that Milwaukee newspapers were in league with the suburbs against the city. It cited its record on the reapportionment battle and the fact that it had urged large annexations.[134]

The editorial of the *Journal* had a cold, angry, almost contemptuous tone. In an editorial entitled "Let Water Committee Proceed," on September 29, 1956, the paper asserted that because the governor did talk to Mayor Zeidler, this in effect was talking to him officially. The paper characterized my reaction as a hotheaded one. The *Journal* said, "The emptiness and absurdity of his complaint becomes stronger than ever. The City Hall's obsessive jealousy over its waterworks is getting just too tiresome. Adult behavior would let the governor's committee proceed in peace and let it assemble the facts which can lead to right conclusions." It said that after that the city could make its case. The *Journal* had obviously joined the side of the suburbs that wanted Milwaukee's waterworks for their own tax-free islands. This was a switch from its previous policy, and I concluded that the reason for the switch was that the paper was fighting for circulation in the suburbs and it would never do for the paper to oppose suburban demands on the city for services.[135]

The mystery of who put the pressure on Governor Kohler—whom, I repeat, was a decent and honorable man in my opinion—grew stronger. I tried to secure from Phil Drotning the names of the persons who had asked the governor for the creation of this study committee. The reply to my question came via the *Milwaukee Journal*. Howard J. Tobin, president of the Greater Milwaukee Committee, disclosed that the delegation to the governor consisted of two Iron Ring attorneys of long standing and the publisher of the *Milwaukee Journal*. The attorneys were Edmund B. Shea, chairman of the Greater Milwaukee Committee's subcommittee on metropolitan problems, and Maxwell H. Herriott, the subcommittee's vice chairman. Mr. Irwin Maier, executive vice-president and publisher of the *Milwaukee Journal*, accompanied them at the request of Mr. Tobin.

Mr. Tobin said that the group had gone to the governor because of the failure of the Committee of 21 to make progress. The Iron Ring crowd, using the Greater Milwaukee Committee as its agent, had inveigled the *Milwaukee Journal* into taking sides against the very city whose name it bore on its masthead.

I never fully understood why the *Journal* or the *Sentinel* were so busy promoting the cause of the suburbs, even from the point of view of circulation. Their chief asset in trade was the word "Milwaukee" on the masthead, and yet they were busy helping the Iron Ring crowd try to pull the city apart, stop its growth and harass city officials in their struggle against the forces of the suburbs. They would have been better off if they had called themselves the "Suburban Milwaukee Advocate" or some such title as it would have been a truer expression of their policy and their feelings.

The suburbs were not slow in getting before the governor's committee to apply pressure for taking over control of the Milwaukee waterworks. Early in October, a delegation consisting of Irvin Knoebel, comptroller of West Allis; H.O. Wolfe, village attorney for Shorewood; Theodore Kunz, comptroller of Wauwatosa; and Samuel Gates, a Wauwatosa engineer, appeared before the committee and expounded the suburban policy.

Once again the suburbs opposed a statewide study of the area because, no doubt, they thought they could check Milwaukee by their numbers and superior propaganda influence in Milwaukee County. They proposed that the county Committee of 21, dominated by their own people, should make a study of the area. Their argument was that Milwaukee problems were unique. They said Milwaukee suburbanites were proud of their communities and that Milwaukee's distrust of the Iron Ring was simply too bad. They again asserted that the suburbs were willing to cooperate, but the city had hamstrung them. They probably meant that the suburbs were willing to accept any services the city was willing to give, but that this cooperation toward Milwaukee would not extend as far as their permitting an equalized tax burden. They said they were not against a raise in water rates, but that they did not want to be discriminated against. What this statement said in effect was that the suburbs saw no reason why they should not pay water rates the same as those paid by Milwaukee people living inside the city boundaries and closer to the source of the system. The suburban leaders said they should pay costs plus a reasonable profit and that political boundaries should not determine rates. However, from the city's experience, the suburbs were ready to fight any change in rates at all and were uniformly unwilling to pay reasonable rates.

The suburban officials charged that Milwaukee used its waterworks as a weapon to coerce annexation, and that was wrong as a municipal policy. They asserted that a metropolitan water system (which incidentally they would control) could provide better service than the city-owned utility. They then expressed opposition to a state study of the area by the Legislature and said that the Legislature should tell Milwaukee to solve its own problems. Hubert O. Wolfe made the additional assertion that he doubted that industry would leave Milwaukee for the suburbs to get a tax savings, which of course was what industry had been doing for decades in moving to West Milwaukee, West Allis and Glendale. The suburbs, however, made it clear that while they wanted to control the Milwaukee waterworks, they were going to reserve the right for the north shore suburbs to build their own waterworks in their own separate water district carved out of Milwaukee's district.[136]

This attitude so persistently and tenaciously held by the suburbs—that "what's mine is mine and what's yours is mine also"—was never deviated from. Their view reminded me of the stubborn claims of Soviet leaders on international issues to keeping what was theirs and to demanding control of others. The suburbs had no shame about enunciating their philosophy and they had a great cunning and wiliness in making this philosophy sound utterly reasonable so that Milwaukeeans opposed to giving the suburbs what they needed seemed most selfish. Suburban leaders clearly wanted to be involved in Milwaukee's affairs; Milwaukeeans should stay out of suburban affairs, however.

The county Committee of 21, under the leadership of Supervisor Bert B. Busby of West Milwaukee, was vainly trying to get control of a study of metropolitan problems to prevent the city from making an effective case. A proposal was made by the committee to study 28 separate functions of local government in order to see how the city government could be made to help the suburbs in those functions in which they were deficient, but in no case, as I recall it, was there any demand on the part of the suburbs to study the problems of the city, such as its minority problem, slum clearance problem or relief problem. The suburbs were in a mood to take and not to give. The proposal came to the Common Council where a study of 16 of the 28 functions was given some consideration. After a discussion, the council voted narrowly, 10 to 9, to permit the city representatives on the Committee of 21 to vote for a study of the 16 services in question, and the Committee of 21 decided to find out how much a survey of those 16 services would cost.[137]

Before any of these actions could begin, there occurred an event known as "The Battle of Green Bay," which had a serious effect on subsequent city-suburban relations.

In October of 1956, the League of Wisconsin Municipalities held its annual meeting at Green Bay. Into this session, Alderman Matt Schimenz of Milwaukee introduced a resolution asking for a statewide study by the Legislature of problems confronting metropolitan areas. This resolution was backed by the league's Resolutions Committee although E.G. Teschan, village manager of Fox Point, protested. Teschan described the Schimenz proposal as controversial and asked that Milwaukee County be deleted from the study. Teschan said the Committee of 21 in Milwaukee County "knows best the existing problem there." Schimenz replied, "We can study until doomsday in the Committee of 21 and unless the Legislature accepts what is done, it's all wasted time."

Another vocal protester against Schimenz's resolution was Anthony X. Basile, father of the Oak Creek bill and at that time city attorney of Oak Creek. He called the Schimenz resolution an attempt by Milwaukee to obtain complete amalgamation of all municipalities in Milwaukee County, and he said, "We fear such a study from many points of view. This resolution asks a blank check. It will force the league to lobby for a law to see how small communities can be cut up to make big communities bigger."

Alderman Schimenz was supported by Alderman Charles Quirk of Milwaukee, by Mayor Walter G. Koepke of Manitowoc and by Village President H.J. Ellis of Brooklyn, Wisconsin. Concerning the Schimenz proposal, I said to the Resolutions Committee that Milwaukee was "willing to take its chances with the Legislature where we have been stung before, but we feel we can't find a solution to our problem elsewhere."[138]

The Resolutions Committee not only supported the Schimenz proposal but also supported a proposal I had made to study the possibility of creating a state department for municipal affairs. The suburbs were not ready to accept these proposals at all.

Word quickly got around at the convention that the suburbs were preparing to defeat the city on these issues. Extended delegations of people from the suburban Milwaukee area began to appear at the convention and by the morning of Friday, October 19, 1956, the suburbs had brought all kinds of people in to register as voting delegates. There was no limitation on the number of persons from a community who could register as delegates. Oak Creek brought a cemetery official as one of the delegates. That community listed as its delegates four aldermen, the mayor, the city attorney, the fire chief, the assessor, the treasurer, a consulting engineer, the advertising manager of the local paper, a representative of a taxpayers' group, and a member of the cemetery commission.[139]

This was one time when I felt the weakness of my leadership for Milwaukee. I believed it was unethical to pack the meeting as the suburbs did, and officials from the City of Milwaukee made no attempt to do so. A more ruthless man in the office of mayor, fighting on behalf of the people of the city, would have walked out of the packed meeting or fought to pack it himself. Neither course of action, I repeat, was ethical, and so Milwaukee delegates stayed to see themselves disgracefully used, verbally abused and savagely denounced in the balloting process.

Presiding in the chair was Thomas A. Byrne, tax commissioner of the City of Milwaukee, who was most uncomfortable about the situation but who felt he could do nothing to protect the city. The suburban crowd viciously assailed the Schimenz proposal. Leading the pack were William H. Bowman and Anthony X. Basile. Moderate statements on the Schimenz resolution by Alderman Schimenz himself were bitterly assailed and although 65 persons voted for it, the vote against the proposal was more than double. The room was heavily packed with suburban people from all of the Milwaukee suburbs. My proposal for a state department of municipal affairs, for which I made a modest plea, was summarily disposed of by the suburban bloc, 110 to 80. The suburbs then proceeded to elect Hubert O. Wolfe, their elder statesman, as president of the league in a final voting defeat of the city and as a means of arraying the league against Milwaukee.

As one newspaper put it, "Amid shouts and cheers, and led by two suburban attorneys, the municipal league defeated a Milwaukee proposal to support a statewide legislative study of urban area problems, killed a Zeidler resolution for a study of the establishment of a state department of municipal affairs and elected Hubert O. Wolfe, Shorewood village attorney, its new president."[140]

The rough handling the City of Milwaukee received from the suburbs naturally brought with it certain reactions from city officials. Alderman Schimenz made the comment, "If I have never before known what it was to face the lion's den, I've had that opportunity this morning." My own reaction was that it was completely useless to try to carry on negotiations of any type with the suburbs. They wanted everything and would give nothing, and they were led by a band of attorneys who were getting rich in suburban litigation.

After the vote on the Schimenz resolution, I said to the press that the vote was a perfect indication of the kind of treatment that the city would get from the Committee of 21 on any basic issue that affected the city. The committee was dominated by suburban residents and I expressed doubt that the city would continue as a part of the committee for it had weakened the city's position. I said to the press also that the large cities of the state would have to look after their own interest. I said that the election of Hubert O. Wolfe was a "slap in the face for Milwaukee," and I asserted that the implacable animosity exhibited by the suburban committees would not stop us from pressing our demands.

William H. Bowman gloated over the victory. He said the fight "was not a defeat for Milwaukee but only for its top policymakers." He claimed the fight was a victory for people who believed in "municipal cooperation and not municipal assassination." Bowman said that the floor fight was over the issue of whether the City of Milwaukee should be allowed to destroy every suburb in Milwaukee County and he said that the Committee of 21 was ready to tag the city with "complete irresponsibility."[141]

As the day wore on and I thought more about the severe handling the city had received, I amplified the city's position. I stated to the press that I intended to veto the resolution passed 10 to 9 by the Common Council authorizing the Committee of 21 to study 16 functions of local government in the Milwaukee area. I said I might also recommend that the city pull out of the Committee of 21 because "the committee can apparently serve no useful purpose." I said that the suburban officials had "displayed senseless animosity" toward any and all Milwaukee proposals at the league convention. "The violence of anti-Milwaukee feeling expressed at Green Bay demonstrated to me that there is no point in the city trying to talk with the suburbs in the Committee of 21 or anywhere else."

About Hubert O. Wolfe, Shorewood village attorney, the league's new president, I said, "I am not opposed to Mr. Wolfe personally. He himself is a moderate. But the circumstances under which he was elected, with cheering and cat-calling and anti-Milwaukee shouting, were offensive. The same sort of tirade took place when they defeated my own resolution, which I considered innocuous, and the resolution of Alderman Schimenz backing the state study of metropolitan problems." Commenting on the roles of Basile and Bowman, I said,

> Tony Basile and Bill Bowman are lawyers who make their living fighting Milwaukee. It was amazing to me to see how these two lawyers with a financial interest in these matters were able to line up the mayors and the elected officials of other suburbs and outside municipalities to do their bidding.
>
> Bowman announced at the league meeting the suburbs intend to use the Committee of 21 to nail Milwaukee to the wall, cut off the city's growth and prevent us even from appealing to the state. Our language was temperate; theirs was not. We are willing to cooperate; the suburbs will make no concessions of any kind. They claim to be self-sufficient. All they want is our water and an end to our growth. Why Shorewood and West Allis and the other suburbs that now get our water should take such a role against us I do not understand. Bowman and Basile, yes, but why the others?

I concluded that the city could not take its case any longer to informally constituted committees where the representation was weighted against the city. I reiterated our long-established policy of opposing consolidation of individual functions and I again supported complete amalgamation.[142]

In another comment, I said, "The idea that no Iron Ring of suburbs surround the city was smashed completely at Green Bay. There can be no doubt about that now."[143]

In the next few days I sent a veto message to the Common Council on its resolution to permit the city's delegates on the Committee of 21 to support a study to see how 16 special functions of city government could be shared with suburban groups. I said that the passage of the resolution represented a fundamental change in policy that the Common Council was making by an indirect action. I said the Common Council should decide if it desired to abandon the idea of total consolidation in favor of the principle of relinquishing individual functions of the city government, whether to the county or to specially created boards, commissions or service districts. "I do not favor the handing over of any more city functions on an individual basis to other units of government unless the tax inequality that exists between the City of Milwaukee and other units of government is eradicated," I said in the message. I opposed giving single functions to new administrative entities in that it led to further fragmentation of government. I also referred to a recent resolution adopted by the Common Council to ask the suburbs just what services they wanted of Milwaukee. I said that with the exception of those suburbs that wanted city water, there were scarcely any requests for other services of the city. I concluded, "I therefore see no major lack of services which requires the continuance of the Committee of 21 other than the desire of some communities to secure the Milwaukee water system rather than to develop their own."

Of this veto message, Supervisor Bert B. Busby, the chairman of the Committee of 21 and a key suburban leader, was naturally very critical. He stated, "The important work of the committee shall go forward and continue regardless of any intemperate statement or action on the part of any individual." He said the committee would go on with its work even if only 14 members were present and that my statement did not surprise him as it was in line with my past performance of rule or ruin as opposed to cooperation in the study of metropolitan problems.[144]

The reaction to this veto message was immediately followed by a story in the *Sentinel* attempting to keep the Committee of 21 alive by quoting aldermen in support of it. The *Sentinel* also quoted Supervisor Bert Busby as sounding a note of compromise. He said, "Maybe we can come to the study of assessments and collection of taxes first, but we certainly can't narrow down our proposed comprehensive survey to one point."[145]

The veto was sustained by a vote of 16 to 4. Debate on the vote brought a general discussion of whether the Committee of 21 should continue or not and whether the city should stay in it.[146] The committee was seriously weakened by revelations of the intransigence of the Iron Ring at Green Bay.

Late in October, at a meeting of the Public Enterprise Committee at the Milwaukee Turners Hall, I proposed that the north shore suburbs should form into one big city and the southern suburbs should do likewise. "By forming such new cities the suburbs would be able to meet those problems that they now asked Milwaukee to solve for them."[147]

Shortly after the "Battle of Green Bay," Robert Dineen, the chairman of the governor's special study committee, asked the city to list in concise form the problems that needed to be studied. Having heard from the suburbs, and undoubtedly influenced by the city's feeling about what had happened at Green Bay, Mr. Dineen, who completely dominated the committee, probably thought it best to ask the city what it considered important, but the city was told to be brief about it. The city officials said they would cooperate.[148]

Robert Dineen called on me and we had an extensive discussion. Later he appeared at a Common Council committee meeting with some of his own committee.

However, it was soon clear that Dineen's committee already had a good idea of what it would recommend. Dineen asked the City of Milwaukee to extend the water survey currently being made by a consulting firm to cover the entire county. Dineen said the request in no way foreshadowed the ultimate recommendations of the study committee about what should be done with the waterworks, and he made it appear to be a minor thing by saying that the costs of the additional study would be relatively small because the remaining people in the county comprised only 14 percent of the total.

I am afraid I was overly blunt in my response. I said I had little faith in Dineen's assurances that the request did not foreshadow a recommendation that the waterworks be turned over to the county. Moreover, if the consulting firm extended the study of water service, this study would not reflect the true impact of a countywide water service on the Milwaukee taxpayer. The study of water service, I said, could not be divorced from a study of the inequalities of the tax system. Besides, the permission to extend the engineering study, to include how the suburbs could be served, would have to come from the Common Council.[149]

Mr. Dineen made his request before the city could put forth its stand. There was no doubt in my mind that his committee would try to compel the city to serve the suburbs with water without erasing the fundamental tax inequalities.

A few days later in November, I made an announcement that a statement of Milwaukee's attitude toward metropolitan area problems was being drafted and would be ready for the Common Council on November 13. The statement was going to emphasize two points. First, with tax inequalities existing in the metropolitan area, the city should not be asked to extend watermains to communities that had tax advantages over the city and with which the city was in competition. Second, the city had a right to expand and laws should be made more conducive for its growth.[150]

The focal point of the struggle with the suburbs once again shifted. Early in November of 1956, the Wisconsin Supreme Court handed down a decision regarding the contested consolidation of the Town of Granville with the City of Milwaukee. The decision did not resolve the conflict. The court ruled that, for the present, about six of the 22 square miles of the town would remain in Milwaukee and the rest would be in Brown Deer. The six square miles had not been posted by Brown Deer and, therefore, consolidation in that area would stay in effect. In the remaining 16 square miles, the Village of Brown Deer had made annexation postings and had circulated petitions. If the city could prove the Brown Deer annexations invalid, then the city could claim the area. These issues were returned to the Circuit Court.

The state Supreme Court also ruled that the boundaries of the several school districts were not to be changed, including that of the Granville-Brown Deer Union High School. This ruling was soon to prove most troublesome to the City of Milwaukee.

My first reaction to the decision was to state that it was puzzling and would result in many more months of litigation, which happened (and not only months, but years, of litigation). Serious questions of budgeting, tax assessment, reapportionment of assets and rendering of services arose. With the advice of Richard F. Maruszewski, the able assistant city attorney of Milwaukee, I said that the city would recognize the "temporary" jurisdiction of Brown Deer over the disputed area. Mr. Maruszewski pointed out that the ruling gave the city the legal right to answer the claim of Brown Deer to the territory on the basis of claimed annexations.[151]

The Wisconsin Supreme Court decision thrust a group of new problems on the city. The question of how to provide services to the area required and received immediate attention. The city also had to decide what legal action to take to meet the claims of Brown Deer to the disputed territory and even to determine the status of Alderman Vincent A. Schmit who lived in the disputed area. A large part of the territory was included in an annexation called the "Corrigan annexation," named after one of the petitioners.[152]

After a day of discussion between various city officials including Common Council leaders and the city attorney, it was decided to withdraw city services from the contested 16 square miles, allow Brown Deer temporary jurisdiction and challenge the matter in the courts. It was made clear that the city in allowing temporary jurisdiction was not conceding its right to be there and would use every legal means to recover this territory that had come to it in a referendum.[153]

Milwaukee then served notice on the Village of Brown Deer that the city's planned withdrawal from portions of the former Town of Granville would only be temporary. The withdrawal was not an admission that Brown Deer had claim to the area. The letter said that the city was terminating its municipal services due to the court decisions and was turning over to Brown Deer the responsibility to furnish services as a temporary custodian until the courts resolved the matter. The city said it expected no deterioration in municipal services furnished to the area.[154]

Joseph R. Lamping, director of the Community Development Department, stated that the disputed portion of Brown Deer would eventually become part of Milwaukee because Brown Deer's claims were illegal and he pointed to the great school problem caused by school districts being partly in one community and partly in another.[155]

The leading spokesman for Brown Deer was Harold H. Fuhrman, the village attorney. After Fuhrman had received a notice from Virgil H. Hurless, Milwaukee comptroller, that the city was withdrawing and expecting no deterioration of services, Fuhrman replied by saying that city services were not efficient. He also asserted that the city recognized the invalidity of its claims to any of Granville and he claimed the additional six square miles, awarded to Milwaukee by the court, for Brown Deer. The village said it would accept the emergency fire service the city intended to maintain in the area until the village was ready to take over, but only if the village fire chief or some village officer requested it. Any services rendered by the City of Milwaukee in the disputed territory would be considered gratuitous. Fuhrman claimed that this had been the consistent position of the village ever since the city "pretended to exercise jurisdiction over village territory." Moreover Fuhrman said he had a petition of 254 residents calling for patrolling of the village by the sheriff because the Milwaukee Police Department was not doing a good job.[156]

The problem of assessing for school costs in the Granville area had not been resolved by the state Supreme Court decision. The problem was whether the city would add a special tax rate in each of the 10 districts to pay for the costs of each district. This plan would produce 10 different rates in the Granville districts and the remainder of Milwaukee would have another rate. Because some of the Granville districts would have a higher rate than others, very strong opposition developed from the people who would be required to pay higher rates. The special levy for the Granville districts was proposed because the Milwaukee tax commissioner did not feel that he could legally assess the people in Milwaukee school districts for the costs of districts outside the Milwaukee school system, even though those districts were in the city for other municipal purposes. About $360,000 was needed from the Granville districts more than what the City of Milwaukee school tax rate would raise. Naturally the Granville residents developed strong sentiments against the idea of a special tax levy.

Milwaukee and its tax commissioner, Thomas A. Byrne, decided to levy all of the taxes in Granville for 1956 and keep the money in a special fund until the court case was decided. The clerk of the Brown Deer Village Board said that the board agreed not to attempt to levy taxes in its 16 square miles for 1956.[157]

In November of 1956, the Milwaukee Common Council voted reluctantly to suspend city services in the 16 square mile area of the former Town of Granville. The vote was 15 to 5 and the opponent to any withdrawal was Alderman Vincent A. Schmit, who was growing more powerful and influential in the Common Council and came to be known as a rough-and-tumble fighter on the issues he joined.[158]

The comptroller soon asked the city to pursue a rehearing before the Wisconsin Supreme Court because of the seemingly insolvable problems of assessment and collection of taxes caused by the court's division of the former town.[159]

The proposal by the tax commissioner to levy special school taxes in the Granville area as the law required was grist for the political mill of Fuhrman, the Brown Deer village attorney. Fuhrman announced that the proposal would be protested and litigated by aggrieved taxpayers and he claimed that the dual levy was illegal, branding it high-handed. Fuhrman, like several other suburban representatives, was given to inflammatory language about Milwaukee. He was quoted as saying, "The recent crucifixion of the Town of Lake by Milwaukee tax authorities stands as a stark example of the loving kindness and tender mercies which citizens of any other municipality can expect to receive should they be so unfortunate as to fall under Milwaukee domination." It was reported that 1,800 Town of Lake residents had protested increased assessments and after a review, many of the assessments were lowered by up to 15 percent, but that 200 cases were still in litigation.[160] This would be juicy business for the attorney who could draw up similar litigation in the Granville area.

The governor's special study committee and the consolidation issue made continuous hot copy in the press. The Milwaukee Board of Realtors, for example, featured a discussion on consolidation by Virgil H. Hurless, city comptroller; Arthur

Saltzstein, administrative secretary to the mayor; and George A. Schmus of West Allis. The Milwaukee officials wanted some consolidation and Schmus, of course, wanted none.[161]

The study committee, its proposed report and the legislation that ultimately arose from it were subjects that would consume the attention of the city for the next four years.

On November 11, 1956, city officials released a preliminary report to be sent to Robert E. Dineen, chairman of the governor's special study committee. This was the concise report that the Dineen committee had requested of the city. The report was drafted by Shepard A. Magidson, administrative assistant to the comptroller; Arthur Saltzstein, administrative secretary to the mayor; and George Saffran, the wise counselor and director of the budget.

The city's report said that the city required areas suitable for planned growth. Whenever a suburb enjoyed a tax advantage and desired a major service from the city, that suburb should join the city to get that major service. No special districts or single countywide consolidation of a function or service should be implemented because such consolidations served to perpetuate existing inequalities. Formation of special districts might appear to spread costs, but they did not affect the current system of unbalanced revenue. The report said, "It follows that any action that will be taken to promote, extend, intensify or prolong the present inefficient, wasteful political disorganization of the metropolitan area must be opposed by Milwaukee, not only as detrimental to its own interests, but as a matter of vital necessity to its continued fiscal soundness." Extension of city services might help the suburbs for a while but would not be advantageous to Milwaukee.

The city's statement pointed out that the area's financial resources were not available to meet areawide problems. The city suffered the most because it could not spread its costs of municipal services equitably over all the people who benefited from them. The state deprived the city of certain logical major sources of revenue and placed the city in an economic competition with state-subsidized tax colonies. The city's property tax was weighted against the city because of the state's method of sharing taxes. The city was at a disadvantage to "retain, let alone improve, its industrial and commercial tax base" because the state was financing intrastate tax competition between its citizens by favoring some communities. The policy of the state needed revision. Revenue produced in a metropolitan area should be made available to solve the problems of the entire area. The Milwaukee metropolitan area was fragmented in terms of its political organization yet the area was really a unit for all other purposes.

The report made by the city reiterated its position that a statewide study of metropolitan problems should be made because local officials would not be "completely objective."[162]

The Milwaukee Common Council now turned its attention to the coming session of the Legislature to obtain a statewide legislative study of metropolitan area problems. The Judiciary Committee of the Common Council recommended that the city attorney draft a bill calling for such a study. A proposal was made in this committee to ask the county Committee of 21 to support the city's request for a state rather than a local study of urban area problems, but the majority of the council committee felt it was pointless to ask for support from this group. Alderman Hass, who more or less favored the Committee of 21 and was not strongly in favor of a state study, said he would vote against the city's position. Alderman Fred Meyers threatened him with impeachment if he did.[163]

Alderman Mortier and Alderman Schimenz introduced a resolution in the Common Council early in December to ask other Wisconsin cities to support a statewide legislative study of metropolitan problems. It was proposed to name a city committee to contact other municipal officials in the state and seek their help in forming a legislative committee to study urban problems.[164]

The fall elections for state and federal office had been completed, and the interested pressure groups throughout the state were busy preparing legislative measures. This was also true of the city and suburban officials on the problem of the waterworks, tax equality and other metropolitan area issues. The Committee of 21, for example, once again discussed how to study metropolitan problems.

At a meeting in December, the Committee of 21 went through another of its stormy sessions at which collapse of the group was threatened. After considerable acrimonious debate, Harold Fuhrman, the village attorney of Brown Deer, made a motion to have the committee go ahead with a sweeping study of some 18 municipal functions as a "test of the responsibilities of the Common Council." This motion failed to get a two-thirds vote necessary for passage. A motion by Common Council President Martin Schreiber for a state study was also turned down. Alderman Hass then moved to disband the committee but the chairman ruled him out of order.[165]

The report of the governor's committee—the "Dineen committee" on metropolitan problems and the waterworks—was now due. The report was made in four parts with a release appearing in the press each day from December 16 to December 19, 1956. The report itself was released on Saturday, December 15, so that it would get the proper press display on the following Sunday.

A two-tier banner headline appeared in the *Milwaukee Journal* on December 16 and the text brought no profound surprise to any city official: "City Water for Metropolitan Area is Recommended by Study Group."[166]

A lengthy account of the report followed, mostly hostile to the city. The essence of the report was that there should be a metropolitan water system for the Milwaukee suburbs, and if Milwaukee did not supply it, then the Legislature should form a metropolitan district and take the Milwaukee waterworks away from the city. The first sentence of the news story was thus: "The Milwaukee waterworks should have the first chance to supply water for Milwaukee County and the entire metropolitan district." Implied in this slick piece of journalism was the impression that somehow this was a great opportunity for Milwaukee if it gave the suburbs water, and that if the city did not take the opportunity then the Legislature should take the waterworks away from the city.

The Dineen report said that Milwaukee should reevaluate its basic policy under which a suburb must become a part of the city to obtain city water, and that the city and suburbs should begin at the earliest time "through cooperative arrangement" to make an areawide engineering study of the water problem to establish a factual basis for a "long-range water policy." This talk of cooperation, in my view, meant that the city should serve the suburbs and the suburbs should have a say in the city waterworks.

The report called for city water policy to be shaped by a citizens' advisory board, appointed by the mayor and confirmed by the Common Council. The report further said that the advisory board should include people from outside the city to show that the city was cooperating with the suburbs. It also recommended that steps be taken to modernize the water utility. These two proposals were unnecessary as the city had already created a water board composed of the Common Council's Utility Committee and waterworks officials, and a major improvement and expansion of the waterworks was already underway.

The Dineen report was critical of the city for failing to expand the waterworks and asserted that there was a lack of leadership and direction in meeting the water problem. The report criticized the city for limiting its current basic engineering study of waterworks expansion only to the city and those suburbs already served by the city. It further stated that if the city did not expand its system to provide more service to the suburbs, the state Legislature should create a water district for the area. The report echoed another suburban criticism of the waterworks by saying that the city was liable to alienate the suburbs because of the political approach used in the expansion of the waterworks.

The committee's report was especially critical of the city's lack of organized growth in its annexations. It criticized the city for using water service as an annexation policy and said that the city could no longer expand anyway. The report also took issue with the rate Milwaukee set for the sale of its water.

The Dineen report attacked the city's fundamental position, namely that the water supply kept industries within the city. It said that water supply was not attracting industry to Wisconsin and that the state's tax structure was a deterrent to new industry. This was a shrewd contention; at one and the same time, it served the interests of the big income groups in Wisconsin by attacking Milwaukee's closely held waterworks, which kept industry in the city, while it also propagandized for lower state taxes for industry. The report further said that citizens were moving into the suburbs and if the city did not provide water, the suburbs would serve themselves — which, of course, was not the case because they were not going to tax themselves for their own waterworks if they could use Milwaukee's waterworks instead.

In proposing to give the waterworks to a metropolitan group, the committee said it was not "stealing" the waterworks away from Milwaukee. The Sewerage Commission, for example, had been set up on a metropolitan basis and nobody charged the state officials or suburban officials with stealing the sewerage system. The report generously promised the city a voice in its own waterworks.

Thus the report came out with the complete line of arguments used by the Iron Ring without a deviation. The Iron Ring now had the prestige of an official report to claim the waterworks and to fortify themselves at the Legislature.

The leading members of the Common Council and myself immediately took issue with the report of the governor's special committee. The suburbs of course favored it.

The main point of our opposition was the proposal that Milwaukee supply water to the suburbs without getting any tax equality or anything else in its favor in return. I stated that the report was not as critical as it had started out to be because it included some comments that gave a more favorable aspect to the city's position than had been voiced at the start by some members of the committee. However, I said that some of the conclusions were erroneous and I objected to the report's implication that the state Legislature should take the waterworks away from Milwaukee. I said I understood there was a well-financed move underway to strip Milwaukee of its waterworks and I promised to check further into this issue. I agreed with that part of the report that said that a citizens' advisory board should be set up, because the city already had such an advisory board. I did not, however, agree to suburban representation on it.

I took direct issue with the committee's suggestion that extension of water service to the suburbs would bring greater cooperation with those suburbs and the eventual annexation or consolidation of such communities with the city. Once a suburb got Milwaukee water and became self sufficient, the desire for municipal cooperation ceased. I cited West Milwaukee as an example. I said it was unfortunate that the committee had limited its efforts to the narrow scope of the water problem without considering the entire metropolitan problem. If suburbs accessed the city water supply, industry would tend to leave, and the city would further lose its tax base, and thus more industry would leave and so a vicious cycle would be set up. Until the city was assured that the loss of its water system to "suburban tax-free pockets" would not mean a loss of industry, the city would have to follow its present course.

I also disagreed with the view that Milwaukee was missing out on good customers for water in the suburbs and that the city could realize a profit on the sale. The suburbs had opposed and would continue to oppose any city proposals for rate increases. The suburbs had chosen to set up their own governments instead of joining the City of Milwaukee. It was presumed that they were ready to provide service for their residents. They were not helpless. I said, "They chose not to make the necessary capital expenditure to provide their own water from wells or from the lake and expected the capital costs to be borne by Milwaukee water users." I also asked how far the committee wanted water service to be extended. Should the service be brought to Waukesha County and, if so, who should pay the costs of extending mains and increasing filter capacity?

The committee had stated that it had a "deep-seated aversion to economic coercion," by which it meant that Milwaukee should not compel people who wanted its water supply to join the city. I replied that Milwaukee also had a deep-seated aversion to "coercion which forces the city to give its water supply to its municipal competitors who are seeking to attract Milwaukee's industrial tax base from it."

The committee's report argued that annexation and consolidation were things of the past. I said that annexation and consolidation would be obsolete only if Milwaukee lost control of its water system. The suburban communities wanted only one major service from Milwaukee other than what they were getting and that was water.

In response to the charge that the city had demonstrated a lack of leadership in expanding, I said that the city's first difficulty with water supply had appeared in 1952 at the start of the city's greatest expansion. Suburban harassment had prevented the city from having an organized growth, had made planning unpredictable and had precipitated water difficulties. I said there was some validity to the charge that the city had not acted quickly enough when the first suggestion had been made for an engineering survey of the waterworks. For some reason, I said, there was community resistance to surveys of city needs being made by consultants, and one newspaper (the *Sentinel*) had made this an issue of the 1956 campaign. This had made the Common Council wary about ordering surveys.

In regard to rate increases, I noted that water rates had been kept low because of complaints from industry about state income taxes and property taxes.

Alderman Martin Schreiber joined in expressing opposition to any effort to establish a metropolitan water district. Alderman Schimenz told about the terrific fight with the superintendent of the waterworks to expand the system (which is another story), yet Schimenz expressed a willingness to expand the system if the suburbs ever showed a willingness to cooperate with Milwaukee.

The mayor of Wauwatosa, whose administration had failed to supply that city with enough water after its own expansion and had pressured Milwaukee to carry the costs of its expansion, said the report confirmed his own position and that it was "the only conclusion that disinterested and intelligent persons could come to." He said that the thinking of the City of Milwaukee was "shortsighted, medieval, archaic and chaotic" and that a fight would occur in the Legislature on the water issue. Anthony X. Basile, the attorney of Oak Creek, said the report was in the right direction. The mayor of Glendale then said that his city did not care about a metropolitan water system; it was going ahead with creating its own.[167]

The more I thought about this report of the governor's committee, the more it occurred to me that it was an indictment of the suburbs for failure to plan for their own water needs. I stated to the press that the committee in effect charged Milwaukee with the failure to anticipate the expansion of the suburbs. I asked if it was logical to ask Milwaukee to plan for such expansion and subsequently plan the extension of Milwaukee services to these suburbs. I stated that the city was charged with failing to plan for suburbs that had not existed at the time the planning was supposed to have occurred. Some of the suburbs had not wanted to expand but then suddenly switched their policies—Wauwatosa and West Allis particularly—and they acquired, with their expansion, water service problems. Was the City of Milwaukee to be charged with the failure to predict the actions of these suburbs?

I also said that if a metropolitan scheme of service distribution was good for water supply why should such a scheme not be good for all other facilities? Why did the committee not take the next step and propose a single unit of government with a single tax base and a just distribution of services and costs? Of course, I said, this would be unacceptable to the tax-free suburbs.

The reporters then called the mayor of West Allis, Arnold Klentz, who said that West Allis had told Milwaukee what it was going to do in expansion. An alderman of Wauwatosa, Clarence A. Muth, said that a metropolitan water district was necessary because the suburbs could not go on sinking wells and that it was incongruous with Wauwatosa being only six miles from the lake. The policy of Wauwatosa officials thus was to make Milwaukee bring water from the lake so that they could avoid paying for the capital expansion of the Wauwatosa system; they were not going to spend their own money drilling wells or even build their own main to the lake. Officials of the north shore suburbs said they were going ahead with their own waterworks no matter what. The chairman of the committee that had made the report, Robert Dineen, having met the demands of the suburbs, said nothing.[168]

The second in the series of reports from the Dineen committee received smaller headlines. The committee's main purpose had been served. The second report dealt with the problems of the sewers. The report said that the sewerage district should include eastern Waukesha County and parts of Washington County and Ozaukee County. The report faulted the city for not separating storm and sanitary sewers in the older combined sewerage system in the city. On the whole, the report complimented the Sewerage Commission.

Milwaukee's commissioner of public works, Lloyd D. Knapp, criticized the report about separating sewers in the combined district. He said it would cost at least $250 million and was not economically justified. He also said that no one from the committee had come to see him about the subject.

It occurred to me that the whole report was hastily put together to justify taking away the waterworks, and that the sewer study was not necessary because the Sewerage Commission was already in the early stages of a $52 million expansion program based on its own engineering report and recommendations. The "study" of the sewerage problems had been added by the committee to disguise its main concern for taking the Milwaukee waterworks for the suburbs.

About the second report I said that I agreed basically with the need to expand the sewerage district, but I wanted to know who would pay for the expansion—the people in Milwaukee or the people in the suburbs.[169]

In the third report in the series, the committee members got in another lick against Milwaukee and once again completely followed the suburban "party" line. The committee recommended a citizens' commission of not more than 15 people from the Milwaukee area to study local metropolitan problems. The proposed commission, naturally, would study all problems except those phases of taxation with a statewide implication. The report said that there might be major structural changes in government, but the time, in its opinion, had not arrived for the people or the Legislature to be ready to consider such changes. It said that a statewide study on local problems was premature and that Milwaukee had its own peculiar problems. It suggested that the commission be composed of men of good intentions. The report proposed provision of certain common services on an areawide basis, effectively and efficiently, fair sharing of costs between municipalities and unincorporated areas, a maximum of local expression and participation in control. The report said there was a need to alleviate tensions.

This was the complete party line. The report was proposing that a commission, dominated by suburbanites, study the problems of the area except the tax inequalities that favored the suburbs. It proposed common services, by which it meant that the city should give to the suburbs the services they might want. The expression of fair sharing of cost between municipalities meant in suburban parlance that the city would carry the cost. "Maximum of local expression" meant that the suburbs would tell the city what they wanted it to do, but that the city should keep its influence out of the suburbs. "Participation in control" meant the suburbanites should serve on city boards and commissions.

The city's response was hostile. I said that the proposed commission would be an "areacrat" body that would study how Milwaukee could be "made to give up its services for the benefit of the suburbs." I noted that the reports made in the last three days were proposing a new doctrine of government that would mean the end of orderly municipal growth. I stated,

> We ought not to lose sight of the main trend of the report of the governor's committee up to now. It has said, in effect, that whenever a suburban fringe is strong enough politically to force an essential community service out of a core city, it should be able to do so by compelling the core city to provide service.
>
> This is a doctrine fraught with evil consequences for orderly municipal government. If a suburban fringe can force out of the core city sewer and water services, then the same principle can apply to fire and health and education services. Thus the suburban fringe can pick and choose from among the services rendered by the core city those services it desires without sharing the responsibility for any of the rest of the core city's problems.
>
> If this doctrine prevails it means the end of orderly municipal growth in Wisconsin and the proliferation of chaotic suburban fringe areas. This chaotic condition would apply equally to the largest cities and to the smallest incorporated villages.

I also opposed the formation of commissions and committees such as the one suggested. I said, "They are weighted in favor of the suburbs even though the bulk of

146

the population resides in Milwaukee. As a result, the committees always attempt to figure out how Milwaukee can be made to give up its services for the benefit of the suburbs."

A surprising response to the report came from George Schmus of West Allis. He was suspicious of it.[170]

The fourth and final report of the Dineen committee received considerably less prominence than the others, and it was somewhat of a surprise. This report recommended a study of the distribution formulas of state shared taxes. "No formula is sacred," it said. The report included a letter of the City of Milwaukee, sent under my name, and a joint letter of Mayor William B. Knuese of Wauwatosa and George Schmus, who were respectively president and secretary of the Milwaukee County League of Municipalities. These letters stated the positions of the opponents in the city-suburban struggle.

The letter from the City of Milwaukee stated the city's position as described earlier. The Knuese-Schmus letter attacked the city's water policy. The suburban letter said that many services were countywide and that the city did not carry the full burden of government services. The letter then made a charge, subsequently repeated again and again by suburbanites, that Milwaukee paid only 65 percent of the relief load while its citizens received 83 percent of relief and that, therefore, the suburbs were carrying the load for the city. The Knuese-Schmus letter repeated that the suburbs had governments close to the people, and advanced the view that the state, by returning tax money to local suburbs, was not sharing taxes, but merely collecting them for the suburbs.

This latter statement was in response to the city's charge that the areas of the county with greatest ability to pay had been granted greatest property tax relief by the state formulas of sharing. The suburbs said that their residential areas had to rely on property taxes and special assessments while the city could put most of its burden on the general property tax.[171]

The response of officials in Milwaukee, of course, was that the tax study proposed by the Dineen committee's report was welcome. I called the suggestion of the report a "sound conclusion," and said it should have been evident by now that the one reason Milwaukee did not want to give away its waterworks was to avoid enhancing the attractiveness of suburbs to industry, thereby pulling that industry out of Milwaukee. I said again that the city was not being vindictive; it was protecting itself.

Alderman James Mortier said that if the tax laws were rectified, debate over water and sewers would end. The mayor of Wauwatosa declined to comment, but said that the suburbs were "entitled to historic revenues." No comment was received from the mayor of West Allis.[172]

Governor Kohler was apparently pleased with the full report from the committee he had appointed. He called it a "very fair, impartial, dispassionate and objective report." He felt this was the case because both the city and suburbs took issue with it.[173]

A move was made at once by the County Board's Legislative Committee to have control of any metropolitan water district that might be created as a result of the Dineen report. The Legislative Committee proposed to ask each unit of government to send representatives to discuss the creation of a metropolitan water utility system. The county resolution asked the Legislature to grant the county "mandatory authority" over such a system. The county was to have the right to create such a utility at the permission of other units of government or at their request.

My response was that this proposal by the county was hostile to Milwaukee and was another device by means of which the Milwaukee water user would pay for the capital cost of expansion of the water system to suburban communities that did not want to pay for their own. The fact that Supervisor Bert Busby's name was attached to the proposal indicated that there would be no accompanying consideration of a tax equalization program.[174] This was because Supervisor Busby represented a community (West Milwaukee) staunchly opposed to tax equalization.[175]

One day after the last report of the governor's committee was published, a news dispatch from Madison stated that the Wisconsin Legislative Council voted unanimously in favor of a statewide study of the problems of urban growth and that it was agreed to recommend to the 1957 session of the state Legislature a bill to establish a governor's committee on urban expansion for all areas of Wisconsin, not just Milwaukee. David Carley, public member of the Legislature's Urban Development Committee, made the proposal. Carley, who was from the Wisconsin State Chamber of Commerce, called the proposal for a limited study "abominable" and he said that 15 other cities had the same problems as Milwaukee.[176]

However, on the same day, there was an announcement in the *Milwaukee Journal* that legislative bills to implement the studies of the governor's committee on water and sewers would be introduced into the 1957 session of the state Legislature. The chairman, Robert E. Dineen, who was uncommunicative to the press during most of the time the studies were being made, declined to disclose who would prepare the bills and when they would be introduced.[177]

No doubt was in my mind that these bills were being drafted by the Iron Ring attorneys. As the city had feared, the Dineen report was being used to formulate legislation hostile to Milwaukee. I immediately raised the question as to whether or not a well-financed organization had been set up to take over Milwaukee's waterworks for the metropolitan area. I wanted to know who was preparing the bills to carry out the report of the Dineen committee and I stated that I could not understand Mr. Dineen's secrecy—why should he keep from the public the name or names of persons preparing the bills? This action followed the pattern of organization of the committee itself, which had been created in a secret maneuver.[178]

I used to marvel at Mr. Dineen's immunity from adverse press comment. The meetings of his group were conducted in secret. He refused to disclose matters to the press and held vital public business close to his bosom in such a way that it would have brought ringing denunciations if anyone else had followed that course of conduct. Mr. Dineen apparently knew the strength of his own position. The press knew he would recommend that the city waterworks be given to the suburbs and this was enough to overlook any slights the press might have felt in the way of newsgathering.

The *Milwaukee Sentinel* got its licks in for the suburbs. In an editorial on December 21, 1956, the *Sentinel* said, "The commendable and constructive report of the governor's Metropolitan Study Committee headed by Robert E. Dineen has highlighted the dissentions and conflicts of interest that exist in this community of a million people. Even if it had done nothing more than that, the report would have been of value." (As if the issues had not been brought out before!) The editorial said that the value of the report could be found in the reactions of the public officials who denounced it. Public officials were too biased toward their own communities and had no dedication to a broader general welfare. The committee members, however, were men of good will, and local officials were therefore not dedicated to the public welfare if they disagreed with the report.[179]

One interesting bit of support for the city position came from the village president of Little Chute who defended Milwaukee's position opposing a metropolitan water system. He sent me a letter saying that the city was correct in insisting that the suburbs build their own water utilities rather than pass along part of the costs to city taxpayers. He said people were building near but not inside cities in the belief that they could be served with sewers, water and fire protection at city expense. He said that the motives of taxpayers adjoining a city to get a free ride should be defeated, and he noted similar problems in Appleton, Neenah, Oshkosh and other state communities.[180]

At the end of 1956, the total area of the city had reached 80.555 square miles as a result that year of one consolidation of 6.71 square miles in the Granville area, due to a favorable court decision, as well as 26 small annexations and one detachment. Thereafter, for all practical purposes, annexations stopped, although very tiny ones were consummated in each of the years 1956 to 1960. In 1959, Milwaukee tentatively gained 11.15 square miles through a Milwaukee County Circuit Court decision on the Granville consolidation. This case was the subject of years of litigation, which Milwaukee ultimately won in a state Supreme Court decision in 1962.

Apart from continuing to press forward with the Granville litigation, the struggle of the city was now to preserve its tax base and to keep its services from leaking to the tax islands in the suburbs.

The year of 1957 was spent by the city in trying to solve the problem of serving the former Granville territory consolidated with Milwaukee, in meeting the tax problem caused by school districts in that area and in fighting to prevent a suburban-dominated metropolitan study commission from being created.

Early in the year, the Committee of 21, probably to forestall the creation of a new committee to study metropolitan problems, agreed to make a detailed survey of tax structures in Milwaukee County, although one of the city representatives, Alderman Martin Schreiber, said the city preferred that a study of metropolitan problems be made by the Legislature.[181] Five aldermen were reported as wanting the city to withdraw from the Committee of 21 because of the proposal to make it a statutory body. They were unhappy that Milwaukee would not have representation based on population and that there would be an infringement of non-elected officials on the duties of elected officials.[182]

The City of Milwaukee published an official reply to the report of the Dineen committee. This reply received a kind of "brush-off" from the *Milwaukee Journal*. A story in the *Journal* said that the reply was a polished-up restatement of objections voiced by city officials when the report was issued. Already the press was beginning to take the attitude that there was no further need to hear from the city, an attitude that was contrary to its earlier editorial advice that the city should keep still until the report was made. The powerful corroding effect of the report was already at work eating away at the city's position.

The city in its reply objected to extending water service and said that such a requirement could only result in eroding the city's tax base and unraveling the city's financial structure. It was not enough to offer Milwaukee merely a study in exchange for its waterworks. The city's statement replied to the committee's claim that Milwaukee was using economic coercion. The city said that taking its waterworks from city control or forcing expansion of its service without dealing with the problem of taxes was an economic weapon against the city. The city's statement was critical of the study commission for artificially dividing its limited study into four areas. The city claimed this approach was fundamentally unsound and called for a comprehensive study of metropolitan problems on a statewide basis. The city declared that it would not change its water policy without an equitable distribution of tax resources in the metropolitan area.[183]

The *Milwaukee Sentinel* gave an editorial nod to the city's reply. Evidently it felt it had overstepped itself in giving support to the suburbs. It said on January 10, 1957, that the city had made a strong reply to the Dineen committee on metropolitan problems, that it was encouraging to find the problems studied from all points of view and that the process would be easier if everyone were sincere.[184]

Governor Walter Kohler had left office at the end of December, 1956, since he did not stand for re-election. He was succeeded by Vernon Thomson, a stalwart Republican. In his opening remarks to the Legislature, Governor Thomson said that the metropolitan problems were most acute in Milwaukee and that he was recommending the Dineen committee's report for the establishment of a central fact-finding group to study urban problems. I said I was pleased that the governor had recognized the existence of the urban-suburban problem but that the city desired a study to be made by the Legislature. Mr. Dineen was gratified of course at the governor's endorsement in his message of the main points of the Dineen committee's report. The suburban forces were on the move.

Supervisor Bert Busby offered the services of the Committee of 21 to make the study, if given the authority.[185]

Recognizing the struggle ahead in the Legislature, Alderman Peter H. Hoffman, chairman of the Judiciary-Legislation Committee of the Common Council, announced that selling the Legislature on a statewide study of metropolitan problems and defending the city against any attempt to take away Milwaukee's waterworks would be top objectives of the city's 1957 legislative program. He also said the city wanted an adjustment of public utilities' tax distribution, which had caused some suburbs to become tax islands.[186]

The representatives of the suburbs arranged a hearing at a county legislative meeting to get legislation to develop a county water utility. Harold Fuhrman, Brown Deer village attorney, originally petitioned the county to create the utility and representatives of eight suburbs supported his petition. Arthur Saltzstein, my administrative secretary, had the task of countering them. He said that Milwaukee had no objections to the suburbs setting up their own water utilities but asked that the county be left out of it. He got the admission from Anthony X. Basile, Oak Creek attorney, that the suburbs wanted the county's credit rating to finance the system. Saltzstein suggested that the suburbs ought to turn in their charters to the county and let the county provide all the services to them. He further asserted that Wauwatosa's water shortage, which was now growing serious, was self-induced by their annexation efforts, and he said that Wauwatosa had yet to ask Milwaukee for a right-of-way access to Lake Michigan for its own system.[187]

The vehemence of the suburbs was not dying down. On January 20, 1957, the *West Allis Star* ran an editorial against me entitled "Does He Want to Be King?" The editorial labeled me "King Frank I" because I pressed for consolidation of governments in the metropolitan area.

At this time also, the *Milwaukee Journal* ran an article by one of its competent staff writers, Robert H. Wills, on urban-suburban relationships. Wills quoted Professor Charles D. Goff of the University of Wisconsin-Milwaukee as saying that "the suburbs are making 18 first downs to the city's 15." Goff noted that in legislative action, metropolitan study reports, annexation policies, court cases involving expansion and attempts to work with other communities the city was time and again losing to the suburbs. Goff stated that it was unrealistic to expect the suburban communities to consolidate with the central city, that there was no combination that could crush the suburbs and that their political advantages would increase.[188]

The story also noted that I said the city would not turn its functions over to the county, which was loosely governed by a group of chieftains. Anthony X. Basile was quoted as saying the more cities that existed around a central city the better. Harold Fuhrman said there was no immediate necessity for areawide services. Thus the propaganda war continued, with the legislators observing and shaping their minds.

An attempt was made to formulate a policy toward the study of urban expansion by the Wisconsin Legislative Council. It introduced a bill to study problems throughout the state and proposed a committee consisting of seven legislators and eight other members, all appointed by the governor, to study tax inequalities. Milwaukee officials naturally said they would support the bill.[489]

At the same time I said to a group of Milwaukee County Democrats that there was a question whether the Legislature would take steps bold enough to solve the problems but this bill would be in the right direction. One of the greatest needs in metropolitan areas, I asserted, was for planning beyond the city's boundaries.[190]

Keeping up my efforts to tell the city's side of the story, I made a talk at the Press Club on January 31, 1957, in which I proposed a development in the metropolitan concept of government, preferring one unit of government but willing to see the consolidation of smaller ones into new units. I proposed better planning for reduction of vulnerability to air attack by relocating industry and this required an extension of metropolitan area boundaries beyond the city and an equalization of taxes throughout the district.

I made other proposals not directly related to urban expansion such as the necessity of bomb shelters, an improved building code to reduce the flammability of cities, a motor vehicle system separated from pedestrian traffic, high taxes on cars, a more efficient sewage disposal system, introduction of green spaces, reduction of atmospheric pollution, improvement of public transit and a neighborhood redevelopment program. These were all somewhat radical ideas and not especially likely to endear me to most suburban people.[191]

Yet another fragment of territory with indescribably confused boundaries was now to be incorporated. William H. Bowman's attempt to incorporate the town of Greenfield as a third-class city became successful in February of 1957 when a charter was issued by state officials. In September of 1956, 3,251 persons had voted for incorporation and 972 had voted against. A victory dance was announced and an election for city officials was scheduled for March 19, 1957.

I called this incorporation "ill advised" and "another minor tragedy in municipal administration." I said Greenfield would be a burden to itself and that its administrative problems could have been best solved in the city where most of the residents undoubtedly were employed. I said that the incorporation pointed out the deficiencies of the state annexation laws and that it did not make sense for the Legislature to allow these cities to come into existence.[192]

A belated editorial now appeared in the *Milwaukee Journal* on this incorporation. In an editorial of February 18, 1957, the *Journal* said,

> The Greenfield incorporation merely writes the last chapter in the planless and chaotic urbanization of government in the metropolitan county. The whole picture is indeed tragic in the sense that it is frustrating, inefficient, expensive and unintelligent.
>
> The real import of the Greenfield move is that every last acre of Milwaukee County is now incorporated—in a jumble of 10 cities and nine villages, all being one community, really. In the space of just three years, town government has suddenly vanished. In the last 14 months alone, the five remaining towns were scratched off the map.
>
> Now it's done, and the best hope must be that it is a turn in the road, a point of new departure.

The editorial hoped that the state Legislature would see this unique situation and that the development might "jerk the County Board into this century." The editorial lamented that the word "metropolitan" had become an inflammatory word lately.[193]

The problem of how to collect school taxes in Granville was a serious one for the various school districts, which were now in whole or in part in the City of Milwaukee. Milwaukee officials would not pay money collected in the Milwaukee school districts into the Granville school districts in the consolidated area on the grounds that a taxpayer suit existed at the time challenging the city's right to collect the taxes. The school districts in Granville had hired an attorney, Ervin V. Novotny, to secure the money from the city.[194]

The Granville situation was naturally aggravating to Alderman Vincent A. Schmit. He was uncertain of his own status and no doubt there was considerable pressure on him to produce money for the Granville school districts without a special levy. Schmit and Alderman Bernard B. Kroenke, a close friend of Schmit, joined in offering a resolution that demanded that the city attorney, Walter J. Mattison, submit forthwith the name of an attorney to act as special counsel in the Granville suits. Schmit said that the Granville case was the most important to Milwaukee in 25 years and that the city attorney could not put a man on the case full time.[195] Despite Schmit's pressure, the Granville case was handled by the city attorney's office without a special counsel.

At about the same time, the Metropolitan Sewerage Commission was pushing a legislative bill to extend its authority to include Oak Creek, Franklin and other parts of southern Milwaukee County. The commission arranged to have hearings on the matter. At one such hearing with the Milwaukee Common Council's Judiciary Committee, I said that in terms of engineering this system could be justified, but economically the City of Milwaukee did not want to pay for sewers to be installed in Oak Creek and Franklin. There was also some opposition by aldermen. The extension of the sewerage district had been endorsed by the Dineen committee, but this extension had been contemplated for a long time by the Sewerage Commission.[196]

Matters on the proposed study of metropolitan problems were rapidly shaping up for a final consideration by the Legislature. The Committee of 21, apparently feeling that the Dineen report would be favored by a Republican governor and Legislature at the behest of the north shore suburbs, came to a decision in March of 1957 to favor two legislative bills. One called for a study of governmental problems in the metropolitan area. The other bill asked for a statewide study on taxation and shared aids. The spearheads for this action were Harold Fuhrman, Brown Deer village attorney; Herbert Mount, the committee's special counsel and a Wauwatosa resident; Patrick Fass, a county supervisor from Milwaukee's 18th Ward; and Alderman Alfred C. Hass.

Milwaukee aldermen on the Committee of 21 were divided over whether to support the suburban position favoring a bill to create a metropolitan study commission. Three aldermen—Martin Schreiber, Ralph Kelly and George Whittow—opposed the bill.[197] Alderman Hass and Alderman John Budzien voted on the

153

Committee of 21 for the bill and were criticized for "riding the fence" and "pussy footing" on the city's policy by other aldermen.[198] The Common Council temporarily postponed a showdown on the issue.[199]

The bill to create a metropolitan study commission was known as bill 182-S. It was sponsored by the Greater Milwaukee Committee, which had aided the suburbs in creating the Dineen committee. Bill 182-S was introduced by Senator Busby and a co-sponsor was Senator Kirby Hendee of Milwaukee's north shore suburbs. The bill proposed to set up an official commission of 15 people to examine the problems experienced by the various governments within Milwaukee County. The 15-member commission would consist of 12 citizens and three officials—one from the City of Milwaukee, one from another city in the county and one from a village or town. The bill was thus heavily loaded against the city—even if the appointing officer, the governor, wanted to put on the committee a strong Milwaukee supporter as the city's only official representative.

The city, of course, took issue with the bill not only on the composition of the commission, which would favor the suburbs, but also because the bill would not include a study of state aids and shared taxes, which the suburbs and the well-to-do members of the Greater Milwaukee Committee did not want. This objection was serious enough that the *Milwaukee Sentinel* tried to read into the language of the bill that the commission could make this study if it wanted, but it was the city's contention that even if it could, the commission would not, and as a matter of fact, it never did.[200]

Bill 182-S was not the only bill before the Legislature to study urban problems. There were several bills presented on the same subject. Bill 5-S, introduced by the Wisconsin Legislative Council, called for a general revision and reorganization of state laws dealing with incorporation and annexation, consolidation and detachment of municipal territory. Bill 30-S proposed to create a statewide committee on urban expansion consisting of three senators, four assemblymen and eight citizens-at-large to study urban problems in the entire state. This bill was introduced by the Legislative Council and it was one favorable to the City of Milwaukee's position. Senator Allen Busby, the brother of Supervisor Bert Busby, put in an amendment to exempt Milwaukee County from the bill for the obvious reason of maintaining suburban control of the county. Bill 183-S, introduced by Senator Walter Merten of Milwaukee and Senator Kirby Hendee of Shorewood, called for the creation of an interim local government tax study committee comprised of two senators, three assemblymen and four citizens to study distribution of state aids to local communities. This was also a bill resulting from the Dineen committee.

The city favored bills 30-S and 183-S and opposed 182-S. An extensive hearing was held on all these bills in March and, as was to be expected, the economic and social power of the Greater Milwaukee Committee and the Milwaukee Association of Commerce opposed the city at every point. Industry was not going to give up its tax advantages, big wealth was not going to give up its tax advantages, but both were determined to get city services.[201]

In a sneak maneuver, four members of the Greater Milwaukee Committee went to the Milwaukee County Board to get it to go on record favoring bill 182-S without giving any notice to the City of Milwaukee. A supervisor from a city district, Supervisor Edward Mertz, stopped the group and accused them of coming in with unclean hands because they had not notified the City of Milwaukee of their intentions. The members of the Greater Milwaukee Committee who came to the meeting were Rudolph A. Schoenecker, executive director; Herbert Kurth, vice president; Clifford Randall and Edward Gerhardy, both past presidents. Supervisor Mertz notified City of Milwaukee officials. Alderman Mortier, Alderman Quirk and Arthur Saltzstein, the administrative secretary to the mayor, showed up at the meeting. The County Board voted to stop the hearing and send the issue back to committee.[202]

The County Board's Legislative Committee debated the issue of the board's endorsement of a local study commission. Edmund B. Shea, an Iron Ring attorney, was the principal spokesman on this occasion.[203] A few weeks later the committee voted four to three to support the study of the metropolitan area under the bill confining it only to the Milwaukee area. The Iron Ring had won another victory in the County Board.[204]

It was becoming apparent also that the Greater Milwaukee Committee, the Iron Ring lobby and the Milwaukee press were going to run over the city with ease in the Legislature. The Committee of 21, seeing the handwriting on the wall for its own hopes of making the metropolitan study, adjourned indefinitely in April of 1957 after endorsing the two Greater Milwaukee Committee bills calling for suburban-controlled studies of Milwaukee.[205]

It was now almost a foregone conclusion that the city was about to be defeated once again by the power of the wealthy suburbs. A state Senate committee recommended the passage of the Greater Milwaukee Committee bill and provided an appropriation of $30,000. The study commission was charged with studying property tax assessments, traffic, water supply (of course!), sewage, planning, civil defense and other services, and it was to determine which of these governmental services could be rendered most adequately and efficiently on a local or countywide basis. The city fully expected that these studies would be used to give the suburbs access to city facilities without requiring the suburbs to pay an equal cost. In the legislative hearing, the suburbs went as far afield as to enlist the support of a Waukesha attorney, William G. Callow, as one of their spokesmen. Callow was prominent in Waukesha politics and had joined the Iron Ring group of attorneys.[206]

Alderman Schreiber and I made public our expression of disappointment over the approval by the Senate committee of this bill. I said, "This is the suburban and West Milwaukee bill, and I am not at all hopeful that impartial findings can come from it. The bill has the same defects that marked the governor's metropolitan study committee. Unless the governor gives due consideration to Milwaukee's population and unless he secures champions of the city's interests, Milwaukee will not be justly treated."[207]

The bill ultimately passed in April of 1957.

The closing of the Iron Ring on Milwaukee began to have a detrimental effect not only on Milwaukee but on the builders. They were mostly hostile to the city and were constantly fighting the city administration over public housing, slum clearance and sewer and water assessments. The Iron Ring posed a problem for the builders because the suburbs did not want many houses or many people due to the increased cost of sewers, water lines, schools and other public services. The suburbs began to use zoning laws to prohibit middle-income housing. In most suburbs, houses had to be placed on no less than a third of an acre of land, and this market was already well saturated. More affordable houses—five, six or seven to the acre—were zoned out of existence. The builders were therefore eager to overcome this disadvantage and wanted to have a single-function countywide government to control zoning, or to lodge the power in the county in order to break the restrictive subdivisions.

This situation brought forth a confused complaint from William A. Norris, my opponent, who shaped *Sentinel* policy on municipal government. Reasoning in his tortuous fashion, Norris attempted to blame me and my annexation drive for the problems of the builders, the suburbs and the low-income people. He said I annexed land to help low-income families—which I did. Norris wrote,

> Through annexations the City of Milwaukee has almost doubled its area. Most of the annexed land has been subdivided for low and middle-low income homes. Far too little of it has been revenue-producing industrial or commercial land. Mayor Zeidler— always a champion of the low-income family—has encouraged this type of annexation. Belatedly, we have discovered that such annex- ations and developments in the long run tend to defeat their own purpose—which is to provide good homes for the low and middle- low income families.

These people, Norris continued, did not pay their way. Milwaukee was too generous with builders who built for low-income families. Suburbs did not want low-income families in their areas and so they had zoned the land to keep low-income families and builders out and to keep taxes down.[206]

Norris repeated this viewpoint on other occasions to justify the suburbs slamming the door on low-income families. The reason for citing this viewpoint here is to demonstrate the contempt shown by the Iron Ring for low-income families and the degree to which low-income people were not wanted. At the same time, the suburbs fought to prevent the city from expanding to provide housing for the people for whom the suburbs themselves were unwilling to provide. Class discrimination, social snobbishness and the absolute repression of low-income families were also factors in the creation of metropolitan study legislation, and Norris, who at one time favored annexation, now became a spokesman for the economic class interests of the suburbs.

A minor flurry between Milwaukee and its suburbs occurred in May of 1957. Joseph R. Lamping, director of the Community Development Department, released a report indicating that seven suburbs had incorporated since 1951. The report predicted that they would eventually join the City of Milwaukee because of the problems they would have. These suburbs were St. Francis, Hales Corners, Greenfield, Brown Deer, Greendale, Oak Creek and Franklin. Mr. Lamping noted gross deficiencies in their services and he cited mounting tax costs.[209]

This report brought cries of derision from the suburbs.[210] Not the least of the sarcastic comments came from the *West Allis Star*, which editorially criticized Lamping, myself, taxes and other and sundry practices of the City of Milwaukee.[211]

In addition to its defeat on the metropolitan study bill in the 1957 Legislature, the city failed to have the Oak Creek law repealed, and no final action was taken on annexation laws. Even if any action had been taken, it was too late for the city.[212]

In July of 1957, I testified on behalf of the United States Conference of Mayors before a House of Representatives subcommittee on intergovernmental relations. I pointed out how state legislatures, dominated by rural politics, had been hostile to the big cities, and that the states had been slow, unwilling or unable to help their cities, which had found it necessary to go to the federal government for help. I warned that any attempt of the states to cut off certain types of federal aid under the cloak of states' rights would be fought by the cities. This conflict had been happening not only in Milwaukee but across the country.[213]

Also in July of 1957, there appeared in the *Socialist Call*, the national publication of the Socialist Party-Social Democratic Federation of the United States, an article in which I expressed concern about the attempt to turn the cities away from the federal government and keep them completely under the domination of the state. In this article I said,

> The net effect of the 'states' rights' theory in the past has been to deny great classes of people equal rights and privileges under the law. The emphasis on state supremacy also has meant the denial of proportional representation in many state legislatures. By this device most large urban communities are cut off from effectively presenting their problems to the legislatures through lack of voice. The following of the theory of states' rights has meant the establishment of a one-party system in many states of the nation to the detriment of the flourishing of democracy.[214]

In the middle of July, 1957, Governor Vernon Thomson signed into law the Greater Milwaukee Committee's metropolitan study bill that the city had so vigorously opposed. This was the bill that gave the city only one representative on a 15-member commission. The newspaper account of the governor's signing recorded that three state senators looked on, along with Rudolph Schoenecker, executive director of the Greater Milwaukee Committee. The state senators were Kirby Hendee of Shorewood, Allen Busby of West Milwaukee and Walter Merten from Milwaukee's northwest side. The signing was an occasion of triumph over the city. If there were any city representatives present I do not know, but certainly no one was asked officially to attend this ceremony celebrating our defeat.[215]

An article a few days later in the *Public Enterprise Record* was quite critical of the whole business. It said that this bill was "a conscious rejection of the city's plea to be studied in connection with other municipalities in the state" and was "designed to keep the city of Milwaukee from such aid as it might receive from Madison, Green Bay, Racine and other cities with suburban problems." The city had fought vainly for a statewide study so that the city could have pooled its interests with that of other central cities with similar growth problems.

The article charged that the study of taxes had died in the state Legislature because the suburbs did not want tax equalization, and it said, "If the present governor follows the pattern of the last governor, the committee will be weighted against the city." The *Record* said also that the study "sets the stage for non-city residents to recommend again to the Legislature that the city yield up its waterworks, stop its growth and remain quiescent while its industry runs away to the tax-free suburbs."[216]

The governor did not appoint the committee members immediately upon signing the bill. He waited several weeks. In the meantime, the next issue of the *Public Enterprise Record*, in August of 1957, brought forth the idea of creating a borough system for the Milwaukee area if a single government could not be developed. Such a borough system, the *Record* pointed out, could plan on an areawide basis, control population density and create green spaces and satellite cities. The article suggested that Whitefish Bay, Fox Point, Glendale, River Hills, Bayside and Brown Deer be amalgamated in one borough and West Allis, West Milwaukee and parts of Brookfield as another, while Wauwatosa, Elm Grove and part of Brookfield could be made into still another borough.[217]

This article sparked another flare-up from the suburbs. George Schmus, the West Allis city attorney, responded by saying, "The idea of a borough system for governmental units of Milwaukee County is largely theoretical. This is a typical slide rule approach to government. I don't think the slide rule approach to democratic government is the proper one. It doesn't take into consideration human values and the needs of the people." Schmus added that the net effect of the system would be to advance Zeidler's power at City Hall. My statement on Schmus' reaction was that his comment indicated the Iron Ring group was not prepared to give up anything to contribute to the progress of the community as a whole. The members of the Iron Ring would try to get from Milwaukee what services they could on a piecemeal basis, but they would make no fundamental alterations to improve the metropolitan setup.[218]

Mayor William B. Knuese of Wauwatosa was quoted as saying that the suburbs did not want Milwaukee services. I then asked if the City of Wauwatosa was prepared to call off the hearing it was pressing to get water from the Milwaukee waterworks. "Suburban communities," I said, "like to express the idea they are sovereign and absolutely independent of surrounding communities, but this is more fiction than fact, for all of us in the metropolitan area are more or less interdependent."[219]

The people at City Hall were apprehensive of the upcoming appointments to the Metropolitan Study Commission. Unlike Governor Kohler, Governor Thomson was not going to mention anything to the City of Milwaukee about what he was going to do. Before the governor appointed the commission, I tried to encourage the continuation of city expansion. At an informal meeting of the aldermen which preceded a Common Council session early in September, I said, "Some of the problems you talk about, like the street improvements, are a result of the expansion program, but if you go out into the 5th, 11th and 15th Wards and see the wonderful new home and business sites available, you realize that we are making progress." I told the Common Council that providing adequate living space for city dwellers had given people positive recreational opportunities, had helped to reduce juvenile delinquency and had lessened traffic problems. I said, "If the city is to be healthy and survive and not have the terrible slums that Philadelphia and Chicago have, its expansion must go on."

I told the aldermen that if the city was going to carry on its expansion, it had to sell the people of Milwaukee the idea that an upgrading of their living areas came with a cost, that the government was not an ogre devouring their substance and that their city provided vital facilities such as water, sewers, streets, schools and other municipal services without which they could not live.

I tried to paint for the aldermen a vision of the future city. This city should have well-defined neighborhoods in which pedestrian and vehicular traffic were separated. There must be improved public transportation, and there must be new sites for industry. I said the people were not looking for cheap taxes, but for a government in which they had confidence.[220]

Also prior to the governor appointing the study commission, I made a suggestion publicly that metropolitan central cities should set up their own study commissions to solve the problems of growth. I said that the central cities should be the principal source of financial encouragement and support for study groups. This was one way for central cities to protect themselves from loaded study committees dominated by suburbs.[221]

All the comments on the needs of the central cities, all the pleas and all the hints that the central cities would seek help from the federal government did not influence Governor Vernon Thomson in the least, it seemed, in appointing the Metropolitan Study Commission. In October, the governor appointed a group that was heavily weighted in favor of the suburbs. The city's representative was Dr. George A. Parkinson of the University of Wisconsin-Milwaukee. He was the part-time director of civil defense for Milwaukee. He was an able man, and while no doubt the governor intended to slight the city by appointing a part-time city official, Dr. Parkinson would later propose that the Milwaukee area take steps toward a metropolitan government. For this suggestion, incidentally, Dr. Parkinson was ultimately maneuvered off the commission.

Enthusiastic approval of the packed committee of course came from the press and suburban leaders.[222]

Criticism about Governor Thomson's appointments came from other city and county officials. His study committee consisted largely of people from the north shore suburbs. The south side of Milwaukee was not represented. There was no representation from county government and there was no major city official on the committee. The aldermen especially felt slighted. The *CIO News* stated that the appointment of one labor man, Harold E. Beck, an able man and a liberal, was window dressing because the committee had been stacked against the wage earners.[223]

The character of this new study commission was discussed by the *Capital Times* in Madison. The *Capital Times* was a paper opposed to reactionary Republicans and it saw in the Milwaukee experience a threat to the central city of Madison, which was facing similar problems with its affluent suburbs, such as Maple Bluff. The *Capital Times*, in a story on October 14, 1957, said, "The fact that Thomson guaranteed a committee majority to suburban representatives and that he personally went to Milwaukee to participate in their first deliberations indicates that Thomson is throwing the weight of the executive office on the side of the suburbs and against the expressed desire of Mayor Frank Zeidler of Milwaukee."[224]

In an editorial on the same date, the *Capital Times* repeated its criticism of the governor's study commission as a manifestation of the weakening of home rule in local units of government. The editorial said,

> The suburbs are making burdensome demands on the city in the way of services and Mayor Zeidler and other city officials, who are elected to watch out for the city's interests, are insisting that the suburbs accept responsibility along with the services. It was bad enough that the Legislature intervened to impose this committee on the city of Milwaukee, it remained for the governor to top off this assault on home rule in the appointments he made to the committee. Out of the 15-member committee, only six came from Milwaukee which stands to lose millions from the recommendations made by the group.

Nine of the committee members, the editorial pointed out, were from suburbs that were insisting that Milwaukee provide even more services than it already did. The Milwaukee representatives, with minor exceptions, reflected the business viewpoint, which was friendly to the suburban side. The chairman of the group, the editorial noted, was a suburbanite. The mayor of Milwaukee, who carried the primary responsibility for the city's interests, was not a member of the committee. The editorial concluded, "If ever a committee was stacked, this is one."[225]

In a radio talk a short time later, William T. Evjue, editor of the *Capital Times*, repeated the charges and noted the parallel between the action of the Legislature in foisting the study commission onto Milwaukee and a bill passed by the Legislature forbidding Madison from constructing a civic center designed by Frank Lloyd Wright.[226]

The *Milwaukee Sentinel* published an editorial defending this packed committee. It praised the appointments to the group, praised the Republican suburban senators who put the bill through and said that no one on the committee was the type "given to narrow, sectional bias," which, of course, was simply not so. The editorial said, "It is unfortunate that Mayor Zeidler and a few other city officials already have sought to undermine public confidence in the commission by expressing doubts as to its impartiality. Certainly it should be given a chance to start working on its tremendous assignment, and to come to some conclusions, before being subjected to public criticism." This was the same old line—create a stacked committee, demand that there be no criticism of its composition, allow it to prepare a biased report and then, on the basis of the biased report, demand legislative action against the city. The concept of fair play simply did not enter into the suburban manner of doing things, and again they reminded me of the Soviet politicians in their mode of action—never give the other fellow a fair break.[227]

Faced with such a loaded committee empowered by official legislative sanction, the city government had to develop an official position on the metropolitan area problem. An announcement was made that such a policy would be drafted to serve as a guide especially for Dr. Parkinson, the city's representative. The major emphasis in the policy was of course the waterworks. The city would fight any attempt to take control of the waterworks or to force the city to supply other municipal customers against its wishes. The city wanted the opportunity to grow either by annexation or consolidation. Milwaukee did not want industry to flee. If other communities wanted services from Milwaukee they should get those services by amalgamating. Parkinson was advised by several aldermen that he was the "mouthpiece" of the city as well as a member of the study commission.[228]

Later in 1957, when I appeared in Chicago before a subcommittee of the United States Senate Banking and Currency Committee, I spoke to the press and said that the federation of the great cities in the Milwaukee-Chicago-Calumet area might prove beneficial, since this region was likely to become one of the great metropolitan areas of the world.[229]

The problem of Milwaukee's consolidation with Granville continued in 1957. The case of the consolidation was still in the courts. The problem of different tax rates in each of the Granville school districts, which had not been consolidated with Milwaukee and which were in some instances partly in and partly out of Milwaukee, was as yet unsolved, although the city had paid the bill at the last budget without a challenge from taxpayers. Vincent A. Schmit, the alderman for the consolidated Granville territory, announced in October that he would oppose plans to vary the tax rate in the area according to school district. He said that varying tax rates would be unfair and that the people who had voted to come into Milwaukee were entitled to the same treatment as the rest of the city. He demanded a public hearing. However, Carl Kennell, an assistant city attorney noted for his meticulousness, and Thomas A. Byrne, the tax commissioner, insisted that the city did not have jurisdiction in the matter because the Granville school districts had not merged with the Milwaukee school system.[230]

In response to Alderman Schmit's pressure, a plan was devised to equalize the tax costs in the Granville school districts by spreading the extra cost throughout the city. This plan was created following Common Council resolutions introduced by Alderman Schmit.[231] I proposed that the city accept the certifications of the school boards as to their needs for 1958. Harry G. Slater, deputy city attorney, acknowledged that the city could not be sure it would avoid a lawsuit if it accepted or rejected the certifications, and there was a fear that the entire tax roll would be attacked.[232]

In December of 1957, the city gained a court victory in the Granville consolidation. Ruling on appeals generated by a Circuit Court case, the Wisconsin Supreme Court rejected Brown Deer's claims that the consolidation ordinances of Granville and Milwaukee were invalid. This decision finally gave Milwaukee the parts of Granville where no Brown Deer annexation proceedings had been instituted. This area was about six square miles.

However, in regard to an additional disputed area of 16 square miles, the court ruled that the City of Milwaukee could not challenge Brown Deer's annexations by claiming that the village could not handle them. This ruling in effect confirmed the status quo of a previous state Supreme Court ruling that had given Brown Deer temporary jurisdiction over the 16 square miles. The way was open for Milwaukee once again to challenge the validity of Brown Deer's annexation of this area in the Circuit Court.[233]

The immediate result of this decision was that both sides claimed gains. Harold Fuhrman, the Brown Deer attorney, said the decision cleared the air and would reduce the issues to those which could be handled in a Circuit Court trial. Of the ruling, Joseph R. Lamping, Milwaukee's community development director, said, "We have found the Brown Deer annexations faulty and we will be prepared to prove it."[234]

The effect of this decision was also to bring a halt to some unofficial talks between city officials and Brown Deer. I was not a participant in these talks, but apparently subdividers and land developers had been trying to get the city's elected officials and Brown Deer officials to divide up the territory. A Brown Deer trustee asserted that this negotiation had been going on for two years but nothing had come of it.[235] I hastened to agree to cut off these talks.

Later, after I left office, talks between Milwaukee and Brown Deer were revived. At issue was the so-called "Corrigan annexation" to Brown Deer. Milwaukee's challenge to this annexation was worked on extensively by Richard F. Maruszewski and several other assistant city attorneys, including John Cook. This was a most tedious case, which Milwaukee won in the Circuit Court before Judge William I. O'Neill in 1959. During a lengthy appeals process, Milwaukee and Brown Deer negotiated in an attempt to draw a line independent of the decision of the Circuit Court. Legislation was obtained by the city in the 1961 Legislature to permit this negotiation because of its doubtful legality. The issue was not finally solved until a Wisconsin Supreme Court ruling in Milwaukee's favor in 1962.

In the early part of 1958, with the Iron Ring definitely closed on the city, Milwaukee was reduced to trying to retain its services, despite the efforts of the suburbs and the Metropolitan Study Commission, and to trying to work up sentiment for further consolidation with some of the more deficient suburbs.

In January of 1958, Joseph R. Lamping, the community development director, said that citizens in five suburbs were in favor of consolidation with Milwaukee. I then asked Richard F. Maruszewski, the assistant city attorney who specialized in annexation matters, to prepare a list of advantages and disadvantages of consolidation for both the suburbs and Milwaukee. I also asked the urban renewal coordinator, Sol Ackerman, and the director of the Housing Authority to make projections of future urban growth because the lot restrictions in the suburbs would compel Milwaukee to increase the number of low-income people it could accommodate.[236]

For my part, I began to advocate the federated or borough form of government to solve metropolitan problems if a single consolidated unit could not be obtained. I felt a borough system could help relieve city taxpayers of the unequal burden they were carrying for some services. To my surprise I discovered in a debate with William H. Bowman, city attorney for Franklin and Greenfield, that he was advocating something similar. Why this was the case, I do not know, except perhaps that Bowman thought the services in which Greenfield and Franklin were deficient could be obtained through a federated or metropolitan form of government.[237]

Mr. Lamping's consolidation policies did not sit well with certain aldermen. Some of them opposed the policies because they felt the next areas to consolidate would be deficient areas and they did not want these areas to compete with their wards for funds. Mr. Lamping's department, which was responsible to the Common Council, apparently circulated a tabloid in a Greenfield city election on behalf of candidates in the city who favored consolidation with Milwaukee. Two aldermen— Vincent A. Schmit and Peter Hoffman—challenged Lamping, and Schmit suggested a resolution to restudy consolidation policies.[238]

In May of 1958, I proposed in a letter to Aldermen Martin Schreiber and Peter Hoffman that four studies be made for legislative action. I said a study was needed on a plan to form an executive department in the county government in order to strengthen that government as it took on more urban functions and received a bigger slice of the tax dollar. I also suggested that studies be made of a state department of urban affairs, of state grants in aid for urban renewal and housing and of a repeal of the Oak Creek law.[239]

The city's attention was drawn for the next couple of months to the work of the Metropolitan Study Commission. Among the proposals that the city put before the commission was a proposal to change the system of state shared taxes so that no community could get more than 50 percent of its combined levy in shared taxes. This proposal came from Shepard A. Magidson, administrative assistant in the office of Virgil H. Hurless, city comptroller. Of course, suburbs such as Glendale, Oak Creek,

Wauwatosa, Bayside, Fox Point and Whitefish Bay went into sharp attack, as this was the means by which these suburbs enjoyed very low property taxes.[240]

The matter of sewer district extension was considered by the Metropolitan Study Commission and this time the city, after earnest consideration, decided to change its stand and support the extension because of the gravity of the sewage problems outside of the city. This stand was taken even though it meant a further cost to the city taxpayer for sewer extensions in the hostile suburbs. The city took the occasion of its support for an enlarged sewer district to plead in vain for a metropolitan government to cover the entire area.[241] The sewer district was ultimately extended.

In July of 1958, the City of Greenfield, which at its inception had held a victory dance to celebrate its independence from Milwaukee, came around to asking the city for water. Upon hearing this request, I urged the Common Council to explore the possibility of consolidating with Greenfield. "The request for a single service from the city government broadens the opportunity for discussion with Greenfield of the various merits of consolidation," I said. I pointed out that there existed between Milwaukee and Greenfield a boundary almost impossible to describe because of its irregularity. I said it would be unfortunate if this irregular boundary, which made the administration of services very difficult, was permitted to survive. I also said that there was some doubt that Greenfield was a city. It had gone through the incorporation proceeding as a 15-square-mile fourth-class city on February 7, 1957.[242]

This statement of mine brought from Mayor Robert M. Owens of Greenfield the comment that the last two elections held in Greenfield had demonstrated that its citizens did not want to become a part of Milwaukee. He said that I was asking Greenfield officials "to betray the voters and commit hari-kari for water." He then noted that Joseph Lamping, Milwaukee's community development director, had been permitted by me to spend thousands of dollars trying to elect a slate of Greenfield candidates, but that Lamping's slate had lost by a 3-to-1 margin. Mayor Owens was heartened that Lamping had been called before the Milwaukee aldermen for spending funds. Owens was also pleased that some aldermen had come to the conclusion that my policies had been detrimental to Milwaukee and by the fact that some aldermen openly opposed my attempts to minimize suburban recognition.[243]

In August of 1958, the suburbs finally broke the back of Milwaukee's resistance to selling water to the suburbs. The sudden change occurred because the Public Service Commission, which was dominated by Republicans, ordered Milwaukee to sell water to Wauwatosa on the grounds that Milwaukee was a water utility and therefore had to serve Wauwatosa. This ruling came despite the fact that the PSC had previously permitted three north shore suburbs to form their own water district separate from the Milwaukee district by ruling that Milwaukee was not a water utility — an absolute contradiction.

The aldermen and I were in favor of fighting the PSC order at first. However, I was advised by an assistant city attorney that if Milwaukee lost its challenge of the order, the city could be sued for damages, which might run into the millions of dollars. I felt that the PSC order would be sustained not on its merits but on the political power of the suburbs and then we could be sued. Based on the advice of the city attorney's office, I ultimately vetoed a Common Council resolution challenging the PSC order.

I also came around to feeling that Milwaukee should serve Wauwatosa with water because the lethargy and indifference of the Wauwatosa city government about furnishing water to its own citizens was so great as to jeopardize the health of the metropolitan area. The Wauwatosa government was a clever one politically, but terribly poor administratively in furnishing vital services. It always seemed to be looking for a free ride on its neighbors.

The breaking of the Milwaukee water policy had many effects, including an impact on the life of the Metropolitan Study Commission. This impact was best described in an issue of the *Public Enterprise Record* in August of 1958. The *Record* predicted that the suburbs would become increasingly hostile to the commission. After breaking Milwaukee's policy against selling water, and with an expanded sewerage district handling outlying sewerage problems, the suburbs would have "little interest in any further recommendations of the commission." The *Record* noted that future proposals would look toward administrative improvement and tax equity, which none of the suburbs wanted. The commission might recommend a metro-politan form of government, but this the suburbs would try to defeat. The *Record* predicted that the commission, weighted with suburban representatives, would learn what it was to experience the hostility of the suburbs.

The *Record* further argued that the city would need to fight for tax equalization either by amalgamation, consolidation or a borough system of government. Without tax equalization, Milwaukee would become a slum for low-income people, while the industries, shopping centers and wealthy people located elsewhere. The article warned that a new session of the Legislature might try to take away the Port of Milwaukee and the waterworks while ignoring reapportionment.

Since the Metropolitan Study Commission was now left with the objective of trying to find some method of getting the suburbs to meet their metropolitan responsibilities, the attitude of the city began to change toward the commission. When it appeared that the commission could not raise funds, a resolution was sponsored in the Milwaukee Common Council by Aldermen Schimenz and Whittow to have the council share a per capita cost of the commission. This action was partly taken to offset the influence of the Milwaukee Association of Commerce, which conducted a drive to raise money for the commission.[244]

The Common Council finally gave about $23,000 for the Metropolitan Study Commission to continue its work.[245]

In September of 1958, I spoke to the Milwaukee Advertising Club on the idea of a metropolitan government. I described the evolution of London's government, and I pointed out that in a federated government people can have some sense of identity with their neighborhood while being able to cooperate on a larger basis. I listed some of the local problems that crossed municipal boundaries — problems such as sewage disposal, water pollution and public and private transportation. The key question to be answered was: "Can community cooperation be obtained at the same time communities are allowed to retain their local identities?" Concerning the Metropolitan Study Commission, I said now that the water victory was won by the suburbs, nothing but good could come of the commission.[246] In this, however, I was mistaken for the commission later came out with recommendations to give the suburbs control of the library and further control of the waterworks.

The *Milwaukee Journal*, which had editorially opposed my efforts for amalgamation, found the idea of federation acceptable.[247]

The idea of a metropolitan government was latent in the minds of some county supervisors while the city and suburbs were struggling with each other. In October of 1958, three county supervisors—Gerald Kops, Patrick Fass and Earl Keegan—asked the County Board to press for a home rule amendment to the Wisconsin Constitution that would enable Milwaukee County to establish a metropolitan government. They introduced a resolution that would have prepared a detailed study of the amendment for submission to the 1959 Legislature. This resolution asked for a broad grant of powers and made great sense. However, Supervisor John Doyne opposed the idea of home rule and wanted specific functions of the county spelled out by the Legislature. Doyne and other supervisors wanted to avoid the form of urban county government found in Dade County, Florida. They somehow felt that Milwaukee County government was superior.[248]

City and suburban officials reacted against the proposal. The city was unwilling to transfer any of its functions to the county on a piecemeal basis, and the suburbs did not want to lose any functions that might diminish their sense of importance. Alderman Schreiber of Milwaukee said the idea was premature. I said the home rule concept of county government did not entirely solve metropolitan problems, although the proposal did represent some advancement. I noted that there was a trend toward metropolitan government. However, I said that the powers of metropolitan government should not rest in the county government. The county should confine itself to its historic function and municipal functions should be administered by a specially chartered municipal agency. The major defect in the county government was that its powers were not centralized. Another defect in the proposal was that the area of the county was not coterminous with the metropolitan area, but I repeated that the idea was an advance.

Supervisor Bert Busby, the suburban leader, said the proposal was untimely and noted that the West Allis Common Council opposed the resolution saying it "ignores, nullifies and short circuits the work of the Metropolitan Study Commission and constitutes a power grab on the part of the County Board at the expense of suburban government."[249]

The Metropolitan Study Commission, apparently sensing that it was losing some suburban support, or in an attempt for an end run around the City of Milwaukee, requested the services of Assistant City Attorney Harry G. Slater to advise the commission on the legal ramifications of its studies. The commission probably wanted to have its work bear the imprimatur of an able assistant city attorney in order to forestall Milwaukee's objections to any recommendations by the commission to hand out city services. After a Common Council dispute, a vote of 15 to 3 permitted Mr. Slater to serve as an advisor. The principal objector was Alderman Fred P. Meyers who saw a threat of metropolitan government arising out of the commission's studies.[250]

In November of 1958, the Metropolitan Study Commission began to release reports on the issues of sewers, water and assessments. I said the reports contained "broad hints" that the City of Milwaukee was responsible for these metropolitan problems—if Milwaukee would have solved the problems of the suburbs, then none of those problems would have existed. However, I also noted that by addressing the problems of sewers and water in the suburbs, and the variations in assessment practices, the commission was beginning to touch upon the evils that resulted from fragmented government, and that the reports therefore were making the strongest possible suggestions that an amalgamated government was essential for the Milwaukee area.

About one of these reports, George A. Schmus, West Allis city attorney, said that the suburbs would support creation of an authority to handle major areawide services but would oppose consolidation of municipalities. In other words, West Allis was in favor of giving Milwaukee's waterworks to a special government, but West Allis would not consolidate.

These comments were contained in an article in the *Milwaukee Journal* on November 26, 1958, under the title "Mayor Plans to Counteract 'Slur' at City." The story said that the city would set up a special committee to evaluate the reports from the Metropolitan Study Commission because of hints that the city was the cause of the problems.

This headline was not supported by the story and I found it necessary in the issue of the *Milwaukee Sentinel* the next day to say that I did not consider the series of reports issued by the Metropolitan Study Commission a "slur" against the city. I said the reports were good and I was not taking exception to their recital of metropolitan problems, but to the impression created in newspaper comment and speeches by other officials that the City of Milwaukee was responsible for those problems.[251]

The Common Council ultimately created a special committee consisting of the mayor, the council president, the city attorney, the city comptroller, the city treasurer and the chairmen of all council standing committees to weigh the reports.[252]

The *Milwaukee Labor Press*, which was ordinarily silent on matters between the city and suburbs, commended the idea of a metropolitan government.[253]

All of this was going on while the city was again trying to solve the problem of separate taxes in the Granville school districts. The issue was raised in October of 1958 when the Common Council's Budget Committee cut out of the budget a special amount designated for residents of five Granville school districts. The committee members had been told that their personal property was liable to seizure and that they would be held responsible for sums illegally appropriated. The aldermen were afraid because in previous years the city had made appropriations that might not have been sustained if they had been challenged in the courts.

Alderman Vincent Schmit of the 20th Ward said he would resign if the Common Council did not restore the budget cut.[254]

The continuing problem in Granville was the result of a clear deficiency in Wisconsin's annexation laws and I pointed out the need for a new state law making a city's boundaries coterminous with its school districts. I said that the City of Milwaukee was not trying to avoid its obligations to Granville residents, but it was trying to conform with the decisions of the courts, and only when a clear-cut court decision was rendered would there be an answer to the Granville situation.[255]

In response to this situation, the Common Council's Judiciary Committee recommended that Milwaukee appeal to State Superintendent of Schools G.E. Watson to set aside a Milwaukee County School Committee order that kept intact the existing school districts in Granville whether portions were in Milwaukee or not. Alderman Schmit introduced a resolution to create a special Common Council fund from which money could be drawn to pay Granville taxes, as a means around the dilemma.[256]

I sent a letter to the County School Committee asking it to detach the Granville school districts from Brown Deer and to attach them to Milwaukee. I also asked the city attorney about the legality of taxing people in one portion of a city to relieve people in another portion from a tax burden imposed by a separate agency of government. Schmit protested my letter. He was determined to override the legal issue.[257]

The Common Council's Finance Committee recommended equalization for taxes in Granville and proposed a transfer of $180,000 to a special fund to pay joint costs.[258]

Assistant City Attorney Richard F. Maruszewski called this action illegal and warned the aldermen that they might be personally liable if they voted for such a plan. Alderman Schmit, however, said that this opinion gave sanction to an injustice and he strongly urged his fellow councilmen to pass the resolution. He said that the city attorney had once written an opinion that the Granville consolidation also consolidated the respective school systems.[259]

I said I would veto the creation of a special fund by the Common Council because such a fund could put the entire tax roll in jeopardy. I said it was not a matter of what the Common Council wanted but what the City of Milwaukee could legally do. The aldermen in voting to support Alderman Schmit said that they were carrying out the promises of the city to the area.[260]

The story that appeared in the *Milwaukee Journal* carrying my statement said I had "denounced" the Common Council's vote on the Granville school matter.[261] This was a poor choice of words by the newspaper and I felt compelled to immediately disclaim that I had "denounced" the Common Council. I said in the *Milwaukee Sentinel*, "I want it clear that I am not denouncing the council, nor am I opposed to relief for the 20th Ward." I pointed out that the council decision would not bring proper relief for Granville residents because it might result in tying up the entire city tax roll for 1959 and the city would be left without funds to operate. I suggested that the sums of money required for tax equalization be lumped in the Common Council contingent fund without being earmarked. If the Legislature later passed a law to legalize the expenditure, then the expenditure could be made. I also said that a still better method would be for the Milwaukee County School Committee to detach to the city's school system the 6.5 square miles of the Granville territory awarded by the Wisconsin Supreme Court to the city. Several hundred residents of the area jammed a meeting at 5300 W. Villard Avenue to voice their concerns.[262]

My statements about vetoing the Common Council action and putting the Granville school tax equalization money in the council contingent fund brought the charge from Alderman Schmit that I was playing politics and was more concerned about the taxpayers in Milwaukee than those in the Granville school districts. I replied that Schmit was trying to solve a very delicate legal problem with a bludgeon. Schmit said my veto would be an injustice if there were no uniformity of taxes. I said that my primary concern was not tax relief but making sure that the problem was resolved in a manner that would not force city officials to act contrary to law. I said that Schmit's implication that this was a political test was categorically wrong.[263]

A Granville citizens' committee urged me not to veto the Schmit resolution. However, I ultimately did veto the Schmit resolution, the funds were put in the council contingent fund and later, as I recall, paid out of that fund without taxpayer protest.[264]

The serious difficulty that the fragmentation of the Granville area showed in administration caught the editorial attention of the *Milwaukee Journal*. The paper recognized the dangers to the aldermen in voting an expenditure of very doubtful legality and supported my suggestion as to the means of relief. It said, "Here is a most dismaying instance of how people can get lost in the governmental jungle here—58 taxing units in one natural community." Yet the paper would not support amalgamated government.[265]

The County School Committee agreed to appoint a study committee to see how to unravel the tangled school district problems after giving me a hearing on this idea.[266]

As these events were unfolding in the Granville area, the City of Milwaukee was busy at the south end of the county contesting the authority of the Town of Oak Creek to incorporate as a fourth-class city. Milwaukee had challenged the Oak Creek law in court and a decision was finally forthcoming. Circuit Court Judge William F. Shaughnessy ruled that the Oak Creek law was valid. The City of Milwaukee had argued that the law unfairly and arbitrarily targeted Milwaukee by facilitating incorporations next to cities of the first class—the only such city in the state was Milwaukee. Judge Shaughnessy ruled that "this argument is without merit for the reason that other industrial or commercial municipalities may well become cities of the first class in the future as population grows."

Then the judge proceeded to unburden himself as to why suburbs are better than central cities. He said,

> The Legislature must have recognized the tendency today on
> the part of people employed in metropolitan areas to establish

residences in the suburbs. Consideration of health, fresh air and the opportunity for physical exercise, the convenience of modern transportation are but a few of the considerations that recommend to people whose work is in the city the advantages of a residence outside of the metropolitan area.

The establishment of residence and convenient commercial areas beyond the metropolitan limits create the necessity for fire and police protection and local government. Obviously people who own homes or establish residences or businesses in such outside districts are entitled to plan, organize and incorporate some form of municipal government.

The court has concluded that the determination by the Legislature to establish the classification included in Section 60.81 of the statutes was not arbitrary but a reasonable and a constitutional classification with which the court has no power to interfere.

This decision was naturally a cause of rejoicing in the suburbs. William H. Bowman, wearing another of his suburban hats as special attorney for Oak Creek, said, "Oh, that's fine. I'm delighted." He said this was not an isolated phenomenon and that the incorporation of suburbs had gone on all over the United States.[267]

My comment was that the law slammed down a kind of suburban iron curtain on the city and I predicted that towns would rush to become cities and that counties would seek urban powers. I felt the decision spelled a difficult future for existing cities.[268]

The judge's preference for suburbs (he lived in one himself) also caught my attention. I was rather interested in the judge's implication that suburban life was better than city life, and I said that I trusted that such a belief was not the legal basis for his decision.[269]

The suburbs were giving the city difficulty on another matter. They were not meeting their share of the burden of reciprocal firefighting services. Shorewood, Whitefish Bay, River Hills, Glendale and West Allis were allegedly not paying their fair share of the costs nor were they being cooperative. A recommendation was made that the city policy of providing them with such service be reviewed.[270] The suburbs had a tendency to be slow about paying for reciprocal service rendered and were reluctant to make expenditures to keep their fire fighting equipment up to Milwaukee standards.

Partly as a result of these problems, Alderman Vincent Schmit proposed a state law to require new suburbs to prove they were self-sustaining before they incorporated. He also proposed a law requiring Milwaukee County to charge suburbs for police protection and other municipal services that the county provided to the suburbs.[271]

When 1959 began, the prospects of annexation were gone for Milwaukee, consolidation was remote, metropolitan federation doubtful, but the attempt to grab the waterworks and other city services by the suburbs was as real as ever. The Legislature was in session.

The leadership of the Iron Ring seemed now to revolve around George Schmus, the city attorney of West Allis, who was given to inflammatory expression, much like William H. Bowman. Schmus made a speech to the Milwaukee County League of Municipalities (the Iron Ring) asking the members to "muster the shock troops" and "besiege the Legislature" to keep in place "the rivets of the iron ring" around the central city. Schmus in his speech said,

> Milwaukee City Hall itself was a substantial contributor to the bootless condition of hostility that strangled governmental progress in the metropolitan area for the long decades before now. But it has been steadily, if slowly and painfully, working itself out of that shell, as suburban leadership must know. In recent months for the first time, some metropolitan progress has seemed to be in real prospect.

This was undoubtedly an allusion to the victory of the suburbs in gaining the city's water supply and in the defeat the city suffered in Oak Creek. The *Milwaukee Journal* criticized Schmus for this speech.[272]

The city government took up the matter of what approach to take before the Metropolitan Study Commission on the form of government in the area. Diverse views appeared. Alderman Vincent Schmit advocated a countywide referendum on forming a single metropolitan government from city or county government. Alderman Charles Quirk and Alderman Fred P. Meyers said the city should preserve its own integrity and not push for any form of metropolitan government, not even complete consolidation. Alderman John Budzien said that equitable taxation was the first problem and that all who wanted city services should consolidate with the city. Alderman Matt Schimenz said the mayor-council form of government had proved itself and the people who were receiving metropolitan services should pay full costs.[273]

A special Common Council committee drew up a proposal calling for an entire contiguous urban area of the Milwaukee region to be governed by a single municipal unit of government with power to expand as the population growth required.[274]

The Common Council finally adopted, by vote of 16 to 1, an official policy statement that urged the city to form the basis of a metropolitan unit of government. The statement argued that it would be a step backward to strip the city of its functions and to transfer them to other forms of government. Suburbs that were unable to furnish necessary services to their residents were urged to consolidate with the city to obtain those services. The statement said that a county government could not meet the needs of the Milwaukee area.

Before the statement was adopted, an attempt was made to declare that equitable tax distribution was the primary concern of the city. This was beaten on a vote of 12 to 5. Alderman Schmit's proposal for a merged city-county form of government with a combination of aldermen and supervisors and a mayor elected at large throughout the county also was beaten.

The Common Council's statement was in effect a return to the city's long-maintained position of one unit of government for the metropolitan area with a municipal, and not county, form of government.[275]

The Common Council also turned its attention to appealing Judge Shaughnessy's ruling that the City of Milwaukee had no right to challenge the Granville school district decision made by the County School Committee. The sentiment of the Common Council was in favor of the appeal, but I said I would veto it because it would effectively prevent detaching parts of these school districts to Milwaukee, since the remaining parts would be too weak to stand by themselves.[276] The city attorney apparently was reluctant to make the appeal because it was of doubtful validity.

One original idea was proposed about metropolitan government. In a hearing before the Metropolitan Study Commission, Mayor Robert MacDonald of Franklin proposed a metropolitan council composed of heads of all communities. All the other communities stood by their previous positions. I urged the commission to come up with some form of metropolitan government.[277]

The suburbs, having beaten Milwaukee on the issue of city expansion, now focused their attack on the city's most vital service. A proposal was shortly offered by the Metropolitan Study Commission to set up a Milwaukee water authority with five members appointed by the City of Milwaukee and two appointed by the governor. But even this proposal was not satisfactory to the partisan *West Allis Star*, which demanded that the entire water system be taken from Milwaukee. The *Star* denounced the study commission's proposal as window dressing and it praised West Allis City Comptroller Irvin Knoebel and Alderman Le Roy Farness as statesmen because they demanded that a metropolitan water authority take over the Milwaukee waterworks.[278]

A proposal was forthcoming from the Metropolitan Study Commission in April of 1959 to form a limited metropolitan government. A leading advocate of this proposal was the vice-chairman of the commission, Dr. George A. Parkinson, who was the official city representative appointed by Governor Thomson. As usual the suburban spokesmen violently opposed this proposal. Their views were aired in the *West Allis Star*, which angrily condemned Parkinson and accused him of ramming the proposals through the committee in the absence of the West Allis city comptroller who was becoming more and more the anchorman for the suburbs on the Metropolitan Study Commission.[279]

The *Star* also took umbrage with the Metropolitan Milwaukee Citizens' Conference held on April 17, 1959, at the Pfister Hotel. At this conference, I represented the City of Milwaukee, Supervisor John Doyne represented the County Board and Evan C. Schwemer, village president of Fox Point, represented the suburbs. The discussion was a reiteration of the viewpoint of the respective groups. I opposed giving up single functions of city government to the suburbs. Supervisor Doyne advocated giving the functions to the county and Schwemer defended the suburbs' separate existence. He said it was not in the public interest to eliminate them and that they were not parasitical as charged. He also opposed changes in the tax structure. Even these public discussions the *Star* found offensive as discussion encouraged people to think about metropolitan problems. The *Star* noted with satisfaction Parkinson's resignation from the Metropolitan Study Commission.[280]

The *West Allis Star* was a perfect echo of the inner strategy of the Iron Ring, and it was apparent that the Iron Ring members were feeling their strength on the basis of their victories over the city. The Legislature was in session and the suburbs were poised to enjoy substantial gains.

The city proposed to introduce bills in the Legislature. One of these would have taken away free sheriff service from Milwaukee County municipalities that did not provide their own. Another bill would have prohibited municipal water customers from forming their own water utility as Whitefish Bay and Fox Point did when they joined with Glendale to form their own water district. A third bill would have made all territory in the City of Milwaukee a part of the Milwaukee school system. These bills were unsuccessful.[281]

The biggest victory the suburbs gained was over Alderman Matt Schimenz. Schimenz appeared to Governor Gaylord Nelson to be a good appointee to the Wisconsin Public Service Commission, which had long been dominated by the utilities and the suburbs. Schimenz was an attorney, a fellow Democrat and had worked for the election of the governor. Governor Nelson's appointment of Schimenz was immediately challenged by the suburbs and they demanded his rejection in a hearing before the state Senate. Among those leading the fight were Mayor William Knuese of Wauwatosa and H.O. Wolfe, the Shorewood village attorney whose forces had defeated Schimenz in the "Battle of Green Bay." Schimenz, who was probably more willing than any other alderman to give the suburbs water, had once made a statement that Wauwatosa would get water only over his dead body, and this the suburbs held against him. Senator Kirby Hendee also attacked Schimenz for playing a leading role in the divisive Kohler shipping case of 1955 in which a strike at the docks in Sheboygan and Milwaukee prevented two ships from delivering clay to the Kohler Company. Schimenz was also questioned because of his past labor connections. His appointment was defeated on an 18-to-14 vote.

I expressed public disapproval of the suburbs for their action and said that no one from Milwaukee would ever have a chance on the Public Service Commission. I pointed out that Schimenz was a moderating influence between the city and suburbs. Schimenz, however, was not particularly grateful for my support. He wanted the position and so he disclaimed my support and criticized me. After a tentative action by the governor to reappoint Schimenz to the Public Service Commission, the governor named him to the Industrial Commission; the suburbs accepted this move and the appointment was confirmed.

That was some kind of lesson for me.[282]

I had two occasions in 1959 to speak on the subject of metropolitan problems before a national forum. In June of 1959, I testified before the Joint Government

Operations Committee of Congress on the creation of a permanent intergovernmental relations committee. I pointed out the need for states being alert to help metropolitan areas create master plans that would result in the orderly development of an entire area. I cited the frequent deficiencies of suburban governments and I expressed approval of a bill to create a federal department of urban affairs.[283]

I also attended the meeting of the United States Conference of Mayors in Los Angeles in July of 1959. One of the sessions of this conference was devoted to urban-suburban relations. Some mayors advocated municipal cooperation on a voluntary basis between the central city and suburbs. I came out flatly for annexation and consolidation. It was apparent from the meeting that many other cities were also plagued by suburban parasitism and obstructionism. My position of course brought disapproval from the press of the Iron Ring.[284]

In the Wisconsin Legislature, the skillful Richard Cutler was busy, this time against the easy incorporation of communities. A bill was introduced, in which he had a hand, as far as I can recollect, which was to set new standards for creating cities and villages to prevent the disorganized metropolitan development that had occurred in the Milwaukee area. The bill was drafted by the Wisconsin Legislative Council's Urban Problems Committee and had been stalled for some months. The measure set a minimum population and area requirement for incorporations and required the approval of the state director of regional planning. The bill ultimately passed, but too late to help Milwaukee.[285]

The city had another tiff with the Metropolitan Study Commission. One of the commission's subcommittees, under the chairmanship of Robert T. Foote, had proposed, in a secret letter to community leaders active in water matters, to find out what equity if any Milwaukee residents had in their water utility and what payment should be made to the city if ownership passed to a water authority. This move was obviously an attempt to build a legal basis to take away the waterworks, which was what the Iron Ring had been advocating all along. The letter also asked for comment on how the proposed authority should be administered and whether rates should be higher for outlying areas than for those closer to the waterworks.

I immediately said that this was a move to justify the north shore suburbs' desire to build their own water utility and at the same time to take away the city's water utility. I charged the commission with again promoting metropolitan fragmentation instead of metropolitan unity. The suburbs were busy trying to make a case for taking over the waterworks since they were obviously not satisfied with the original commission report that had proposed to give them two out of seven water commissioners.

Foote declined to comment on the issue but said that only Richard Cutler, the commission strongman, could comment.[286]

This situation also stirred Milwaukee aldermen who renewed charges that the commission was dominated by suburban interests. A majority of aldermen started a resolution to ask Governor Nelson and the Legislature to abolish the commission. Alderman Mortier charged that Charles Goff, a University of Wisconsin-Milwaukee

174

professor, had been fired because he was too objective for the commission. Goff blamed his difficulties with the commission on Richard Cutler.[287]

Apparently the Metropolitan Study Commission was concerned about the city's reaction. It voted to meet with city officials to convince them that the commission had no bias against the city. Foote explained that he had sent the letter around merely to settle any doubts that might remain about the water report and to obtain additional information. I said that the city's retention of its own waterworks was necessary to give the city a good bargaining position with the suburbs.[288] If the waterworks were taken from the city, all hopes of metropolitan cooperation would disappear.

Harry G. Slater, deputy city attorney, said the questions that Foote asked in his letter were not in the province of the commission since the waterworks was a proprietary operation of the city.

I said that once and for all we wanted to dispel the impression that we were hostile to the people of the suburbs. We were not, I said, but we were opposed to their leaders who wanted to take over our services piecemeal.[289]

The fires of battle over annexation and consolidation, however, were dying down at the latter end of 1959. The suburbs were sated with victory upon victory, and although the Metropolitan Study Commission proposed to give certain additional facilities such as city libraries to the suburbs, the torpor that comes from a full meal engulfed the suburbs. The one exception was Brown Deer, which continued litigating with Milwaukee over the Granville consolidation until 1962 when the state Supreme Court gave Milwaukee a victory. The Granville school issue eventually died down with the city finding a way to pay for the school taxes without jeopardizing the entire tax roll.[290]

The new tack of the suburbs that appeared to be developing was based on the notion that the suburbs had the right to participate in Milwaukee elections and gain control of Milwaukee policies through boards and commissions and inside political friendships. Although I was not running for office myself in 1960, having declared my intention not to run in the fall of 1959, I noted with apprehension the prominent role played by suburban advisors to two of the leading candidates—George A. Bowman, the Republican assistant city attorney, and Henry W. Maier, the Democratic state senator and ultimately the winning candidate for mayor. Each had a suburban leader as his most prominent advisor. I publicly voiced my concern, and the answer to my complaint was made by the *Milwaukee Times* in the issue of December 3, 1959. The *Times*, specializing in south side news, had an owner living in Wauwatosa and its chief editorial writer living in one of the north shore suburbs. The *Times* asserted that persons with vast financial interests in Milwaukee could not be denied the right to voice their opinions or take interest in Milwaukee elections. They had "every right" to be interested in Milwaukee's government so long as they did not overstep their bounds.

Platforms of the Public Enterprise Committee issued around this time for the city and county urged expansion of metropolitan powers for the county.[291] It was beginning to appear that the only way out of the impasse was to strengthen the county government administratively and give it metropolitan powers.

I had the opportunity to speak as mayor twice more before major groups on the subject of metropolitan problems, which for some curious reason, now that the battle had been lost by the city, was arousing popular interest. In January of 1960, I spoke at the 46th annual meeting of the Citizens' Governmental Research Bureau and advocated the creation of a department of urban affairs in Wisconsin government. I also proposed that the classification of cities should include a new category for a metropolitan community. I advocated a federal study of urban defense, regional planning for transportation and orderly industrial and residential development. Concerning the extension of powers to counties, I said that highly urbanized counties must either be given power to expand at the expense of neighboring counties, or else they must be confined to their historic functions, and the areawide functions extending beyond a single county must be given to a metropolitan agency created by the state. I doubted if voluntary cooperation between local governments would work fast enough.[292]

In March I appeared on a panel program with Supervisor Doyne and George Schmus, city attorney of West Allis, at Milwaukee Lutheran High School to discuss metropolitan problems. I stated again my belief that area problems could not be handled by fragmented governments and that there must be a metropolitan government. Doyne asserted that the metropolitan government was already here; it was the county government. George Schmus said that suburban governments would cooperate on specific problems but would not give up their identity. We were at the point we started in 1947, but the suburbs had won all the major battles.[293]

*   *   *   *   *

During the period of 1948 to 1960, almost everything the city feared about the waterworks and metropolitan developments came to pass. The Iron Ring closed tightly, the north shore suburbs carved a piece of the Milwaukee water service area for themselves and the city was forced to serve the suburbs with water without getting any tax equality, thereby causing the people of Milwaukee to pay much higher rates.

The report of the Dineen committee was a major factor causing those events to happen. The Dineen report encouraged the Legislature to set up a study commission that was dominated by suburbanites and that targeted Milwaukee and its waterworks. The city was never able to counter the damage inflicted by the Dineen report.

As the city had predicted, the Metropolitan Study Commission spent much of its time figuring out how Milwaukee could give its services to the suburbs. When it became certain that Milwaukee would have to serve the suburbs, the work of the Metropolitan Study Commission lost merit in the eyes of the Iron Ring. Having received water, the suburbs were not interested in learning of their obligations to the metropolitan community at large, and by 1961 they succeeded in killing the commission in the Wisconsin Legislature. Some of the press and some civic leaders who had played the game of the Iron Ring in forming the commission were bitterly disappointed, but they had been warned in advance that on the day the suburbs got water, the study commission was dead as far as the suburbs were concerned.

Great forces were at work and the struggles between the city and suburbs were the result of these great forces. During this time, the population of Wisconsin increased, mostly around the metropolitan center of Milwaukee. In common with other industrial places, Milwaukee grew at the expense of other smaller communities in the atomic age. The attempt of the city to control and regulate this growth was frustrated by several factors. One was the insufficiency of state laws to provide orderly metropolitan growth. Another retarding factor was the failure of the Legislature to recognize what was happening in the urban areas. Still another factor was the process of people segregating themselves according to income and class status in the urban areas. These factors ultimately combined to choke off Milwaukee's growth as a city and to give it an unduly high proportion of low-income people with a relatively poor tax base.

Most central cities in the nation failed to take steps to expand their borders. As a result of Milwaukee's expansion, the city went from 13th in population in the nation in 1950 to 11th in 1960 and counteracted the decay of the inner city by providing new lands for growth.

The struggle to expand was also a struggle to provide decent homesites for the families of working men and women. The suburbs seemed to prefer to see such people hemmed in by tenements and ghettoes. The city's struggle for raw land for modest subdivisions helped to provide quality housing for many hundreds of thousands of people.

Was the policy of expansion right or wrong? No expansion could have been fast enough to reduce the city as an atomic target, for the weapons of atomic destruction far outpaced the pattern of urban dispersal. However, the city's expansion did produce good results in terms of providing healthful living conditions for the people, and I am as much an opponent of fragmentation at the end of the period as I was at the first. What would conditions have been like if Milwaukee had 10 to 20 more suburbs because the city would not annex? Milwaukee itself would have been a ghetto of the poor and nothing else. Instead it had room for new homes, for new industry and for commercial centers. The city gained living space so that slum clearance could be accomplished without tearing down houses of people who had no place to go.

The attitude of the aldermen was most favorable. They could see the issues and they supported the city's position for the most part faithfully. The city comptroller, Virgil H. Hurless, aided annexation. A strong supporter was George C. Saffran, the budget supervisor, who was a guide for the council and a kind of mentor to all. The council president, Martin Schreiber, met the issues of annexation, as did Aldermen Mortier, Schimenz, Meyers and even the two aldermen from annexed territory,

Vincent Schmit and John Budzien. The city should have no regrets for its expansion. It was in the interest of a healthy community for the suburbs as well as the city.

In making this extensive report on the course of annexation and consolidation by Milwaukee and its struggle with the suburbs, I could by no means be truly exhaustive. The report was necessarily as I saw and remembered events. An immense amount of work was done by other departments and agencies of city government. The Annexation Department and later the Community Development Department actually had to do the fieldwork, and the report of their efforts would make for a lengthy account in itself. Special note should be made of the work of Arthur M. Werba and Joseph R. Lamping, the two directors of annexation; of Henry Oetzmann, one of the staff of the department; and of the annexation solicitors.

The city attorney's office fought numerous protracted lawsuits. The work of the city attorney's staff, especially that of Richard F. Maruszewski, deserves its own chronicle for the scholar who is interested in the twists and turns of the annexation struggle.

These were all good people to work with in the crucial problems that faced the city. Their work meant light and air and gardens for people, and playgrounds for children, and green spaces, and freedom from excessive traffic that congestion would otherwise have brought. Theirs was a life-giving work.[294]

A statement from my annual message to the Milwaukee Common Council on April 19, 1955, is worth repeating here as a conclusion to this account:

> Our Community Development Department proved its worth again and again by obtaining, in the face of great obstacles, the necessary building sites for our expanded population. Just imagine the crowding and blight which would have occurred if this expanding population had been compelled to find shelter within the existing boundaries of the community. Instead it was possible, because of our program, for families to secure a residence on an individual plot of ground—a fact which has distinct advantages for family life, for the raising of children and for the development of human personality.

Author's Acknowledgements

This manuscript was prepared with the assistance of historical material supplied by Mr. Richard W.E. Perrin and Frank Polidori of the City of Milwaukee, and by Mr. Peter J. McCormick and Mr. Orval Liljequist of the Milwaukee Public Library. The staff of the library was most helpful.

NOTES FOR CHAPTER 3

1. See "The Maier Platform for Practical Leadership," circa March, 1960. In this publication, Henry W. Maier called for a city-suburb water committee to advise the Common Council on water policy, an issue the city had previously resisted as leading to suburban control of the waterworks.

2. See "Platform for Milwaukee's Future," Municipal Enterprise Committee, December 6, 1947; inaugural address of Frank P. Zeidler, April, 1948.

3. Arthur M. Werba and John L. Grunwald. *Making Milwaukee Mightier, A Record of Annexation and Consolidation and a Study of Unification of Government Here and Elsewhere.* Milwaukee: Board of Public Land Commissioners, 1929.

4. A subdivision that aroused comment on this score was one in the vicinity of N. 92nd Street and W. Keefe Avenue. City installations in this subdivision were mostly unused for two decades because the city did not expand in this area until the 1950s.

5. *Milwaukee Annual Report.* William L. Slayton, editor. City of Milwaukee, 1946.

6. For a statement of the beliefs of Milwaukee officials and planners, see Werba and Grunwald, op cit.

7. See *Municipal Campaign Book*, published by the County Central Committee, Social-Democratic Party, Milwaukee, 1912. This campaign handbook describes the Socialists' interests in a clean city, planning, parks and playgrounds. On page 45, there is the following, "Many cities of this nation have become aware of the necessity that our growth must be directed along comprehensive and well-planned lines. This administration has taken a live interest in this problem. The city treasurer has put in his entire spare time on the work." The city treasurer was Charles B. Whitnall, who was described as a "florist and landscape gardener." He was a member of both the City Planning Commission and the County Park Commission from their inception.

8. See *City Planning for Milwaukee* by Dr. Werner Hegemann, February, 1916. Hegemann was a famous German planner who made this report to certain Milwaukee organizations interested in planning. It featured European ideas of the center of the city and of workers' suburbs.

9. See *What Progress Costs Milwaukee*, Charles B. Whitnall, Milwaukee, April, 1935. This pamphlet contains some of Mr. Whitnall's later ideas on planning and land use.

10. "Annexation is Water Price," *Milwaukee Journal*, May 1, 1942; "Ampco Plant to Get Water," *Milwaukee Journal*, May 5, 1942. Subsequently other plants along Port Washington Road in the Town of Milwaukee also received water service for defense reasons. This area later provided the main reason for the incorporation of Glendale.

11. "'Sales Talks' for Granville," *Milwaukee Journal*, October 25, 1946.

12. "Town of Milwaukee on Way to Becoming City, Riverside," *Milwaukee Journal*, November 22, 1946. The name "Riverside" was later dropped for "Glendale."

13. "Point Butler Way to Water," *Milwaukee Journal*, December 14, 1946; "Werba Sees Annexation of Hampton Road Area," *Milwaukee Sentinel*, December 15, 1946.

14. See "Delay Survey of Annexation," *Milwaukee Journal*, January 2, 1947, and "Annexation of New Territory Called Only Remedy," *Milwaukee Sentinel*, January 3, 1947.

15. For an account of the typical methods of opposition, see "Blocks Action on Annexation," *Milwaukee Journal*, January 3, 1947. C.R. Dineen, attorney for the Town of Wauwatosa, was reported as having obtained a petition of 54 names of persons who withdrew their signatures from another petition for annexation in the vicinity of N. 90th Street and W. Blue Mound Road. With respect to pressure, it was alleged by three businessmen in the Town of Lake that the town constable intimidated them because they favored annexation of lands to the City of Milwaukee. See "Pressure Told in Annexation," *Milwaukee Journal*, April 6, 1947.

16. "Towns Battle Against a Bill on Annexation," *Milwaukee Journal*, March 5, 1947.

17. "City May Get 100 Acres Plot," *Milwaukee Journal*, February 17, 1947; "Disputed Tract Ruled by Two Governments," *Milwaukee Journal*, July 10, 1947.

18. "Annexation Housing OK'd," *Milwaukee Sentinel*, August 27, 1947; "City Should Annex New Areas to Build," *Milwaukee Journal*, August 28, 1947. The latter was an editorial encouraging annexation for home building purposes.

19. "City, Towns Start to Spar on Annexing," *Milwaukee Journal*, February 9, 1948.
20. "Annexations Since 1946 Add 3.9 Square Miles: More Changes Slated in Near Future," *Milwaukee Journal*, August 1, 1948. This story by a veteran reporter, Lloyd Gladfelter, recounts some of the annexations and the problems accompanying them.
21. See "Fight Started on Annexation," *Milwaukee Journal*, January 14, 1949, and "McParland Offers Bills to Stymie Annexation," *Milwaukee Sentinel*, January 27, 1949, for a discussion of the contents of the bills. The *Journal* felt compelled to editorialize twice on these bills; see "Mr. McParland's Nonsense," February 12, 1949, and "Annexation Is Only Way City Can Provide Housing," April 2, 1949. The *Journal* still was a supporter of annexation at this time.
22. "Decide Annexation Issue, Zeidler Asks Legislators," *Milwaukee Journal*, April 7, 1949; "Zeidler Seeks Annex Policy," *Milwaukee Sentinel*, April 7, 1949.
23. "Advance Curb on Annexation," *Milwaukee Journal*, May 4, 1949; "Senate Given Annexing Bill," *Milwaukee Journal*, June 3, 1949.
24. "Factory Land Lack Choking Industry Here," *Milwaukee Journal*, April 24, 1949.
25. "Vote $25,000 for Land Deals," *Milwaukee Journal*, April 12, 1949.
26. "Annexing Hits School Funds," *Milwaukee Journal*, June 18, 1949.
27. "Judge Upholds City's Addition of Butler Area," *Milwaukee Sentinel*, March 7, 1950.
28. "City Expansion Views Differ," *Milwaukee Journal*, July 16, 1950, and "Milwaukee—Our City," a column in the *Milwaukee Sentinel* by William A. Norris on July 23, 1950, and July 31, 1950.
29. "City Told to Spread Across County Line," *Milwaukee Journal*, March 11, 1951.
30. "'New Milwaukee' Plans Include Five Counties," *Milwaukee Journal*, February 1, 1951.
31. "High Court Ruling Blocks City's Plan," *Milwaukee Journal*, April 3, 1951. "Top Court Kills Annexations," *Milwaukee Sentinel*, April 4, 1951; "Seek to Save City's Powers of Annexing," *Milwaukee Journal*, April 4, 1951; "9 'Befriend' High Court in Annexation Battle," *Milwaukee Sentinel*, April 9, 1951. The latter story is an account of nine suburban attorneys versus a lone assistant City of Milwaukee attorney, Richard F. Maruszewski, on the annexation case.
32. "City Speeds to Annex Greenfield Industry," *Milwaukee Journal*, April 22, 1950; "Both City and Village Move to Annex Area," *Milwaukee Journal*, June 6, 1950; "West Milwaukee Wins Suit for Land," *Milwaukee Journal*, February 26, 1951. The malting houses went into West Milwaukee on a ruling by Circuit Court Judge Gustave E. Gehrz.
33. "Parts of Town of Wauwatosa Will be Annexed by the City," *Milwaukee Sentinel*, July 14, 1950.
34. "Population Outruns Annexation Program," *Milwaukee Sentinel*, June 24, 1960.
35. "Milwaukeeans Accuse Repealer Bill Backers," *Milwaukee Sentinel*, March 28, 1951.
36. "Bills Drafted for Aiding City on Annexation," *Milwaukee Journal*, April 10, 1951.
37. "Argue Points of Annexation," *Milwaukee Journal*, April 13, 1951.
38. "Assembly Unit Looks at City," *Milwaukee Sentinel*, April 27, 1951; "Suburbs Shine for Lawmakers," *Milwaukee Journal*, May 3, 1951.
39. "Change Urged in Annexation," *Milwaukee Journal*, June 1, 1951; "Bill Is Passed on Annexation," *Milwaukee Journal*, June 13, 1951. This bill was due in part to the work of Assemblyman Arthur Mockrud who had a good sense of proportion on municipal matters. It was signed by Governor Walter J. Kohler on July 8, 1951.
40. "Join Glendale in New Move," *Milwaukee Journal*, August 4, 1951.
41. "Would Block Any Expansion by St. Francis," *Milwaukee Sentinel*, August 2, 1951; "Move Started to End Towns," *Milwaukee Journal*, August 5, 1951.
42. "Plan Annexing to Aid Transit," *Milwaukee Journal*, September 15, 1951; "Rural Reactions Varied at Move for Annexations," *Milwaukee Journal*, September 16, 1951; "Zeidler Calls 38 Mile Annexations a Big Order," *Milwaukee Sentinel*, September 16, 1951; "Major Revolution in Annexation Planned," column by William A. Norris, *Milwaukee Sentinel*, September 19, 1951; "Plans Collapse on Annexations," *Milwaukee Journal*, October 5, 1951.
43. See "2nd Big Annexation Project Would Add Granville to City," *Milwaukee Sentinel*, September 22, 1951; "Suburbs Plan to Annex Large Tracts," *Milwaukee Journal*, September 28, 1951; "Meeting Urged on Granville," *Milwaukee Sentinel*, September 23, 1951; "Steps Outlined in Annexation," *Milwaukee Journal*, September 24, 1951.
44. "Urges Master Plan as Need for Annexing," *Milwaukee Journal*, September 24, 1951.

45. "Posting Clash in Greenfield Opens Battle," *Milwaukee Journal*, October 2, 1951.
46. A letter dated March 15, 1952, was sent to Mr. Earl Sackse, secretary of the Wisconsin Legislative Council, on the matter of the posting race in Granville. This letter was sent after a call to the governor's office on the problem. A copy of the letter is in the Frank P. Zeidler Collection at the Milwaukee Public Library.
47. See *Minutes, Regular Meeting of the Legislative Council, Public Hearing*, June 16, 1952. A copy can be obtained in the Frank P. Zeidler Collection at the Milwaukee Public Library.
48. *Planning*, 1952, Proceedings of the Annual National Planning Conference held in Boston, Massachusetts, October 5-9, 1952, American Society of Planning Officials, Chicago, Illinois. See also "Mayor Urges Master Plan," *Milwaukee Journal*, October 9, 1952.
49. "Zeidler Takes City's Woes to Kohler," *Milwaukee Sentinel*, January 10, 1953.
50. "Zeidler Asks Federal Aid in Area Fight," *Milwaukee Journal*, January 31, 1953.
51. "Suburbs Rap Zeidler Views," *Milwaukee Journal*, February 5, 1953.
52. Ibid.
53. "The Uncooperative Mr. Zeidler," *West Allis Star*, Feb. 12, 1953.
54. Werba and Grunwald, op cit, p. 18.
55. "Mayor Jabs at 'Iron Ring,'" *Milwaukee Journal*, April 6, 1952.
56. *Planning*, 1952, op cit.
57. "Bill of Rights of Cities Urged," *Milwaukee Journal*, May 22, 1953.
58. "The Milwaukee Way," *1953 Annual Report of Milwaukee for the Year 1952*, City of Milwaukee; "City Upheld in Annexation Test Case," *Milwaukee Sentinel*, February 3, 1954.
59. "Mayor Thinks Annexations Should Stop," *Milwaukee Sentinel*, January 16, 1954.
60. "Zeidler Fears New Suburb," *Milwaukee Journal*, January 8, 1954; "Granville Cityhood Feared by Zeidler," *Milwaukee Sentinel*, January 8, 1954.
61. I have been unable to locate the original of this letter in the Frank P. Zeidler Collection at the Milwaukee Public Library.
62. "Our Answer to Mayor Zeidler's Charges," *West Allis Star*, February 25, 1954, editorial.
63. "Strength of U.S. Depends on Cities, Zeidler Says," *Milwaukee Journal*, March 21, 1954.
64. "Zeidler Raps State Control," *Milwaukee Journal*, May 27, 1954.
65. "Cites Benefit of Annexation," *Milwaukee Journal*, February 11, 1955.
66. "Mayor Is Asked to Halt Annexation," *Milwaukee Journal*, February 17, 1955.
67. "Two Civic Groups Back 21 Committee Proposal," *Milwaukee Journal*, February 27, 1955.
68. "'21' Bill Opposed by Council Unit," *Milwaukee Sentinel*, March 1, 1955.
69. "Council Votes for State-Wide Urban Studies," *Milwaukee Journal*, March 5, 1955.
70. "21 Group Votes to Back Busby Bill at Madison," *Milwaukee Sentinel*, March 29, 1955.
71. If memory serves me, the legal expenses of Oak Creek during this period came perhaps to $50,000.
72. "Oak Creek Bill Snagged in Assembly," *Milwaukee Sentinel*, June 16, 1955.
73. "City Fared Poorly in State Legislature," *Milwaukee Journal*, June 26, 1955.
74. "Mayor Urges Veto of Bills Aimed at City," *Milwaukee Sentinel*, June 17, 1955.
75. "City Alienates Town, Claim," *Milwaukee Journal*, March 28, 1955.
76. "Zeidler Urges Granville Consolidation," *Milwaukee Sentinel*, July 7, 1955.
77. "Oak Creek Bill Signed: Growth of City in Peril," *Milwaukee Journal*, July 26, 1955; "Kohler Signs Oak Creek Bill," *Milwaukee Sentinel*, July 26, 1955.
78. "Law to Let Oak Creek Be a City is Blow at All Urban Areas," *Milwaukee Journal*, July 27, 1955.
79. "Act as a City, Attorney Says to Oak Creek," *Milwaukee Journal*, November 10, 1955.
80. "Block Oak City Incorporation Plan," *Milwaukee Sentinel*, November 10, 1955; "Thomson, Governor Seek a Test of Law in State High Court," *Milwaukee Journal*, November 9, 1955.
81. "It Is Now a City Oak Creek Asserts," *Milwaukee Journal*, November 11, 1955.
82. "Officials of Oak Creek Agree to a Court Test," *Milwaukee Journal*, November 23, 1955; "Kohler Calls on Oak Creek to Test of City Status," *Milwaukee Sentinel*, November 24, 1955.
83. "Facts About Milwaukee," *1956 Report of 1955*, City of Milwaukee.
84. "Outline Plans for Annexing," *Milwaukee Journal*, September 13, 1955.
85. This event took place in August, 1955.

86. The *West Allis Star* plunged into a heated denunciation of this comment in its issue of September 29, 1955. In an editorial entitled "Another Suburb Hater," the *Star* called this statement "tripe, from the pipe," "hypocrisy," "prattling," "inane" — which provided a good indication of the tenor of official suburban hostility toward Milwaukee.

87. "Cooperate as Equals, Say Suburbs," *Milwaukee Sentinel*, November 17, 1955.

88. See "Milwaukee's Growth Was Double Madison's Rate," *Capital Times*, October 27, 1955, for a brief comment on this phase of city policy in expanding.

89. "Mayor Talks 'Elbow Room,'" *Milwaukee Journal*, December 8, 1955.

90. "City Ready to Talk Granville Merger," *Milwaukee Sentinel*, January 12, 1956; "City Invites Granville to Talk It Over," *Milwaukee Journal*, January 12, 1956. The report favoring consolidation with Milwaukee was made by Griffenhagen and Associates.

91. "Merger Is a Possibility for Granville and City," *Milwaukee Journal*, January 15, 1956.

92. "Doubt April 3 Merger Vote," *Milwaukee Journal*, January 19, 1956.

93. "Merger Talks Asked of City by Granville," *Milwaukee Journal*, January 27, 1956.

94. "Petition Filed For Granville," *Milwaukee Journal*, January 29, 1956.

95. "Granville is 'Welcomed,'" *Milwaukee Journal*, March 17, 1956.

96. "Granville, Key to a Greater Milwaukee," *Milwaukee Sentinel*, April 11, 1956. I always had the feeling that in this column Norris was consoling himself because his candidate for mayor, Alderman Milton J. McGuire, lost the race. In the election campaign, incidentally, Norris had attacked me for pressing for annexation.

97. "Annexation Plans Land in Mayor's Lap," *Milwaukee Sentinel*, March 7, 1956.

98. "Zeidler Tells Plans for New Area,"*Milwaukee Journal*, March 7, 1956.

99. "Foresee Profit in Annexing," *Milwaukee Journal*, March 13, 1956.

100. "State Aid Asked to Solve City Annexation Problems," *Milwaukee Sentinel*, January 17, 1956.

101. "Zeidler Raps 'State Rights,'" *Milwaukee Journal*, May 16, 1956.

102. "City's Policy on Suburbs Unchanged — Zeidler Affirms that Aim is Government for Whole Metropolitan Area," *Milwaukee Journal*, May 20, 1956.

103. "Mr. Zeidler's One World," *West Allis Star*, May 25, 1956.

104. "Mr. Zeidler Objects," *West Allis Star*, June 7, 1956.

105. "Ask Review of Annexation," *Milwaukee Journal*, June 5, 1956.

106. "Boost in Assessments Stirs Anger in Old Town of Lake," *Milwaukee Journal*, July 6, 1956.

107. "Town of Lake Petition Hits Tax Increases," *Milwaukee Sentinel*, July 12, 1956.

108. "Seek to Restore Town of Lake," *Milwaukee Sentinel*, July 29, 1956.

109. "Outgo in Former Town Exceeds Income to City," *Milwaukee Journal*, August 28, 1956.

110. "Mayor Hit on Lake Tax Statements," *Milwaukee Sentinel*, August 30, 1956.

111. "Zeidler Shuns 'Lake' Debate," *Milwaukee Journal*, September 7, 1956; "Mayor Hits Tax Protest Tactics," *Milwaukee Sentinel*, September 8, 1956.

112. "Call Mayor for Quiz on Lake Taxes," *Milwaukee Sentinel*, September 9, 1956; "Mayor Served with Subpoena," *Milwaukee Journal*, September 9, 1956.

113. "Mayor Denies Secret Record," *Milwaukee Journal*, September 27, 1956.

114. "Granville Consolidation Ruled Void," *Milwaukee Journal*, July 10, 1956.

115. Ibid.

116. "City Starts Action in Court to Reopen Granville Case," *Milwaukee Journal*, July 11, 1956.

117. "Fight Inroads by Neighbors, City Proposes," *Milwaukee Journal*, July 24, 1956.

118. "Zeidler Raps 'Suburb Bill,'" *Milwaukee Sentinel*, August 18, 1956.

119. "Mayor Seeks County Unity," *Milwaukee Journal*, August 26, 1956.

120. "Aldermen Will Support State Study of Problems," *Milwaukee Journal*, July 11, 1956.

121. "Committee of 21 Minus 8 May Decide to Disband," *Milwaukee Journal*, July 24, 1956.

122. "Town Urged to Incorporate," *Milwaukee Journal*, September 8, 1956.

123. "Critics of Water Study 'Ridiculous' Kohler Says," *Milwaukee Sentinel*, September 11, 1956.

124. "Mayor to Press Metropolitan Study by State," *Milwaukee Sentinel*, September 12, 1956.

125. "Study Group Will Limit Probe to Water, Sewers," *Milwaukee Journal*, September 21, 1956.

126. Ibid.

127. "Provincialism," *Milwaukee Sentinel*, September 12, 1956.

128. "City's Watchdog Barks Up Wrong Tree," *Milwaukee Sentinel*, September 12, 1956.
129. "Is Governor Kohler Cooperating in an Effort to Turn Milwaukee's Water System over to the Suburbs?" *Capital Times*, September 13, 1956.
130. "Water Group Given OK of Mayor, View," *Milwaukee Journal*, September 27, 1956; "Mayor Insists City Study 'A Surprise,'" *Milwaukee Sentinel*, September 28, 1956.
131. Ibid.
132. *Public Enterprise Record*, September, 1956.
133. "Pre-Judging," *Milwaukee Sentinel*, September 28, 1956.
134. "Short Memory," *Milwaukee Sentinel*, September 29, 1956.
135. "Let Water Committee Proceed," *Milwaukee Journal*, September 29, 1956.
136. "District Water System Gets Suburbs' Backing," *Milwaukee Journal*, October 3, 1956; "Municipal League Flays '21' Group on Water Issue," *Milwaukee Sentinel*, October 11, 1956.
137. "Council Splits on Committee of 21," *Milwaukee Journal*, October 3, 1956; "Council Votes Study by Committee of 21," *Milwaukee Journal*, October 10, 1956; "'21' Committee Orders Survey Cost Study," *Milwaukee Sentinel*, October 16, 1956.
138. "Metropolitan Quiz Backed by League," *Milwaukee Sentinel*, October 19, 1956.
139. "Suburbs' Delegates Top City's Group," *Milwaukee Sentinel*, October 26, 1956.
140. "Veto Vowed for 21 Study," *Milwaukee Journal*, October 20, 1956.
141. "No Increase in Taxes on Property Advised—Municipalities League Defeats Plan to Back State-Wide Study of City Problems," *Milwaukee Journal*, October 20, 1956.
142. "Veto Vowed for 21 Study," *Milwaukee Journal*, October 20, 1956.
143. "City May Pull Out of Committee of 21," *Milwaukee Sentinel*, October 20, 1956. For the Iron Ring comment on this issue, see "They've Earned Bitterness," *West Allis Star*, October 25, 1956.
144. "Mayor Vetoes City Study OK," *Milwaukee Journal*, October 22, 1956.
145. "City Expected to Remain with Committee of 21," *Milwaukee Sentinel*, October 23, 1956; "Busby Hails City Staying in 21 Group," *Milwaukee Sentinel*, October 23, 1956.
146. "Council Backs Mayor on '21,'" *Milwaukee Journal*, October 26, 1956.
147. "Suburbs Get Unity Advice," *Milwaukee Journal*, October 26, 1956.
148. "City Is Asked for Problems," *Milwaukee Journal*, October 23, 1956.
149. "City Is Asked to Extend Its Water Survey," *Milwaukee Journal*, November 3, 1956.
150. "Study of Area Stand Drafted," *Milwaukee Journal*, November 6, 1956.
151. "Granville's Merger Remains Unsettled," *Milwaukee Journal*, November 7, 1956.
152. "Granville Restudy to Begin," *Milwaukee Sentinel*, November 8, 1956.
153. "City Agrees to Withdraw from Town," *Milwaukee Journal*, November 10, 1956; "'Lost' Granville Area Loses City Services," *Milwaukee Sentinel*, November 10, 1956.
154. "Granville Act 'Temporary,'" *Milwaukee Journal*, November 11, 1956.
155. "City Certain Brown Deer Set-up Illegal," *Milwaukee Sentinel*, November 11, 1956.
156. "Brown Deer Answers City," *Milwaukee Journal*, November 12, 1956; "Brown Deer Annex Setup Called Valid," *Milwaukee Sentinel*, November 13, 1956; "Brown Deer Won't Pay for Unasked Service," *Milwaukee Journal*, November 13, 1956.
157. "Uniform City Tax Rate for Granville Gets Nod," *Milwaukee Journal*, November 2, 1956; "Special Levy Charges, Plan for Granville," *Milwaukee Journal*, November 2, 1956; "City to Levy Taxes in All of Granville," *Milwaukee Journal*, November 14, 1956.
158. "City Will Suspend Granville Services," *Milwaukee Journal*, November 14, 1956.
159. "New Hearing Asked on Granville Ruling," *Milwaukee Sentinel*, November 17, 1956.
160. "Sees Granville Tax Litigation," *Milwaukee Journal*, November 25, 1956.
161. "Merger Merits Are Discussed," *Milwaukee Journal*, November 14, 1956.
162. "Sharing Area Costs Is Called City Need," *Milwaukee Journal*, November 11, 1956.
163. "Council Body Urges a State Study of Area," *Milwaukee Journal*, November 19, 1956.
164. "Resolution Asks Urban Study Aid," *Milwaukee Journal*, December 4, 1956.
165. "21 Committee Almost Quits Over Area Study," *Milwaukee Journal*, December 11, 1956.
166. "City Water for Metropolitan Area Is Recommended by Study Group," *Milwaukee Journal*, December 16, 1956.

167. "Mayor and Aldermen Oppose Suburbs Water," *Milwaukee Journal*, December 16, 1956. See also "Governor Named Body to Make Water Study," *Milwaukee Journal*, December 16, 1956.

168. "City, Suburbs Water Battle Steams Anew," *Milwaukee Sentinel*, December 17, 1956.

169. "Sewer District Expansion to Outlying Areas Urged," *Milwaukee Journal*, December 17, 1956.

170. "Maps Way to Study Metropolitan Needs," *Milwaukee Journal*, December 18, 1956.

171. "Study Commission on Taxes Proposed," *Milwaukee Journal*, December 19, 1956.

172. "City Officials Welcome Tax Survey Suggestion," *Milwaukee Journal*, December 19, 1956.

173. "Kohler Lauds Study Report," *Milwaukee Journal*, December 19, 1956.

174. No substantial tax relief was forthcoming for Milwaukee. The tax bill that was passed in December, 1961, while it promised some property tax relief for Milwaukee, shifted much of the burden of higher income tax payments on Milwaukee workers.

175. "Water Talk Invitations Asked," *Milwaukee Journal*, December 19, 1956.

176. "Urban Growth Survey on State-Wide Basis Is Given Approval by Legislative Council," *Milwaukee Journal*, December 20, 1956.

177. "1957 Legislature to Get Bills From Study Report," *Milwaukee Journal*, December 20, 1956.

178. "Zeidler Hints at Big Area Water Lobby," *Milwaukee Sentinel*, December 22, 1956.

179. "Valuable Report," *Milwaukee Sentinel*, December 21, 1956.

180. "Village Head Backs Zeidler on Water," *Milwaukee Sentinel*, December 28, 1956.

181. "O.K. Is Voted on Tax Study," *Milwaukee Journal*, January 8, 1957.

182. "5 Aldermen Ask City to Quit '21,'" *Milwaukee Sentinel*, January 8, 1957. See also "Council Vote on '21' Likely," *Milwaukee Journal*, January 29, 1957.

183. "City's Reply to Report on Area Study Drafted," *Milwaukee Journal*, January 11, 1957.

184. "City's Reply," *Milwaukee Sentinel*, January 10, 1957.

185. "Urban Study Bid 'Please' Zeidler," *Milwaukee Sentinel*, January 11, 1957.

186. "City Lists Legislative Program," *Milwaukee Sentinel*, January 13, 1957.

187. "Suburbs Back County-Sponsored Water Utility," *Milwaukee Sentinel*, January 15, 1957.

188. "Suburbs Will Win Out, UWM Professor Thinks," *Milwaukee Journal*, January 22, 1957.

189. "New Bill Proposes Urban Areas Study," *Milwaukee Journal*, January 23, 1957.

190. Ibid.

191. "Mayor Offers City 16 Point Birthday List," *Milwaukee Journal*, January 31, 1957; "Mayor Zeidler's Vision of a Better Milwaukee," *Milwaukee Journal*, February 10, 1957.

192. "Zeidler Classes Greenfield Incorporation 'Tragedy,'" *Milwaukee Journal*, February 15, 1957; "Greenfield to Dance, But Zeidler's Glum," *Milwaukee Sentinel*, February 15, 1957.

193. "Area Wide Citizenry May Now Have to Cooperate," *Milwaukee Journal*, February 18, 1957.

194. "Granville Tax Levy Release Demanded," *Milwaukee Sentinel*, January 8, 1957.

195. "Seek Counsel on Granville," *Milwaukee Journal*, January 1, 1957.

196. "Mayor Fights Sewer Plan," *Milwaukee Journal*, February 16, 1957.

197. "Group Supports 2 Met Problems Study," *Milwaukee Sentinel*, March 5, 1957.

198. "Play Suburbs Game, Claim," *Milwaukee Journal*, March 7, 1957.

199. "Council Postponed Showdown on '21' Withdrawal," *Milwaukee Sentinel*, March 7, 1957.

200. "Full Study," *Milwaukee Sentinel*, March 8, 1957.

201. "State Units Still Split on Urban Studies," *Milwaukee Sentinel*, March 14, 1957.

202. "County 'Silences' Civic Group at Urban Study Talks," *Milwaukee Sentinel*, March 15, 1957.

203. "No Approval for Study Bill," *Milwaukee Journal*, March 17, 1956.

204. "Backs Survey of Area Needs," *Milwaukee Journal*, April 8, 1957.

205. "Drops City Bills Restudy, 21 Adjourns," *Milwaukee Sentinel*, April 2, 1957.

206. "Senate Group OK's Study of Area Problems," *Milwaukee Journal*, April 4, 1957.

207. "City Fears Senate Survey Bill Support," *Milwaukee Sentinel*, April 5, 1957.

208. "Land Use Bill Dramatizes Housing Plight," *Milwaukee Sentinel*, April 17, 1957.

209. "Report Hints Suburbs Will Join the City," *Milwaukee Journal*, May 20, 1957.

210. "Set to Consolidate? No! Reply Suburbs," *Milwaukee Journal*, May 21, 1957.

211. "Flight to 'Paradise,'" *West Allis Star*, May 23, 1957.

212. "Session of Legislature Didn't 'Damage' City," *Milwaukee Journal*, June 30, 1957; "Mayor Notes Bills Passed," *Milwaukee Journal*, July 1, 1957.

213. "More States' Power Hit," *Milwaukee Journal*, July 5, 1957.
214. "The President Revises the Constitution," *Socialist Call*, July, 1957.
215. "Metropolitan Study Is Sure: Bill Signed, Sets Up Board," *Milwaukee Journal*, July 21, 1957.
216. *Public Enterprise Record*, July, 1957; "Milwaukee Study Bill Hit," *Milwaukee Sentinel*, July 24, 1957; "Assail Thomson for OK of Study," *Milwaukee Journal*, July 24, 1957.
217. *Public Enterprise Record*, August, 1957; "Borough System Gets Support from Zeidler," *Milwaukee Journal*, August 21, 1957.
218. "Borough Idea Hit by West Allis," *Milwaukee Sentinel*, August 22, 1957.
219. "Borough Fight Seen by Mayor," *Milwaukee Sentinel*, August 23, 1957.
220. "Healthy City Needs Taxes, Zeidler Says," *Milwaukee Journal*, September 5, 1957.
221. "Zeidler Asks Local Studies," *Milwaukee Journal*, September 19, 1957.
222. "Study Appointments Receive Warm Praise," *Milwaukee Journal*, October 13, 1957. See also main story on appointments "Governor Names 15 for City Area Study," *Milwaukee Journal*, October 13, 1957.
223. "Metro Unit Declares: Can't Do It All Overnight," *Milwaukee Sentinel*, October 14, 1957; "Aldermen Aim Fire at Study Unit," *Milwaukee Sentinel*, October 16, 1957; "Gov. Thomson Stacks the Deck," *CIO News*, October 18, 1957.
224. "New Threat to Home Rule," *Capital Times*, October 14, 1957.
225. "Milwaukee's Home Rule Rights Also Attacked by State," *Capital Times*, October 14, 1957.
226. "Milwaukee Next in Attack on Home Rule," *Capital Times*, October 20, 1957. Frank Lloyd Wright's Monona Terrace was finally built in Madison after nearly six decades of debate.
227. "Study Group," *Milwaukee Sentinel*, October 17, 1957.
228. "City to Map Its Policy for Study Group," *Milwaukee Journal*, October 23, 1957.
229. "Mayor Zeidler Sees Area Federation," *Chicago American*, November 6, 1957.
230. "Equal Granville Tax Rate Asked," *Milwaukee Sentinel*, October 5, 1957.
231. "20th Ward Tax Equality Plan Asked," *Milwaukee Sentinel*, October 22, 1957; "Council Orders Effort to Aid Ward 20 Taxes," *Milwaukee Sentinel*, October 23, 1957.
232. "Propose Plan in 20th Ward," *Milwaukee Journal*, November 5, 1957.
233. "High Court Dismisses Brown Deer Charges," *Milwaukee Journal*, December 3, 1957.
234. "Brown Deer Fight Victory Claimed by Mayor Zeidler," *Milwaukee Sentinel*, December 4, 1957.
235. "City, Brown Deer Urged to Cease Granville Talks," *Milwaukee Sentinel*, December 30, 1957.
236. "Tells Moves for Merger," *Milwaukee Journal*, January 23, 1958.
237. "Zeidler, Foe 'Close' on Metro Solution," *Milwaukee Journal*, February 17, 1958.
238. "Consolidation Policy Eyed," *Milwaukee Journal*, March 10, 1958. See also "Attack Made on Lamping," *Milwaukee Journal*, May 5, 1958.
239. "Zeidler Asks Study of Problems of City," *Milwaukee Journal*, May 5, 1958.
240. "Suburbs Blast City Stand on Shared Taxes," *Milwaukee Sentinel*, May 10, 1958.
241. "Back Extended Limits for Sewerage District," *Milwaukee Journal*, June 6, 1958; "Full County Sewer Setup Advocated," *Milwaukee Sentinel*, June 6, 1958.
242. "Study Urged on Greenfield," *Milwaukee Journal*, July 27, 1958.
243. "Greenfield Mayor Raps Water Offer," *Milwaukee Sentinel*, July 31, 1958. See also "Suburb Asks City to Report on Vote Fund," *Milwaukee Journal*, March 7, 1958. William H. Bowman demanded a financial statement on city expenditures on a newspaper urging election of pro-consolidation candidates in Greenfield.
244. "Asks Council to Aid Study," *Milwaukee Journal*, September 3, 1958.
245. "City Willing to Aid Study," *Milwaukee Journal*, September 24, 1958; "City, Suburb Seen Paying Study's Cost," *Milwaukee Journal*, October 10, 1958.
246. "Zeidler Predicts City, Suburb Federation," *Milwaukee Sentinel*, September 26, 1958; "Mayor Gives Area Study a Pat on Back," *Milwaukee Journal*, September 26, 1958.
247. "All or Nothing Attitude Not Best Way for Urban Solution," *Milwaukee Journal*, March 4, 1957. In this editorial the *Journal* discussed the failure of a merger plan in Louisville, Kentucky, and said that the experience cast doubt on the realism of the Zeidler approach. See also "Federated Government for Metropolitan Area, Good Idea," *Milwaukee Journal*, September 8, 1958.
248. "Metropolitan Government in County Urged by Officials," *Milwaukee Journal*, October 21, 1958.

249. "County 'Metro' Idea Is Strongly Opposed," *Milwaukee Journal*, October 22, 1958.
250. "Council Lets Slater Advise Study Group," *Milwaukee Journal*, November 10, 1958.
251. "Metro Reports Don't Slur City, Zeidler Says," *Milwaukee Sentinel*, November 27, 1958.
252. "Metro Report Study Urged," *Milwaukee Journal*, December 2, 1958; "Committee Is Created to Study Metro Data," *Milwaukee Journal*, December 10, 1958.
253. "Metropolitan Government," *Milwaukee Labor Press*, December 4, 1958.
254. "May Resign Schmit Says," *Milwaukee Journal*, October 18, 1958.
255. "Put Granville 'Mess' Up to State," *Milwaukee Sentinel*, October 19, 1958.
256. "Urge Granville Schools Appeal," *Milwaukee Sentinel*, October 21, 1958; "Seeks City Tax Rate for Granville," *Milwaukee Sentinel*, October 22, 1958.
257. "Zeidler Offers Plan on 20th Ward Schools," *Milwaukee Sentinel*, October 30, 1958.
258. "Council Unit Asks Relief for Granville," *Milwaukee Journal*, November 3, 1958.
259. "Call Granville Fund Plan Illegal," *Milwaukee Sentinel*, November 8, 1958.
260. "Zeidler Hits 20th Ward Tax Relief," *Milwaukee Journal*, November 13, 1958.
261. Ibid.
262. "Zeidler Denies Attacking Council on Granville Tax," *Milwaukee Sentinel*, November 14, 1958.
263. "Maps Granville Tax Compromise," *Milwaukee Sentinel*, November 16, 1958.
264. "Equal 20th Ward Tax Back Where It Started," *Milwaukee Journal*, November 16, 1958; "Mayor Urged to Shun Veto," *Milwaukee Journal*, November 17, 1958.
265. "Aldermen Face Tough Problem on 20th Ward Taxes," *Milwaukee Journal*, November 14, 1958.
266. "Granville School Tax Study Planned," *Milwaukee Sentinel*, December 10, 1958.
267. "Circuit Judge Upholds the 'Oak Creek' Law," *Milwaukee Journal*, December 18, 1958.
268. Ibid.
269. "Oak Creek Ruling Disappoints City," *Milwaukee Sentinel*, December 19, 1958.
270. "City Eyes Suburbs Fire Aid Changes," *Milwaukee Sentinel*, December 17, 1958.
271. "Proposed Law Asks Suburbs Prove Solvency," *Milwaukee Sentinel*, December 23, 1958.
272. "'Muster Shock Troops' of Suburbs is No Contribution," *Milwaukee Journal*, January 1, 1959.
273. "Aldermen Differ on Countywide Metro Referendum," *Milwaukee Sentinel*, January 30, 1959.
274. "City Proposes Single Government for Area," *Milwaukee Journal*, February 3, 1959.
275. "Council Urges City as Basis of Metro Rule," *Milwaukee Sentinel*, February 14, 1959.
276. "Delay in School Merger Appeal Hit," *Milwaukee Sentinel*, February 18, 1959; "School Merger Appeal Veto Sure," *Milwaukee Sentinel*, February 19, 1959.
277. "'Metro Council' Proposed; Area Heads Would Serve," *Milwaukee Sentinel*, February 26, 1959.
278. "Laud Knoebel, Farness," *West Allis Star*, March 26, 1959.
279. "Stop the Metrocrats," *West Allis Star*, April 9, 1959.
280. "County, Suburbs, City Advance Metro Rule View," *Milwaukee Sentinel*, April 18, 1959; "A Metropolitan Brainwash," *West Allis Star*, April 25, 1959.
281. "City-Suburban Fight Moves to Legislature," *Milwaukee Journal*, March 20, 1959.
282. "'Reject Schimenz' Area Suburbs Say," *West Allis Star*, March 19, 1959; "Schimenz Rejected, 18-14, for PSC by State Senate," *Milwaukee Journal*, March 31, 1959; "Report: Nelson Ready to Rename Schimenz," *Milwaukee Journal*, April 5, 1959; "Vote is Won by Schimenz," *Milwaukee Journal*, June 26, 1959.
283. "Zeidler Tells City Troubles," *Milwaukee Journal*, June 18, 1959.
284. "U.S. Aid Pressed as Need of Cities," *New York Times*, July 15, 1959; "Metro Monsters Still Alive," *West Allis Star*, July 23, 1959.
285. "Bill on New Cities OK'd," *Milwaukee Journal*, July 24, 1959.
286. "Metro Study Body Accused by Zeidler," *Milwaukee Journal*, July 21, 1959.
287. "Seek to End Metro Unit," *Milwaukee Journal*, July 24, 1959.
288. "Study Groups Aim to Show City It Is Fair," *Milwaukee Journal*, July 28, 1959.
289. "Metro Study to Try to End Breach with City," *Milwaukee Sentinel*, July 28, 1959.
290. A minor flare occurred over the jurisdiction of the east Granville school district. See "May Take School Order to Court," *Milwaukee Journal*, August 29, 1959.
291. "Metropolitan Powers Are Urged for County," *Milwaukee Journal*, January 10, 1960. See also "Public Enterprise Committee Program for the County of Milwaukee" and "Public Enterprise

Committee Program for the City of Milwaukee," both published in December of 1959 by the Public Enterprise Committee of Milwaukee County.

292. "State Urged to Set Up Urban Affairs Office," *Milwaukee Journal*, January 28, 1960; "Zeidler Skeptical Counties Can Solve Metro Problems," *Milwaukee Sentinel*, January 28, 1960.
293. "Zeidler Predicts Metro Area Rule," *Milwaukee Sentinel*, March 19, 1960.
294. Additional information on annexation policies may be obtained from the annual messages of the mayor to the Common Council, delivered in April of each year, and from the city's annual report. Decisions on annexation cases and the precise statement of the courts on various issues can be obtained at the office of the city attorney of Milwaukee. The Milwaukee Public Library houses my files on annexation matters and will more precisely delineate some of the events described here. A study of the documents and reports of the Metropolitan Study Commission would also prove interesting in showing the effect of the suburban policy to close the "ring" on the city and gain its services.

Bibliography

Beck, Elmer Axel. Introduction by Frank P. Zeidler. *The Sewer Socialists: A History of the Socialist Party of Wisconsin, 1897-1940.* Fennimore, WI: Westburg Associates Publishers, 1982.

Crosby, Ernest H. *Golden Rule Jones.* Chicago: Public Publishing Company, 1906.

Cuneo, Ernest. *Life With Fiorello.* New York: Macmillan, 1955.

Gurda, John. *The Making of Milwaukee.* Milwaukee: Milwaukee County Historical Society, 1999.

Hegemann, Werner. *City Planning for Milwaukee,* February, 1916.

Hoan, Daniel W. *City Government.* New York: Harcourt, Brace, 1926.

Laidler, Harry W. *American Socialism – Its Aims and Practical Program.* New York: Harper and Brothers, 1937.

———. *A History of Socialist Thought.* New York: Thomas Y. Crowell, 1927.

———. *A Program for Modern America.* New York: Thomas Y. Crowell, 1936.

———. *The Road Ahead.* New York: Thomas Y. Crowell, 1932.

———. *Socialist Planning and a Socialist Program.* New York: Falcon Press, 1932.

———. *Unemployment and Its Remedies.* New York: League for Industrial Democracy, 1931.

Lorenz, Carl. *Tom L. Johnson, Mayor of Cleveland.* New York: Barnes, 1911.

MacMechen, Edgar C., ed. *Robert W. Speer, A City Builder,* Denver: Denver Common Council, 1919.

Muzik, Edward J. "Victor Berger's Early Career," *Historical Messenger,* Milwaukee: Milwaukee County Historical Society, March, 1961.

O'Connor, Edwin. *The Last Hurrah.* Boston: Little, Brown, 1956.

Olson, Frederick. "Trading Post to Metropolis: Milwaukee County's First 150 Years." Ralph M. Aderman, editor. Milwaukee: Milwaukee County Historical Society, 1987.

Page, Kirby. *Capitalism and Its Rivals.* New York: Eddy and Page, 1936.

———. *Individualism and Socialism.* New York: Farrar and Rinehart, 1933.

———. *Must We Go To War.* New York: Farrar and Rinehart, 1937.

———. *National Defense.* New York: Farrar and Rinehart, 1931.

———. *A New Economic Order.* New York: Harcourt, Brace, 1930.

———. *War: Its Causes, Consequences and Cure.* New York: George H. Doran, 1923.

Schmandt, Henry J. and William H. Standing. *The Milwaukee Metropolitan Study Commission.* Bloomington: Indiana University Press, 1965.

Thomas, Norman. *After the New Deal, What?* New York: Macmillan, 1936.
——. *America's Way Out.* New York: Macmillan, 1931.
——. *As I See It.* New York: Macmillan, 1932.
——. *The Challenge of War.* New York: League for Industrial Democracy, 1924.
——. *The Choice Before Us.* New York: Macmillan, 1934.
——. *Human Exploitation in the United States.* New York: Frederick A. Stokes, 1934.
——. *The Socialist Cure for a Sick Society.* New York: John Day, 1932.
——. *War: No Glory, No Profit, No Need.* New York: Frederick A. Stokes, 1935.
Wells, Robert W. *The Milwaukee Journal: An Informal Chronicle of Its First 100 Years.* Milwaukee: Milwaukee Journal Company, 1981.
Werba, Arthur M. and John L. Grunwald *Making Milwaukee Mightier, A Record of Annexation and Consolidation and a Study of Unification of Government Here and Elsewhere.* Milwaukee: Board of Public Land Commissioners, 1929.
Whitnall, Charles B. *What Progress Costs Milwaukee,* Milwaukee: April, 1935.

Index

Industrial Commission, 173
International Association of Machinists, 20,
    36
Iron Ring, 89, 91, 94, 97, 99, 103, 105, 109-
    110, 114, 125, 128, 131, 135-136, 143, 148,
    155-156, 158, 163, 171, 173-174, 176-177
Israel, 61
Italy, 61, 63
Jackson, MS, 73
Jirikowic, Glenn, 36
Joiners Union, 33
Jones, Samuel, 38
Keegan, Earl, 166
Keep Milwaukee Debt-Free Committee,
    8-9
Kelly, Ralph, 83, 153
Kennedy, John, i
Kennell, Carl, 161
Kerwin, Shirley, 64
Khrushchev, Nikita, i, 120-121
Kiefer, Edward, 6
King, Anthony, 36
Klentz, Arnold, 145
Klitzke, Harold, 19, 23, 35, 37, 50
Knapp, Lloyd, 145
Knappe, Edwin, 4, 6
Knights of Pythias, 66
Knoebel, Irvin, 131, 172
Knuese, William, 147, 158, 173
Koepke, Walter, 133
Kohler Company, 114, 173
Kohler, Walter, Jr., 81, 100-102, 111, 113,
    127-128, 131, 147, 150, 159, 181
Kole, John, 59
Kops, Gerald, 166
Korea, 63
Koth, Ervin, 4, 6
Kraft, Wendelin, 41
Kremlin, 120
Krieger, Elmer, 90, 96
Kroenke, Bernard, 83, 153
Krueger, Joseph, 40, 51
Krumbiegel, E.R., 52, 94
Kujawa, Valentine, 80, 83
Kunz, Theodore, 131
Kurth, Herbert, 155
LaFollette, Phil, 3
LaFollette, Robert, Jr., 3, 7, 39-40

Laidler, Harry, 2, 38
Lake Delton, WI, 119
Lake Michigan, 67, 151
Lake, Town of, WI, 90, 93, 95, 98, 104-105,
    107-108, 115, 117, 120, 122-125, 139, 180
Lakeside Power Plant, 90, 107
Lamping, Joseph, 90, 117, 138, 157, 162,
    163-164, 178
Landowski, Ralph, 83
Laocoon, 114
Latvia, 61
Lawrence, David, 73
Layton Park Lions Club, 66
League of Minnesota Municipalities, 74
League of Wisconsin Municipalities, 66-67,
    133
Lebanon, 61
Leitch, Russell, 27
Liljequist, Orval, 179
Little Chute, WI, 149
London, England, 165
Loomis, Orland, 39
Los Angeles, CA, 73, 174
Louisville, KY, 186
Ludwig, Clarence, 74
Lynn, Margaret, 64
MacArthur, Douglas, 28
MacDonald, Robert, 172
Machinists Union, 20, 36
Madison, WI, 4, 111, 119, 127, 129, 148, 158,
    160-161, 186
Magidson, Shepard, 140
Maier, Henry, 13, 16-18, 22, 24, 28, 29, 56,
    70, 76, 115, 175, 180
Maier, Irwin, 131
Malenkov, Georgy, 120
Manitowoc, WI, 133
Mann, George, 39
Maple Bluff, WI, 160
Marquette University, v, 66
Maruszewski, Richard, 116, 119, 138, 162-
    163, 168, 178, 181
Marx, Karl, iii, 27-29
Matthes, Edward, 20, 32, 36-37, 41
Mattison, Walter, 28, 51, 116, 153
McCarthy, Joseph, 7, 39-40
McCarthyism, ii, 50
McCormick, Peter, 179

To Learn More . . .

The following organizations can provide additional information for anyone who would like to learn more about the subjects explored in this book.

City of Milwaukee Legislative Reference Bureau
City Hall, Room B-11
200 E. Wells St.
Milwaukee, WI 53202
414-286-2295
www.city.milwaukee.gov

Interfaith Conference of Greater Milwaukee
1442 N. Farwell Avenue
Milwaukee, WI 53202
414-276-9050
www.interfaithconference.org

Milwaukee County Historical Society
910 N. Old World Third Street
Milwaukee, WI 53203
414-273-8288
www.milwaukeecountyhistsoc.org

Milwaukee County Labor Council AFL-CIO
633 S. Hawley Road
Milwaukee, WI 53214
414-771-7070
www.wisaflcio.org

Milwaukee Journal Sentinel
333 W. State Street
Milwaukee, WI 53203
414-224-2000
www.jsonline.com

Milwaukee Public Library
814 W. Wisconsin Avenue
Milwaukee, WI 53233
414-286-3000
www.mpl.org

Peace Action Wisconsin
1001 E. Keefe Avenue
Milwaukee, WI 53212
414-964-5158
www.peaceactionwi.org
www.peace-action.org

Socialist Party of Wisconsin
1001 E. Keefe Avenue
Milwaukee, WI 53212
414-332-0654
www.sp-usa.org

**United Nations Educational, Scientific
    and Cultural Organization (UNESCO)**
7 Place de Fontenoy
75352 PARIS 07 SP, France
www.unesco.org

United Nations
100 United Nation Plaza
48 Saint & 1st Avenue
New York, NY 10001
212-644-6373
www.un.org

University of Wisconsin-Milwaukee
2200 E. Kenwood Boulevard
Milwaukee, WI 53211
414-229-1122
www.uwm.edu
www.sce.uwm.edu